W9-AUL-264

Student's
Solutions Manual

▪▪▪▪▪▪▪▪▪▪▪▪

Jay R. Schaffer
University of Northern Colorado

Elementary
Statistics
Picturing the World
Third Edition

▪▪▪▪▪▪▪▪▪▪▪▪

Larson • Farber

▪▪▪▪▪▪▪▪▪▪▪▪

PEARSON

Prentice
Hall

Upper Saddle River, NJ 07458

Editor-in-Chief: Sally Yagan
Acquisitions Editor: Petra Recter
Supplements Editor: Joanne Wendelken
Vice President of Production and Manufacturing: David W. Riccardi
Executive Managing Editor: Kathleen Schiaparelli
Assistant Managing Editor: Becca Richter
Production Editor: Allyson Kloss
Assistant Manufacturing Manager: Michael Bell
Manufacturing Buyer: Ilene Kahn
Supplement Cover Designer: Robert Aleman

© 2006 Pearson Education, Inc.
Pearson Prentice Hall
Pearson Education, Inc.
Upper Saddle River, NJ 07458

All rights reserved. No part of this book may be reproduced in any form or by any means, without permission in writing from the publisher.

Pearson Prentice Hall™ is a trademark of Pearson Education, Inc.

The author and publisher of this book have used their best efforts in preparing this book. These efforts include the development, research, and testing of the theories and programs to determine their effectiveness. The author and publisher make no warranty of any kind, expressed or implied, with regard to these programs or the documentation contained in this book. The author and publisher shall not be liable in any event for incidental or consequential damages in connection with, or arising out of, the furnishing, performance, or use of these programs.

This work is protected by United States copyright laws and is provided solely for teaching courses and assessing student learning. Dissemination or sale of any part of this work (including on the World Wide Web) will destroy the integrity of the work and is not permitted. The work and materials from it should never be made available except by instructors using the accompanying text in their classes. All recipients of this work are expected to abide by these restrictions and to honor the intended pedagogical purposes and the needs of other instructors who rely on these materials.

Printed in the United States of America

10 9 8 7 6 5 4 3 2 1

ISBN 0-13-148322-6

Pearson Education Ltd., *London*
Pearson Education Australia Pty. Ltd., *Sydney*
Pearson Education Singapore, Pte. Ltd.
Pearson Education North Asia Ltd., *Hong Kong*
Pearson Education Canada, Inc., *Toronto*
Pearson Educación de Mexico, S.A. de C.V.
Pearson Education—Japan, *Tokyo*
Pearson Education Malaysia, Pte. Ltd.

CONTENTS

CONTENTS

1.1 AN OVERVIEW OF STATISTICS

1.1 Try It Yourself Solutions

1a. The population consists of the prices per gallon of regular gasoline at all gasoline stations in the United States.

b. The sample consists of the prices per gallon of regular gasoline at the 900 surveyed stations.

c. The data set consists of the 900 prices.

2a. Because the numerical measure of $2,130,863,461 is based on the entire collection of player's salaries, it is from a population.

b. Because the numerical measure is a characteristic of a population, it is a parameter.

3a. Descriptive statistics involve the statement "76% of women and 60% of men had a physical examination within the previous year."

b. An inference drawn from the study is that a higher percentage of women had a physical examination within the previous year.

1.1 EXERCISE SOLUTIONS

1. A sample is a subset of a population.

3. A parameter is a numerical description of a population characteristic. A statistic is a numerical description of a sample characteristic.

5. False. A statistic is a measure that describes a sample characteristic.

7. True

9. False. A population is the collection of all outcomes, responses, measurements, or counts that are of interest.

11. The data set is a population since it is a collection of the ages of all the state governors.

13. The data set is a sample since the collection of the 500 students is a subset within the population of the university's 10,000 students.

15. Sample, because the collection of the 20 patients is a subset within the population.

17. Population: Party of registered voters in Bucks County.

Sample: Party of Bucks County voters responding to phone survey.

19. Population: Ages of adults in the United States who own computers.

Sample: Ages of adults in the United States who own Dell computers.

21. Population: Collection of all infants in Italy.

Sample: Collection of the 33,043 infants in the study.

23. Population: Collection of all women in the United States.

Sample: Collection of the 546 U.S. women surveyed.

1

© 2006 Pearson Education, Inc., Upper Saddle River, NJ. All rights reserved. This material is protected under all copyright laws as they currently exist. No portion of this material may be reproduced, in any form or by any means, without permission in writing from the publisher.

25. Statistic. The value $68,000 is a numerical description of a sample of annual salaries.

27. Statistic. 8% is a numerical description of a sample of computer users.

29. Statistic. 47% is a numerical description of a sample of people in the United States.

31. The statement "56% are the primary investor in their household" is an application of descriptive statistics.

    An inference drawn from the sample is that an association exists between U.S. women and being the primary investor in their household.

33. Answers will vary.

35. (a) An inference drawn from the sample is that senior citizens who own luxury cars have more of their natural teeth than senior citizens who do not own luxury cars.

    (b) It implies that if you purchase a luxury car, an individual will keep more of their natural teeth.

37. Answers will vary.

1.2 DATA CLASSIFICATION

1.2 Try It Yourself Solutions

1a. One data set contains names of cities and the other contains city populations.

  b. City: Nonnumerical

     Population: Numerical

  c. City: Qualitative

     Population: Quantitative

2. (1a) The final standings represent a ranking of hockey teams.

    (1b) ordinal

    (2a) The collection of phone numbers represent labels. No mathematical computations can be made.

    (2b) Nominal, because you cannot make calculations on the data.

3. (1a) The data set is the collection of body temperatures.

    (1b) Interval, because the data can be ordered and meaningful differences can be calculated, but it does not make sense writing a ratio using the temperatures.

    (2a) The data set is the collection of heart rates.

    (2b) Ratio, because the data can be ordered, can be written as a ratio, you can calculate meaningful differences, and the data set contains an inherent zero.

1.2 EXERCISE SOLUTIONS

  1. Nominal and ordinal

  3. False. A systematic sample is selected by ordering a population in some way and then selecting members of the population at regular intervals.

© 2006 Pearson Education, Inc., Upper Saddle River, NJ. All rights reserved. This material is protected under all copyright laws as they currently exist.
No portion of this material may be reproduced, in any form or by any means, without permission in writing from the publisher.

5. False. Data at the nominal level simply represent labels. Calculations cannot be performed.

7. Qualitative, because telephone numbers are merely labels.

9. Quantitative, because the scores of a class on an accounting exam are numerical measures.

11. Ordinal. Data can be arranged in order, but differences between data entries make no sense.

13. Nominal. No mathematical computations can be made and data are categorized using names.

15. Ordinal. The data can be arranged in order, but differences between data entries are not meaningful.

17. Ordinal

19. Nominal

21. An inherent zero is a zero that implies "none." Answers will vary.

1.3 EXPERIMENTAL DESIGN

1.3 Try It Yourself Solutions

1. (1a) Focus: Effect of exercise on senior citizens.

(1b) Population: Collection of all senior citizens.

(1c) Experiment

(2a) Focus: Effect of radiation fallout on senior citizens.

(2b) Population: Collection of all senior citizens.

(2c) Sampling

2a. Example: start with the first digits 92630782 . . .

b. 92|63|07|82|40|19|26

c. 63, 7, 40, 19, 26

3. (1a) The sample was selected by only using available students.

(1b) Because the students were readily available in your class, this is convenience sampling.

(2a) The sample was selected by numbering each student in the school, randomly choosing a starting number, and selecting students at regular intervals from the starting number.

(2b) Because the students were ordered in a manner such that every 25th student is selected, this is systematic sampling.

1.3 EXERCISE SOLUTIONS

1. False. Using stratified sampling guarantees that members of each group within a population will be sampled.

3. False. To select a systematic sample, a population is ordered in some way and then members of the population are selected at regular intervals.

5. In this study, you want to measure the effect of a treatment (using a fat substitute) on the human digestive system. So, you would want to perform an experiment.

© 2006 Pearson Education, Inc., Upper Saddle River, NJ. All rights reserved. This material is protected under all copyright laws as they currently exist.
No portion of this material may be reproduced, in any form or by any means, without permission in writing from the publisher.

7. Because it is impractical to create this situation, you would want to use a simulation.

9. Each U.S. telephone number has an equal chance of being dialed and all samples of 1599 phone numbers have an equal chance of being selected, so this is a simple random sample. Telephone sampling only samples those individuals who have telephones, are available, and are willing to respond, so this is a possible source of bias.

11. Because the students were chosen due to their convenience of location (leaving the library), this is a convenience sample. Bias may enter into the sample because the students sampled may not be representative of the population of students. For example, there may be an association between time spent at the library and drinking habits.

13. Because a random sample of out-patients were selected and all samples of 1210 patients had an equal chance of being selected, this is a simple random sample.

15. Because a sample is taken from each one-acre subplot (stratum), this is a stratified sample.

17. Because every ninth name on a list is being selected, this is a systematic sample.

19. Census, since it is relatively easy to obtain the salaries of the 50 employees.

21. Question is biased since it already suggests that drinking fruit juice is good for you. The question might be rewritten as "How does drinking fruit juice affect your health?"

23. Question is unbiased since it does not imply how many hours of sleep are good or bad.

25. The households sampled represent various locations, ethnic groups, and income brackets. Each of these variables is considered a stratum.

27. Open Question
    Advantage: Allows respondent to express some depth and shades of meaning in the answer.
    Disadvantage: Not easily quantified and difficult to compare surveys.

    Closed Question
    Advantage: Easy to analyze results.
    Disadvantage: May not provide appropriate alternatives and may influence the opinion of the respondent.

CHAPTER 1 REVIEW EXERCISE SOLUTIONS

1. Population: Collection of all U.S. adult VCR owners.
   Sample: Collection of the 898 U.S. adult VCR owners that were sampled.

3. Population: Collection of all U.S. ATMs.
   Sample: Collection of 82,188 ATMs that were sampled.

5. The team payroll is a parameter since it is a numerical description of a population (entire baseball team) characteristic.

7. Since "89 students" is describing a characteristic of a population (University of Arizona students), it is a parameter.

9. The average surcharge of $1.48 for withdrawals from a competing bank is representative of the descriptive branch of statistics. An inference drawn from the sample is that all ATMs charge an average $1.48 for withdrawals from a competing bank.

11. Quantitative because monthly salaries are numerical measurements.

13. Quantitative because ages are numerical measurements.

15. Interval. It makes no sense saying that 100 degrees is twice as hot as 50 degrees.

© 2006 Pearson Education, Inc., Upper Saddle River, NJ. All rights reserved. This material is protected under all copyright laws as they currently exist. No portion of this material may be reproduced, in any form or by any means, without permission in writing from the publisher.

17. Nominal. The data is categorical and cannot be arranged in a meaningful order.

19. Because judges keep accurate records of charitable donations, you could take a census.

21. In this study, you want to measure the effect of a treatment (plant hormone) on chrysanthemums. You would want to perform an experiment.

23. Because random telephone numbers were generated and called, this is a simple random sample.

25. Since each community is considered a cluster and every pregnant woman in a selected community is surveyed, this is a cluster sample.

27. Since grades are considered strata and 25 students are sampled from each stratum, this is a stratified sample.

29. Telephone sampling only samples individuals who have telephones, are available, and are willing to respond.

31. The selected communities may not be representative of the entire area.

CHAPTER 1 QUIZ SOLUTIONS

1. Population: Collection of all individuals with sleep disorders.
Sample: Collection of 254 patients in study.

2. (a) Statistic. 53% is a characteristic of a sample of parents.

(b) Parameter. 67% is a characteristic of the entire union (population).

3. (a) Qualitative, since student identification numbers are merely labels.

(b) Quantitative, since a test score is a numerical measure.

4. (a) Nominal. Players may be ordered numerically, but there is no meaning in this order and no mathematical computations can be made.

(b) Ratio. It makes sense to say that the number of products sold during the 1st quarter was twice as many as sold in the 2nd quarter.

(c) Interval because meaningful differences between entries can be calculated, but a zero entry is not an inherent zero.

5. (a) In this study, you want to measure the effect of a treatment (low dietary intake of vitamin C and iron) on lead levels in adults. You want to perform an experiment.

(b) Since it would be difficult to survey every individual within 500 miles of your home, sampling should be used.

6. (a) Because people were chosen due to their convenience of location (on the beach), this is a convenience sample.

(b) Since every fifth part is selected from an assembly line, this is a systematic sample.

(c) Stratified sample because the population is first stratified and then a sample is collected from each strata.

7. Convenience

8. (a) False. A statistic is a numerical measure that describes a sample characteristic.

(b) False. Ratio data represents the highest level of measurement.

© 2006 Pearson Education, Inc., Upper Saddle River, NJ. All rights reserved. This material is protected under all copyright laws as they currently exist. No portion of this material may be reproduced, in any form or by any means, without permission in writing from the publisher.

© 2006 Pearson Education, Inc., Upper Saddle River, NJ. All rights reserved. This material is protected under all copyright laws as they currently exist.
No portion of this material may be reproduced, in any form or by any means, without permission in writing from the publisher.

Descriptive Statistics

2.1 Try It Yourself Solutions

1a. The number of classes (8) is stated in the problem.

b. Min = 0   Max = 72   Class width $= \dfrac{(72 - 0)}{8} = 9$

c.

Lower limit	Upper limit
0	9
10	19
20	29
30	39
40	49
50	59
60	69
70	79

d. See part (e).

e.

Class	Frequency, f
0–9	15
10–19	19
20–29	14
30–39	7
40–49	14
50–59	6
60–69	4
70–79	1

2a. See part (b).

b.

Class	Frequency, f	Midpoint	Relative frequency	Cumulative frequency
0–9	15	4.5	0.1875	15
10–19	19	14.5	0.2375	34
20–29	14	24.5	0.1750	48
30–39	7	34.5	0.0875	55
40–49	14	44.5	0.1750	69
50–59	6	54.5	0.0750	75
60–69	4	64.5	0.0500	79
70–79	1	74.5	0.0125	80
	$N = 80$		$\sum \frac{f}{n} = 1$	

c. 42.5% of the population is under 20 years old. 6.25% of the population is over 59 years old.

3a.

Class Boundaries
−0.5–9.5
9.5–19.5
19.5–29.5
29.5–39.5
39.5–49.5
49.5–59.5
59.5–69.5
69.5–79.5

b. Use class midpoints for the horizontal scale and frequency for the vertical scale.

© 2006 Pearson Education, Inc., Upper Saddle River, NJ. All rights reserved. This material is protected under all copyright laws as they currently exist.
No portion of this material may be reproduced, in any form or by any means, without permission in writing from the publisher.

c.   **Ages of Akhiok Residents**

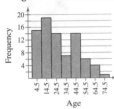

d. 42.5% of the population is under 20 years old. 6.25% of the population is over 59 years old.

4a. Use class midpoints for the horizontal scale and frequency for the vertical scale.

b. See part (c).

c.   **Ages of Ahkiok Residents**

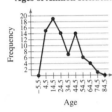

d. The population increases up to the age of 14.5 and then decreases. The population increases again between the ages of 34.5 and 44.5, but then after 44.5, the population decreases.

5abc.   **Ages of Akhiok Residents**

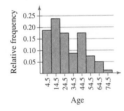

6a. Use upper class boundaries for the horizontal scale and cumulative frequency for the vertical scale.

b. See part (c).

c.   **Ages of Akhiok Residents**

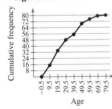

d. Approximately 69 residents are 49 years old or younger.

7ab.

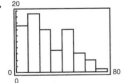

© 2006 Pearson Education, Inc., Upper Saddle River, NJ. All rights reserved. This material is protected under all copyright laws as they currently exist. No portion of this material may be reproduced, in any form or by any means, without permission in writing from the publisher.

2.1 EXERCISE SOLUTIONS

1. By organizing the data into a frequency distribution, patterns within the data may become more evident.

3. Class limits determine which numbers can belong to that class.

Class boundaries are the numbers that separate classes without forming gaps between them.

5. False. The midpoint of a class is the sum of the lower and upper limits of the class divided by two.

7. True

9. (a) Class width = 30 − 20 = 10

(b) and (c)

Class	Frequency, f	Midpoint	Class boundaries
20–29	10	24.5	19.5–29.5
30–39	132	34.5	29.5–39.5
40–49	284	44.5	39.5–49.5
50–59	300	54.5	49.5–59.5
60–69	175	64.5	59.5–69.5
70–79	65	74.5	69.5–79.5
80–89	25	84.5	79.5–89.5
	$\sum f = 991$		

11.

Class	Frequency, f	Midpoint	Relative frequency	Cumulative frequency
20–29	10	24.5	0.01	10
30–39	132	34.5	0.13	142
40–49	284	44.5	0.29	426
50–59	300	54.5	0.30	726
60–69	175	64.5	0.18	901
70–79	65	74.5	0.07	966
80–89	25	84.5	0.03	991
	$\sum f = 991$		$\sum \frac{f}{n} = 1$	

13. (a) Number of classes = 7

(b) Least frequency ≈ 10

(c) Greatest frequency ≈ 300

(d) Class width = 10

15. (a) 50　　(b) 12.5–13.5 lb

17. (a) 24　　(b) 19.5 lb

19. (a) Class with greatest relative frequency: 8–9 in.
Class with least relative frequency: 17–18 in.

(b) Greatest relative frequency ≈ 0.195
Least relative frequency ≈ 0.005

(c) Approximately 0.015

21. Class with greatest frequency: 500–550
Class with least frequency: 250–300 or 700–750

© 2006 Pearson Education, Inc., Upper Saddle River, NJ. All rights reserved. This material is protected under all copyright laws as they currently exist.
No portion of this material may be reproduced, in any form or by any means, without permission in writing from the publisher.

23. Class width $= \dfrac{\text{Max} - \text{Min}}{\text{Number of classes}} = \dfrac{39 - 0}{5} = 7.8 \Rightarrow 8$

Class	Frequency, f	Midpoint	Relative frequency	Cumulative frequency
0–7	8	3.5	0.32	8
8–15	8	11.5	0.32	16
16–23	3	19.5	0.12	19
24–31	3	27.5	0.12	22
32–39	3	35.5	0.12	25
	$\sum f = 25$		$\sum \dfrac{f}{n} = 1$	

25. Class width $= \dfrac{\text{Max} - \text{Min}}{\text{Number of classes}} = \dfrac{7119 - 1000}{6} = 1019.83 \Rightarrow 1020$

Class	Frequency, f	Midpoint	Relative frequency	Cumulative frequency
1000–2019	12	1509.5	0.5455	12
2020–3039	3	2529.5	0.1364	15
3040–4059	2	3549.5	0.0909	17
4060–5079	3	4569.5	0.1364	20
5080–6099	1	5589.5	0.0455	21
6100–7119	1	6609.5	0.0455	22
	$\sum f = 22$		$\sum \dfrac{f}{n} = 1$	

Class with greatest frequency: 1000–2019
Class with least frequency: 5080–6099; 6100–7119

27. Class width $= \dfrac{\text{Max} - \text{Min}}{\text{Number of classes}} = \dfrac{514 - 291}{8} = 27.875 \Rightarrow 28$

Class	Frequency, f	Midpoint	Relative frequency	Cumulative frequency
291–318	5	304.5	0.1667	5
319–346	4	332.5	0.1333	9
347–374	3	360.5	0.1000	12
375–402	5	388.5	0.1667	17
403–430	6	416.5	0.2000	23
431–458	4	444.5	0.1333	27
459–486	1	472.5	0.0455	28
487–514	2	500.5	0.0909	30
	$\sum f = 30$		$\sum \dfrac{f}{n} = 1$	

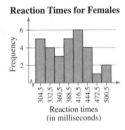

Class with greatest frequency: 403–430
Class with least frequency: 459–486

29. Class width $= \dfrac{\text{Max} - \text{Min}}{\text{Number of classes}} = \dfrac{264 - 146}{5} = 23.6 \Rightarrow 24$

Class	Frequency, f	Midpoint	Relative frequency	Cumulative frequency
146–169	6	157.5	0.2308	6
170–193	9	181.5	0.3462	15
194–217	3	205.5	0.1154	18
218–241	6	229.5	0.2308	24
242–265	2	253.5	0.0769	26
	$\sum f = 26$		$\sum \dfrac{f}{n} = 1$	

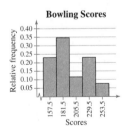

Class with greatest relative frequency: 170–193
Class with least relative frequency: 242–265

© 2006 Pearson Education, Inc., Upper Saddle River, NJ. All rights reserved. This material is protected under all copyright laws as they currently exist. No portion of this material may be reproduced, in any form or by any means, without permission in writing from the publisher.

31. Class width $= \dfrac{\text{Max} - \text{Min}}{\text{Number of classes}} = \dfrac{52 - 33}{5} = 3.8 \Rightarrow 4$

Class	Frequency, f	Midpoint	Relative frequency	Cumulative frequency
33–36	8	34.5	0.3077	8
37–40	6	38.5	0.2308	14
41–44	5	42.5	0.1923	19
45–48	2	46.5	0.0769	21
49–52	5	50.5	0.1923	26
	$\sum f = 26$		$\sum \dfrac{f}{n} = 1$	

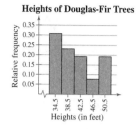

Heights of Douglas-Fir Trees

Class with greatest relative frequency: 33–36
Class with least relative frequency: 45–48

33. Class width $= \dfrac{\text{Max} - \text{Min}}{\text{Number of classes}} = \dfrac{73 - 50}{6} = 3.83 \Rightarrow 4$

Class	Frequency, f	Relative frequency	Cumulative frequency
50–53	1	0.0417	1
54–57	0	0.0000	1
58–61	4	0.1667	5
62–65	9	0.3750	14
66–69	7	0.2917	21
70–73	3	0.1250	24
	$\sum f = 24$	$\sum \dfrac{f}{n} \approx 1$	

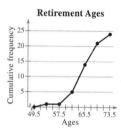

Retirement Ages

Location of the greatest increase in frequency: 62–65

35. Class width $= \dfrac{\text{Max} - \text{Min}}{\text{Number of classes}} = \dfrac{18 - 2}{6} = 2.67 \Rightarrow 3$

Class	Frequency, f	Relative frequency	Cumulative frequency
2–4	9	0.3214	9
5–7	6	0.2143	15
8–10	7	0.2500	22
11–13	3	0.1071	25
14–16	2	0.0714	27
17–19	1	0.0357	28
	$\sum f = 28$	$\sum \dfrac{f}{n} \approx 1$	

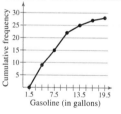

Gallons of Gasoline Purchased

Location of the greatest increase in frequency: 2–4

37. Class width $= \dfrac{\text{Max} - \text{Min}}{\text{Number of classes}} = \dfrac{98 - 47}{5} = 10.2 \Rightarrow 11$

Class	Frequency, f	Midpoint	Relative frequency	Cumulative frequency
47–57	1	52	0.05	1
58–68	1	63	0.05	2
69–79	5	74	0.25	7
80–90	8	85	0.40	15
91–101	5	96	0.25	20
	$\sum f = 20$		$\sum \dfrac{f}{N} = 1$	

Exam Scores

Class with greatest frequency: 80–90
Classes with least frequency: 47–57 and 58–68

© 2006 Pearson Education, Inc., Upper Saddle River, NJ. All rights reserved. This material is protected under all copyright laws as they currently exist. No portion of this material may be reproduced, in any form or by any means, without permission in writing from the publisher.

39. (a) Class width $= \dfrac{\text{Max} - \text{Min}}{\text{Number of classes}} = \dfrac{104 - 61}{8} = 5.375 \Rightarrow 6$

Class	Frequency, f	Midpoint	Relative frequency
61–66	1	63.5	0.0333
67–72	3	69.5	0.1000
73–78	6	75.5	0.2000
79–84	10	81.5	0.3333
85–90	5	87.5	0.1667
91–96	2	93.5	0.0667
97–102	2	99.5	0.0667
103–108	1	105.5	0.0333
	$\sum f = 30$		$\sum \dfrac{f}{N} = 1$

Daily Withdrawals

(b) 16.7%, because the sum of the relative frequencies for the last three classes is 0.167.

(c) $9600, because the sum of the relative frequencies for the last two classes is 0.10.

41.

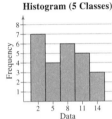

Histogram (5 Classes)

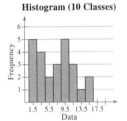

Histogram (10 Classes)

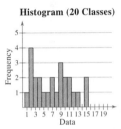

Histogram (20 Classes)

In general, a greater number of classes better-preserves the actual values of the data set, but is not as helpful for observing general trends and making conclusions. When choosing the number of classes, an important consideration is the size of the data set. For instance, you would not want to use 20 classes if your data set contained 20 entries. In this particular example, as the number of classes increases, the histogram shows more fluctuation. The histograms with 10 and 20 classes have classes with zero frequencies. Not much is gained by using more than five classes. Therefore, it appears that five classes would be best.

2.2   MORE GRAPHS AND DISPLAYS

2.2 Try It Yourself Solutions

1a.
```
0 |
1 |
2 |
3 |
4 |
5 |
6 |
7 |
```

b. Key: 3|3 = 33
```
0 | 5 2 7 1 5 3 1 0 1 3 3 9 0 4 5
1 | 8 2 5 6 3 3 7 3 0 7 8 2 3 8 9 3 6 9 9
2 | 5 4 2 0 3 3 4 0 1 5 9 6 6 6
3 | 9 6 9 7 9 9 3
4 | 4 2 4 7 1 8 0 0 1 9 9 5 1 9
5 | 8 3 1 6 8 9
6 | 0 8 7 8
7 | 2
```

© 2006 Pearson Education, Inc., Upper Saddle River, NJ. All rights reserved. This material is protected under all copyright laws as they currently exist. No portion of this material may be reproduced, in any form or by any means, without permission in writing from the publisher.

c. Key: $3|3 = 33$

```
0 | 0 0 1 1 1 2 3 3 3 4 5 5 5 7 9
1 | 0 2 2 3 3 3 3 3 5 6 6 7 7 8 8 8 9 9 9
2 | 0 0 1 2 3 3 4 4 5 5 6 6 6 9
3 | 3 6 7 9 9 9 9
4 | 0 0 1 1 1 2 4 4 5 7 8 9 9 9
5 | 1 3 6 8 8 9
6 | 0 7 8 8
7 | 2
```

d. It appears that the residents of Akhiok are a young population with most of the ages being below 40 years old.

2ab. Key: $3|3 = 33$

```
0 | 0 0 1 1 1 2 3 3 3 4
0 | 5 5 5 7 9
1 | 0 2 2 3 3 3 3 3
1 | 5 6 6 7 7 8 8 8 9 9 9
2 | 0 0 1 2 3 3 4 4
2 | 5 5 6 6 6 9
3 | 3
3 | 6 7 9 9 9 9
4 | 0 0 1 1 1 2 4 4
4 | 5 7 8 9 9 9
5 | 1 3
5 | 6 8 8 9
6 | 0
6 | 7 8 8
7 | 2
7 |
```

3a. Use ages for the horizontal axis.

b. **Ages of Akhiok Residents**

Age (in years)

c. It appears that a large percentage of the population is younger than 40 years old.

4a.

Vehicle type	Killed (frequency)	Relative frequency	Central angle
Cars	22,385	0.6556	$(0.6555)(360°) \approx 236°$
Trucks	8,457	0.2477	$(0.2477)(360°) \approx 89°$
Motorcycles	2,806	0.0822	$(0.0822)(360°) \approx 30°$
Other	497	0.0146	$(0.0146)(360°) \approx 5°$
	$\sum f = 34{,}145$	$\sum \frac{f}{n} \approx 1$	

b. **Motor Vehicle Occupants Killed in 1991**

Trucks 25%
Motorcycles
8%
Other 1%
Cars 66%

c. It appears the percentage of truck occupants killed has increased by 9% while the percentage of car occupants killed has decreased by 10%. The motorcycle deaths for both years is nearly the same.

© 2006 Pearson Education, Inc., Upper Saddle River, NJ. All rights reserved. This material is protected under all copyright laws as they currently exist. No portion of this material may be reproduced, in any form or by any means, without permission in writing from the publisher.

5a.

Cause	Frequency, f
Auto Dealers	14,668
Auto Repair	9,728
Home Furnishing	7,792
Computer Sales	5,733
Dry Cleaning	4,649

b.

c. It appears that the auto industry (dealers and repair shops) account for the largest portion of complaints filed at the BBB.

6ab.

c. It appears that the longer an employee is with the company, the larger his/her salary will be.

7ab.

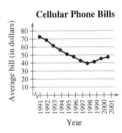

c. It appears that the average monthly bill for cellular telephone subscribers has decreased significantly from 1991 to 1998, then increased from 1998 to 2001.

2.2 EXERCISE SOLUTIONS

1. Quantitative: Stem-and-Leaf Plot, Dot Plot, Histogram, Time Series Chart, Scatter Plot
Qualitative: Pie Chart, Pareto Chart

3. a

5. b

7. 27, 32, 41, 43, 43, 44, 47, 47, 48, 50, 51, 51, 52, 53, 53, 53, 54, 54, 54, 54, 55, 56, 56, 58, 59, 68, 68, 68, 73, 78, 78, 85

Max: 85   Min: 27

9. 13, 13, 14, 14, 14, 15, 15, 15, 15, 15, 16, 17, 17, 18, 19

Max: 19   Min: 13

11. Anheuser-Busch is the top sports advertiser spending approximately $190 million. Honda spends the least. (Answers will vary.)

13. Tailgaters irk drivers the most, while too cautious drivers irk drivers the least. (Answers will vary.)

© 2006 Pearson Education, Inc., Upper Saddle River, NJ. All rights reserved. This material is protected under all copyright laws as they currently exist. No portion of this material may be reproduced, in any form or by any means, without permission in writing from the publisher.

15. Key: $3|3 = 33$

3	233459
4	01134556678
5	133
6	0069

Most elephants tend to drink less than 55 gallons of water per day. (Answers will vary.)

17. Key: $17|5 = 17.5$

16	48
17	113455679
18	13446669
19	0023356
20	18

It appears that most farmers charge 17 to 19 cents per pound of apples. (Answers will vary.)

19.

Housefly Life Spans

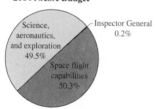

Life span (in days)

It appears that the lifespan of a fly tends to be between 4 and 14 days. (Answers will vary.)

21.

Category	Budget frequency	Relative frequency	Angle
Science, aeronautics, and exploration	7782	0.5031	$(0.5031)(360°) \approx 181°$
Space flight capabilities	7661	0.4952	$(0.4952)(360°) \approx 178°$
Inspector General	26	0.0017	$(0.0017)(360°) \approx 0.6°$
	$\Sigma f = 15{,}469$	$\sum \frac{f}{N} \approx 1$	

2004 NASA Budget

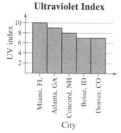

It appears that 50.31% of NASA's budget went to science, aeronautics, and exploration. (Answers will vary.)

23.

Ultraviolet Index

It appears that Boise, ID and Denver, CO have the same UV index. (Answers will vary.)

© 2006 Pearson Education, Inc., Upper Saddle River, NJ. All rights reserved. This material is protected under all copyright laws as they currently exist. No portion of this material may be reproduced, in any form or by any means, without permission in writing from the publisher.

25.

Teachers' Salaries

It appears that a teacher's average salary decreases as the number of students per teacher increases. (Answers will vary.)

27.

Price of Grade A Eggs

It appears the price of eggs peaked in 1996. (Answers will vary.)

29. (a) When data is taken at regular intervals over a period of time, a time series chart should be used. (Answers will vary.)

(b)

Sales for Company A

2.3 MEASURES OF CENTRAL TENDENCY

2.3 Try It Yourself Solutions

1a. $\Sigma x = 578$

b. $\bar{x} = \dfrac{\Sigma x}{n} = \dfrac{578}{14} = 41.3$

c. The typical age of an employee in a department store is 41.3 years old.

2a. 0, 0, 1, 1, 1, 2, 3, 3, 4, 5, 5, 5, 9, 10, 12, 12, 13, 13, 13, 13, 13, 15, 16, 16, 17, 17, 18, 18, 18, 19, 19, 19, 20, 20, 21, 22, 23, 23, 24, 24, 25, 25, 26, 26, 26, 29, 36, 39, 39, 39, 39, 40, 40, 41, 41, 41, 42, 44, 44, 45, 47, 48, 49, 49, 49, 51, 53, 56, 58, 58, 60, 67, 68, 68, 72

b. median = middle entry = 23

3a. 0, 0, 1, 1, 1, 2, 3, 3, 3, 4, 5, 5, 5, 7, 9, 10, 12, 12, 13, 13, 13, 13, 13, 15, 16, 16, 17, 17, 18, 18, 18, 19, 19, 19, 20, 20, 21, 22, 23, 23, 24, 24, 25, 25, 26, 26, 26, 29, 33, 36, 37, 39, 39, 39, 39, 40, 40, 41, 41, 41, 42, 44, 44, 45, 47, 48, 49, 49, 49, 51, 53, 56, 58, 58, 59, 60, 67, 68, 68, 72

© 2006 Pearson Education, Inc., Upper Saddle River, NJ. All rights reserved. This material is protected under all copyright laws as they currently exist. No portion of this material may be reproduced, in any form or by any means, without permission in writing from the publisher.

b. median = mean of two middle entries $\{23, 24\} = 23.5$

c. Half of the residents of Akhiok are younger than 23.5 and half are older than 23.5.

4a. $0, 0, 1, 1, 1, 2, 3, 3, 3, 4, 5, 5, 5, 7, 9, 10, 12, 12, 13, 13, 13, 13, 13, 15, 16, 16, 17, 17, 18, 18, 18, 19,$
$19, 19, 20, 20, 21, 22, 23, 23, 24, 24, 25, 25, 26, 26, 26, 29, 33, 36, 37, 39, 39, 39, 39, 40, 40, 41, 41,$
$41, 42, 44, 44, 45, 47, 48, 49, 49, 49, 51, 53, 56, 58, 58, 59, 60, 67, 68, 68, 72$

b. The age that occurs with the greatest frequency is 13 years old.

c. The mode of the ages of the residents of Akhiok is 13 years old.

5a. "Yes" occurs with the greatest frequency (169).

b. The mode of the responses to the survey is "Yes".

6a. $\bar{x} = \dfrac{\Sigma x}{n} = \dfrac{410}{19} \approx 21.6$

median $= 21$

mode $= 20$

b. The mean in Example 6 ($\bar{x} \approx 23.8$) was heavily influenced by the age 65. Neither the median nor the mode was affected as much by the age 65.

7ab.

Source	x	Score, w	Weight, $x \cdot w$
Test Mean	86	0.50	$(83)(0.50) = 43$
Midterm	96	0.15	$(96)(0.15) = 14.4$
Final	98	0.20	$(98)(0.20) = 19.6$
Computer Lab	98	0.10	$(98)(0.10) = 9.8$
Homework	100	0.05	$(100)(0.05) = 5$
		$\Sigma w = 1.00$	$\Sigma(x \cdot w) = 91.8$

c. $\bar{x} = \dfrac{\Sigma(x \cdot w)}{\Sigma w} = \dfrac{91.8}{1.00} = 91.8$

d. The weighted mean for the course is 91.8.

8abc.

Class	Midpoint, x	Frequency, f	$x \cdot f$
0–9	4.5	15	67.50
10–19	14.5	19	275.50
20–29	24.5	14	343.00
30–39	34.5	7	241.50
40–49	44.5	14	623.00
50–59	54.5	6	327.00
60–69	64.5	4	258.00
70–79	74.5	1	74.50
		$N = 80$	$\Sigma(x \cdot f) = 2210$

d. $\mu = \dfrac{\Sigma(x \cdot f)}{N} = \dfrac{2210}{80} \approx 27.6$

The average age of a resident of Akhiok is approximately 27.6.

© 2006 Pearson Education, Inc., Upper Saddle River, NJ. All rights reserved. This material is protected under all copyright laws as they currently exist.
No portion of this material may be reproduced, in any form or by any means, without permission in writing from the publisher.

2.3 EXERCISE SOLUTIONS

1. False. The mean is the measure of central tendency most likely to be affected by an extreme value (or outlier).

3. False. All quantitative data sets have a median.

5. Answers will vary. A data set with an outlier within it would be an example. For instance, the mean of the prices of existing home sales tends to be "inflated" due to the presence of a few very expensive homes.

7. Skewed right since the "tail" of the distribution extends to the right.

9. Uniform since the bars are approximately the same height.

11. (9), since the distribution values range from 1 to 12 and has (approximately) equal frequencies.

13. (10), since the distribution has a maximum value of 90 and is skewed left due to a few students scoring much lower than the majority of the students.

15. (a) $\bar{x} = \dfrac{\Sigma x}{n} = \dfrac{81}{13} \approx 6.2$

   5 5 5 5 5 5 ⑥ 6 6 7 8 9 9
   └──── middle value ⟹ median = 6

   mode = 5   (occurs 6 times)

   (b) Median appears to be the best measure of central tendency since the distribution is skewed.

17. (a) $\bar{x} = \dfrac{\Sigma x}{n} = \dfrac{32}{7} \approx 4.57$

   3.7 4.0 4.8 ④.8 4.8 4.8 5.1
   └──── middle value ⟹ median = 4.8

   mode = 4.8   (occurs 4 times)

   (b) Median appears to be the best measure of central tendency since there are outliers present.

19. (a) $\bar{x} = \dfrac{\Sigma x}{n} = \dfrac{2720.6}{29} \approx 93.81$

   85.4, 88, 88.7, 89.7, 89.8, 90.1, 90.3, 90.3, 90.7, 91.5,
   91.8, 91.8, 92, 92.8, ⓬92.9, 93.3, 94, 94.2, 94.5, 94.8,
   95.3, 96.7, 97.1, 97.2, 98, 98.2, 102.8, 103.5, 105.2
   └──── middle value ⟹ median = 92.9

   mode = 90.3, 91.8   (occurs 2 times each)

   (b) Median appears to be the best measure of central tendency since the distribution is skewed.

21. (a) $\bar{x}$ = not possible (nominal data)

   median = not possible (nominal data)

   mode = "Worse"

   (b) Mode appears to be the best measure of central tendency since the data is at the nominal level of measurement.

© 2006 Pearson Education, Inc., Upper Saddle River, NJ. All rights reserved. This material is protected under all copyright laws as they currently exist. No portion of this material may be reproduced, in any form or by any means, without permission in writing from the publisher.

23. (a) $\bar{x} = \dfrac{\Sigma x}{n} = \dfrac{1194.4}{7} \approx 170.63$

155.7, 158.1, 162.2, (169.3), 180, 181.8, 187.3

— middle value $\Rightarrow$ median $= 169.3$

mode = none

(b) Mean appears to be the best measure of central tendency since there are no outliers.

25. (a) $\bar{x} = \dfrac{\Sigma x}{n} = \dfrac{226}{10} = 22.6$

14, 14, 15, 177, 18, 20, 22, 25, 40, 41

— two middle values $\Rightarrow$ median $= \dfrac{18 + 20}{2} = 19$

mode = 14   (occurs 2 times)

(b) Median appears to be the best measure of central tendency since the distribution is skewed.

27. (a) $\bar{x} = \dfrac{\Sigma x}{n} = \dfrac{197.5}{14} \approx 14.11$

1.5, 2.5, 2.5, 5, 10.5, 11, 13, 15.5, 16.5, 17.5, 20, 26.5, 27, 28.5

— two middle values $\Rightarrow$ median $= \dfrac{13 + 15.5}{2} = 14.25$

mode = 2.5   (occurs 2 times)

(b) Mean appears to be the best measure of central tendency since there are no outliers.

29. (a) $\bar{x} = \dfrac{\Sigma x}{n} = \dfrac{578}{14} = 41.3$

10, 12, 21, 24, 27, 37, 38, 41, 45, 45, 50, 57, 65, 106

— two middle values $\Rightarrow$ median $= \dfrac{38 + 41}{2} = 39.5$

mode = 4.5   (occurs 2 times)

(b) Median appears to be the best measure of central tendency since the distribution is skewed.

31. (a) $\bar{x} = \dfrac{\Sigma x}{n} = \dfrac{292}{15} \approx 19.5$

5, 8, 10, 15, 15, 15, 17, (20), 21, 22, 22, 25, 28, 32, 37

— middle value $\Rightarrow$ median $= 20$

mode = 15   (occurs 3 times)

(b) Median appears to be the best measure of central tendency since the data is skewed.

33. A = mode (data entry that occurred most often)

B = median (left of mean in skewed right dist.)

C = mean (right of median in skewed right dist.)

35. Mode since the data is nominal.

37. Mean since the data does not contain outliers.

© 2006 Pearson Education, Inc., Upper Saddle River, NJ. All rights reserved. This material is protected under all copyright laws as they currently exist. No portion of this material may be reproduced, in any form or by any means, without permission in writing from the publisher.

39.

Source	Score, x	Weight, w	$x \cdot w$
Homework	85	0.15	$(85)(0.15) = 12.75$
Quiz	80	0.10	$(80)(0.10) = 8$
Quiz	92	0.10	$(92)(0.10) = 9.2$
Quiz	76	0.10	$(76)(0.10) = 7.6$
Project	100	0.15	$(100)(0.15) = 15$
Speech	90	0.15	$(90)(0.15) = 13.5$
Final Exam	93	0.25	$(93)(0.25) = 23.25$
		$\Sigma w = 1$	$\Sigma(x \cdot w) = 89.3$

$$\bar{x} = \frac{\Sigma(x \cdot w)}{\Sigma w} = \frac{89.3}{1} = 89.3$$

41.

Grade	Points, x	Credits, w	$x \cdot w$
B	3	3	$(3)(3) = 9$
B	3	3	$(3)(3) = 9$
A	4	4	$(4)(4) = 16$
D	1	2	$(1)(2) = 2$
C	2	3	$(2)(3) = 6$
		$\Sigma w = 15$	$\Sigma(x \cdot w) = 42$

$$\bar{x} = \frac{\Sigma(x \cdot w)}{\Sigma w} = \frac{42}{15} = 2.8$$

43.

Midpoint, x	Frequency, f	$x \cdot f$
61	3	$(61)(3) = 183$
64	4	$(64)(4) = 256$
67	7	$(67)(7) = 469$
70	2	$(70)(2) = 140$
	$n = 16$	$\Sigma(x \cdot f) = 1048$

$$\bar{x} = \frac{\Sigma(x \cdot f)}{n} = \frac{1048}{16} \approx 65.5$$

45.

Midpoint, x	Frequency, f	$x \cdot f$
4.5	57	$(4.5)(57) = 256.5$
14.5	68	$(14.5)(68) = 986$
24.5	36	$(24.5)(36) = 882$
34.5	55	$(34.5)(55) = 1897.5$
44.5	71	$(44.5)(71) = 3159.5$
54.5	44	$(54.5)(44) = 2398$
64.5	36	$(64.5)(36) = 2322$
74.5	14	$(74.5)(14) = 1043$
84.5	8	$(84.5)(8) = 676$
	$n = 389$	$\Sigma(x \cdot f) = 13620.5$

$$\bar{x} = \frac{\Sigma(x \cdot f)}{n} = \frac{13,620.5}{389} \approx 35.0$$

47. Class width $= \dfrac{\text{Max} - \text{Min}}{\text{Number of classes}} = \dfrac{14 - 3}{6} = 1.83 \Rightarrow 2$

Class	Midpoint, x	Frequency, f
3–4	3.5	3
5–6	5.5	8
7–8	7.5	4
9–10	9.5	2
11–12	11.5	2
13–14	13.5	1
		$\Sigma f = 20$

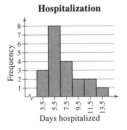

Shape: Positively skewed

© 2006 Pearson Education, Inc., Upper Saddle River, NJ. All rights reserved. This material is protected under all copyright laws as they currently exist. No portion of this material may be reproduced, in any form or by any means, without permission in writing from the publisher.

49. Class width $= \dfrac{\text{Max} - \text{Min}}{\text{Number of classes}} = \dfrac{76 - 62}{5} = 2.8 \Rightarrow 3$

Class	Midpoint, x	Frequency, f
62–64	63	3
65–67	66	7
68–70	69	9
71–73	72	8
74–76	75	3
		$\Sigma f = 30$

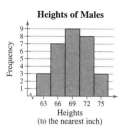

Shape: Symmetric

51. (a) $\bar{x} = \dfrac{\Sigma x}{n} = \dfrac{36.03}{6} = 6.005$

5.59, 5.99, $\underbrace{6,\ 6.02}$, 6.03, 6.4

two middle values $\Rightarrow$ median $= \dfrac{6 + 6.02}{2} = 6.01$

(b) $\bar{x} = \dfrac{\Sigma x}{n} = \dfrac{35.67}{6} = 5.945$

5.59, 5.99, $\underbrace{6,\ 6.02}$, 6.03, 6.4

two middle values $\Rightarrow$ median $= \dfrac{6 + 6.02}{2} = 6.01$

(c) mean

53. (a) Mean should be used since Car A has the highest mean of the three.

(b) Median should be used since Car B has the highest median of the three.

(c) Mode should be used since Car C has the highest mode of the three.

55. (a) $\bar{x} = 49.2\overline{3}$ (b) median = 46.5

(c) Key: 3 | 6 = 36   (d) Positively skewed

```
1 | 1 3
2 | 2 8          ╱median
3 | 6 6 6 7 7 7 8
4 | 1 3 4 6 7
5 | 1 1 1 3      ╲mean
6 | 1 2 3 4
7 | 2 2 4 6
8 | 5
9 | 0
```

57. Two different symbols are needed since they describe a measure of central tendency for two different sets of data (sample is a subset of the population).

© 2006 Pearson Education, Inc., Upper Saddle River, NJ. All rights reserved. This material is protected under all copyright laws as they currently exist. No portion of this material may be reproduced, in any form or by any means, without permission in writing from the publisher.

2.4 Try It Yourself Solutions

1a. Min = 23 or $23,000 and Max = 58 or $58,000

b. Range = max − min = 58 − 23 = 35 or $35,000

c. The range of the starting salaries for Corporation B is 35 or $35,000 (much larger than range of Corporation A).

2a. $\mu = \dfrac{\Sigma x}{N} = \dfrac{415}{10} = 41.5$ or $41,500

b.

Salary, x (1000s of dollars)	Deviation, $x - \mu$ (1000s of dollars)
23	23 − 41.5 = −18.5
29	29 − 41.5 = −12.5
32	32 − 41.5 = −9.5
40	40 − 41.5 = −1.5
41	41 − 41.5 = −0.5
41	41 − 41.5 = −0.5
49	49 − 41.5 = 7.5
50	50 − 41.5 = 8.5
52	52 − 41.5 = 10.5
58	58 − 41.5 = 16.5
$\Sigma x = 415$	$\Sigma(x - \mu) = 0$

3ab. $\mu = 41.5$ or $41,500

Salary, x	$x - \mu$	$(x - \mu)^2$
23	−18.5	$(-18.5)^2 = 342.25$
29	−12.5	$(-12.5)^2 = 156.25$
32	−9.5	$(-9.5)^2 = 90.25$
40	−1.5	$(-1.5)^2 = 2.25$
41	−0.5	$(-0.5)^2 = 0.25$
41	−0.5	$(-0.5)^2 = 0.25$
49	7.5	$(7.5)^2 = 56.25$
50	8.5	$(8.5)^2 = 72.25$
52	10.5	$(10.5)^2 = 110.25$
58	16.5	$(16.5)^2 = 272.25$
$\Sigma x = 415$	$\Sigma(x - \mu) = 0$	$\Sigma(x - \mu)^2 = 1102.5$

c. $\sigma^2 = \dfrac{\Sigma(x - \mu)^2}{N} = \dfrac{1102.5}{10}$

d. $\sigma = \sqrt{\sigma^2} = \sqrt{\dfrac{1102.5}{10}} = 10.5$ or $10,500

e. The population variance is 110.3 and the population standard deviation is 10.5 or $10,500.

© 2006 Pearson Education, Inc., Upper Saddle River, NJ. All rights reserved. This material is protected under all copyright laws as they currently exist. No portion of this material may be reproduced, in any form or by any means, without permission in writing from the publisher.

4a.

Salary, x	$x - \bar{x}$	$(x - \bar{x})^2$
23	-18.5	342.25
29	-12.5	156.25
32	-9.5	90.25
40	-1.5	2.25
41	-0.5	0.25
41	-0.5	0.25
49	7.5	56.25
50	8.5	72.25
52	10.5	110.25
58	16.5	272.25
$\Sigma x = 415$	$\Sigma(x - \bar{x}) = 0$	$\Sigma(x - \bar{x})^2 = 1102.5$

$$SS_x = \Sigma(x - \bar{x})^2 = 1102.5$$

b. $s^2 = \dfrac{\Sigma(x - \bar{x})^2}{(n - 1)} = \dfrac{1102.5}{9} = 122.5$

c. $s = \sqrt{s^2} = \sqrt{122.5} \approx 11.1$ or $\$11,100$

5a. (Enter data in computer or calculator)

b. $\bar{x} = 37.89, \qquad s = 3.98$

6a. $7, 7, 7, 7, 7, 13, 13, 13, 13, 13$

b.

x	$x - \mu$	$(x - \mu)^2$
7	$7 - 10 = -3$	$(-3)^2 = 9$
7	$7 - 10 = -3$	$(-3)^2 = 9$
7	$7 - 10 = -3$	$(-3)^2 = 9$
7	$7 - 10 = -3$	$(-3)^2 = 9$
7	$7 - 10 = -3$	$(-3)^2 = 9$
13	$13 - 10 = 3$	$(3)^2 = 9$
13	$13 - 10 = 3$	$(3)^2 = 9$
13	$13 - 10 = 3$	$(3)^2 = 9$
13	$13 - 10 = 3$	$(3)^2 = 9$
13	$13 - 10 = 3$	$(3)^2 = 9$
$\Sigma x = 100$	$\Sigma(x - \mu) = 0$	$\Sigma(x - \mu)^2 = 90$

$$\mu = \frac{\Sigma x}{N} = \frac{100}{10} = 10$$

$$\sigma = \sqrt{\frac{\Sigma(x - \mu)^2}{N}} = \sqrt{\frac{90}{10}} = \sqrt{9} = 3$$

7a. $64 - 61.25 = 2.75 = 1$ standard deviation

b. 34%

c. The estimated percent of the heights that are between 61.25 and 64 inches is 34%.

8a. $31.6 - 2(19.5) = -7.4 = \; > 0$

b. $31.6 + 2(19.5) = 70.6$

c. $1 - \dfrac{1}{k^2} = 1 - \dfrac{1}{(2)^2} = 1 - \dfrac{1}{4} = 0.75$

At least 75% of the data lie within 2 standard deviations of the mean. At least 75% of the population of Alaska is between 0 and 70.6 years old.

© 2006 Pearson Education, Inc., Upper Saddle River, NJ. All rights reserved. This material is protected under all copyright laws as they currently exist.
No portion of this material may be reproduced, in any form or by any means, without permission in writing from the publisher.

9a.

x	f	xf
0	10	$(0)(10) = 0$
1	19	$(1)(19) = 19$
2	7	$(2)(7) = 14$
3	7	$(3)(7) = 21$
4	5	$(4)(5) = 20$
5	1	$(5)(1) = 5$
6	1	$(6)(1) = 6$
	$n = 50$	$\sum xf = 85$

b. $\bar{x} = \dfrac{\sum xf}{n} = \dfrac{85}{50} = 1.7$

c.

$x - \bar{x}$	$(x - \bar{x})^2$	$(x - \bar{x})^2 \cdot f$
$0 - 1.7 = -1.70$	$(-1.70)^2 = 2.8900$	$(2.8900)(10) = 28.90$
$1 - 1.7 = -0.70$	$(-0.70)^2 = 0.4900$	$(0.4900)(19) = 9.31$
$2 - 1.7 = 0.30$	$(0.30)^2 = 0.0900$	$(0.0900)(7) = 0.63$
$3 - 1.7 = 1.30$	$(1.30)^2 = 1.6900$	$(1.6900)(7) = 11.83$
$4 - 1.7 = 2.30$	$(2.30)^2 = 5.2900$	$(5.2900)(5) = 26.45$
$5 - 1.7 = 3.30$	$(3.30)^2 = 10.9800$	$(10.9800)(1) = 10.89$
$6 - 1.7 = 4.30$	$(4.30)^2 = 18.4900$	$(18.4900)(1) = 18.49$
		$\sum (x - \bar{x})^2 f = 106.5$

d. $s = \sqrt{\dfrac{\sum (x - \bar{x})^2 f}{(n-1)}} = \sqrt{\dfrac{106.5}{49}} = \sqrt{2.17} \approx 1.5$

10a.

Class	x	f	xf
0–99	49.5	380	$(49.5)(380) = 18,810$
100–199	149.5	230	$(149.5)(230) = 34,385$
200–299	249.5	210	$(249.5)(210) = 52,395$
300–399	349.5	50	$(349.5)(50) = 17,475$
400–499	449.5	60	$(449.5)(60) = 26,970$
500+	650.0	70	$(650.0)(70) = 45,500$
		$n = 1000$	$\sum xf = 195,535$

b. $\bar{x} = \dfrac{\sum xf}{n} = \dfrac{195,535}{1000} \approx 195.5$

c.

$x - \bar{x}$	$(x - \bar{x})^2$	$(x - \bar{x})^2 \cdot f$
$49.5 - 195.54 = -146.04$	$(-146.04)^2 = 21,327.68$	$(21,327.68)(380) = 8,104,518.4$
$149.5 - 195.54 = -46.04$	$(-46.04)^2 = 2119.68$	$(2119.68)(230) = 487,526.4$
$249.5 - 195.54 = 53.96$	$(53.96)^2 = 2911.68$	$(2911.68)(210) = 611,452.8$
$349.5 - 195.54 = 153.96$	$(153.96)^2 = 23,703.68$	$(23,703.68)(50) = 1,185,184$
$449.5 - 195.54 = 253.96$	$(253.96)^2 = 64,495.68$	$(64,495.68)(60) = 3,869,740.8$
$650 - 195.54 = 454.96$	$(454.96)^2 = 206,533.89$	$(206,533.89)(70) = 14,457,372.3$
		$\sum (x - \bar{x})^2 f = 28,715,794.7$

d. $s = \sqrt{\dfrac{\sum (x - \bar{x})^2 f}{n-1}} = \sqrt{\dfrac{28,715,794.7}{999}} = \sqrt{28,744.539} \approx 169.5$

© 2006 Pearson Education, Inc., Upper Saddle River, NJ. All rights reserved. This material is protected under all copyright laws as they currently exist. No portion of this material may be reproduced, in any form or by any means, without permission in writing from the publisher.

2.4 EXERCISE SOLUTIONS

1. Range = max − min = 11 − 4 = 7

$$\mu = \frac{\Sigma x}{N} = \frac{81}{10} = 8.1$$

x	$x - \mu$	$(x - \mu)^2$
11	11 − 8.1 = 2.9	$(2.9)^2 = 8.41$
10	10 − 8.1 = 1.9	$(1.9)^2 = 3.61$
8	8 − 8.1 = −0.1	$(-0.1)^2 = 0.01$
4	4 − 8.1 = −4.1	$(-4.1)^2 = 16.81$
6	6 − 8.1 = −2.1	$(-2.1)^2 = 4.41$
7	7 − 8.1 = −1.1	$(-1.1)^2 = 1.21$
11	11 − 8.1 = 2.9	$(2.9)^2 = 8.41$
6	6 − 8.1 = −2.1	$(-2.1)^2 = 4.41$
11	11 − 8.1 = 2.9	$(2.9)^2 = 8.41$
7	7 − 8.1 = −1.1	$(-1.1)^2 = 1.21$
$\Sigma x = 81$	$\Sigma(x - \mu) = 0$	$\Sigma(x - \mu)^2 = 56.9$

$$\sigma^2 = \frac{\Sigma(x - \mu)^2}{N} = \frac{56.9}{10} = 5.69 \approx 5.7$$

$$\sigma = \sqrt{\frac{\Sigma(x - \mu)^2}{N}} = \sqrt{\frac{56.9}{10}} = \sqrt{5.69} \approx 2.4$$

3. Range = max − min = 19 − 5 = 14

$$\bar{x} = \frac{\Sigma x}{n} = \frac{100}{9} \approx 11.1$$

x	$x - \mu$	$(x - \mu)^2$
15	15 − 11.11 = 3.89	$(3.89)^2 = 15.13$
8	8 − 11.11 = −3.11	$(-3.11)^2 = 9.67$
12	12 − 11.11 = 0.89	$(0.89)^2 = 0.79$
5	5 − 11.11 = −6.11	$(-6.11)^2 = 37.33$
19	19 − 11.11 = 7.89	$(7.89)^2 = 62.25$
14	14 − 11.11 = 2.89	$(2.89)^2 = 8.35$
8	8 − 11.11 = −3.11	$(-3.11)^2 = 9.67$
6	6 − 11.11 = −5.11	$(-5.11)^2 = 26.11$
13	13 − 11.11 = 1.89	$(1.89)^2 = 3.57$
$\Sigma x = 100$	$\Sigma(x - \bar{x}) = 0$	$\Sigma(x - \bar{x})^2 = 172.89$

$$s^2 = \frac{\Sigma(x - \bar{x})^2}{n - 1} = \frac{172.89}{8} \approx 21.6$$

$$s = \sqrt{\frac{\Sigma(x - \bar{x})^2}{n - 1}} = \sqrt{\frac{172.89}{8}} \approx 4.6$$

5. Range = max − min = 96 − 23 = 73

7. The range is the difference between the maximum and minimum values of a data set. The advantage of the range is that it is easy to calculate. The disadvantage is that it uses only two entries from the data set.

9. The units of variance are squared. Its units are meaningless. (Ex: dollars^2)

11. (a) Range = max − min = 46.6 − 21.5 = 25.1

   (b) Range = max − min = 66.6 − 21.5 = 45.1

   (c) The range has increased substantially.

© 2006 Pearson Education, Inc., Upper Saddle River, NJ. All rights reserved. This material is protected under all copyright laws as they currently exist. No portion of this material may be reproduced, in any form or by any means, without permission in writing from the publisher.

13. Graph (a) has a standard deviation of 24 and graph (b) has a standard deviation of 16 since graph (a) has more variability.

15. When calculating the population standard deviation, you divide the sum of the squared deviations by n, then take the square root of that value. When calculating the sample standard deviation, you divide the sum of the squared deviations by $n - 1$, then take the square root of that value.

17. Company B. Due to the larger standard deviation in salaries for company B, it would be more likely to be offered a salary of $33,000.

19. (a) LA: range = max − min = 35.9 − 18.3 = 17.6

x	$(x - \bar{x})$	$(x - \bar{x})^2$
20.2	−6.06	36.67
26.1	−0.16	0.02
20.9	−5.36	28.68
32.1	5.84	34.16
35.9	9.64	93.02
23.0	−3.64	10.60
28.2	1.94	3.78
31.6	5.34	28.56
18.3	−7.96	63.29
$\Sigma x = 236.3$		$\Sigma(x - \bar{x})^2 = 298.78$

$$\bar{x} = \frac{\Sigma x}{n} = \frac{236.3}{9} = 26.26$$

$$s^2 = \frac{\Sigma(x - \bar{x})^2}{(n - 1)} = \frac{298.78}{8} \approx 37.35$$

$$s = \sqrt{s^2} \approx 6.11$$

LB: range = max − min = 26.9 − 18.2 = 8.7

x	$(x - \bar{x})$	$(x - \bar{x})^2$
20.9	−1.98	3.91
18.2	−4.68	21.88
20.8	−2.08	4.32
21.1	−1.78	3.16
26.5	3.62	13.12
26.9	4.02	16.18
24.2	1.32	1.75
25.1	2.22	4.94
22.2	−0.68	0.46
$\Sigma x = 205.9$		$\Sigma(x - \bar{x})^2 = 69.72$

$$\bar{x} = \frac{\Sigma x}{n} = \frac{205.9}{9} = 22.88$$

$$s^2 = \frac{\Sigma(x - \bar{x})^2}{(n - 1)} = \frac{69.72}{8} \approx 8.71$$

$$s = \sqrt{s^2} \approx 2.95$$

(b) It appears from the data that the annual salaries in LA are more variable than the salaries in Long Beach.

© 2006 Pearson Education, Inc., Upper Saddle River, NJ. All rights reserved. This material is protected under all copyright laws as they currently exist. No portion of this material may be reproduced, in any form or by any means, without permission in writing from the publisher.

21. (a) M: range = max − min = 1328 − 923 = 405

x	$(x - \bar{x})$	$(x - \bar{x})^2$
1059	−51.13	2,613.77
1328	217.8	47,469.52
1175	64.88	4,208.77
1123	12.88	165.77
923	−187.13	35,015.77
1017	−93.13	8,672.77
1214	103.88	10,790.02
1042	−68.13	4,641.02
$\Sigma x = 8881$		$\Sigma(x - \bar{x})^2 = 113{,}576.88$

$$\bar{x} = \frac{\Sigma x}{n} = \frac{8881}{8} = 1110.13$$

$$s^2 = \frac{\Sigma(x - \bar{x})^2}{(n - 1)} = \frac{113{,}576.9}{7} \approx 16{,}225.3$$

$$s = \sqrt{s^2} \approx 127.4$$

F: range = max − min = 1393 − 841 = 552

x	$(x - \bar{x})$	$(x - \bar{x})^2$
1226	92.50	8,556.25
965	−168.50	28,392.25
841	−292.50	85,556.25
1053	−80.50	6,480.25
1056	−77.50	6,006.25
1393	259.50	67,340.25
1312	178.50	31,862.25
1222	88.50	7,832.25
$\Sigma x = 9068$		$\Sigma(x - \bar{x})^2 = 242{,}026.00$

$$\bar{x} = \frac{\Sigma x}{n} = \frac{9068}{8} = 1133.50$$

$$s^2 = \frac{\Sigma(x - \bar{x})^2}{(n - 1)} = \frac{242{,}026}{7} \approx 34{,}575.1$$

$$s = \sqrt{s^2} \approx 185.9$$

(b) It appears from the data, the SAT scores for females are more variable than the SAT scores for males.

23. (a) Greatest sample standard deviation: (ii)

Data set (ii) has more entries that are farther away from the mean.

Least same standard deviation: (iii)

Data set (iii) has more entries that are close to the mean.

(b) The three data sets have the same mean, but have different standard deviations.

25. (a) Greatest sample standard deviation: (ii)

Data set (ii) has more entries that are farther away from the mean.

Least sample standard deviation: (iii)

Data set (iii) has more entries that are close to the mean.

(b) The three data sets have the same mean, median, and mode, but have different standard deviations.

© 2006 Pearson Education, Inc., Upper Saddle River, NJ. All rights reserved. This material is protected under all copyright laws as they currently exist. No portion of this material may be reproduced, in any form or by any means, without permission in writing from the publisher.

27. Similarity: Both estimate proportions of the data contained within k standard deviations of the mean.

Difference: The Empirical Rule assumes the distribution is bell shaped, Chebychev's Theorem makes no such assumption.

29. $(800, 1200) \rightarrow (1000 - 1(200), 1000 + 1(200)) \rightarrow (\bar{x} - s, \bar{x} + s) \rightarrow (\bar{x}, \bar{x} + 2s)$

68% of the farms value between $800 and $1200 per acre.

31. (a) $n = 75$

$68\%(75) = (0.68)(75) = 51$ farm values will be between $800 and $1200 per acre.

(b) $n = 25$

$68\%(25) = (0.68)(25) = 17$ of these farm values will be between $800 and $1200 per acre.

33. $\bar{x} = 1000$ $\{1250, 1375, 1450, 550\}$ are outliers. They are more than 2 standard deviations from the mean (800, 1200).

$s = 200$

35. $(\bar{x} - 2s, \bar{x} + 2s) \rightarrow (1.14, 5.5)$ are 2 standard deviations from the mean.

$1 - \dfrac{1}{k^2} = 1 - \dfrac{1}{(2)^2} = 1 - \dfrac{1}{4} = 0.75 \Rightarrow$ At least 75% of the eruption times lie between 1.14 and 5.5 minutes.

If $n = 32$, at least $(0.75)(32) = 24$ eruptions will lie between 1.14 and 5.5 minutes.

37.

x	f	xf	$x - \bar{x}$	$(x - \bar{x})^2$	$(x - \bar{x})^2 f$
0	5	0	−2.08	4.31	21.53
1	11	11	−1.08	1.16	12.71
2	7	14	−0.08	0.01	0.04
3	10	30	0.93	0.86	8.56
4	7	28	1.93	3.71	25.94
	$n = 40$	$\sum xf = 83$			$\sum (x - \bar{x})^2 f = 68.78$

$\bar{x} = \dfrac{\sum x}{n} = \dfrac{83}{40} \approx 2.1$

$s = \sqrt{\dfrac{\sum (x - \bar{x})^2 f}{n - 1}} = \sqrt{\dfrac{68.78}{39}} = \sqrt{1.76} \approx 1.3$

39. Class width $= \dfrac{\text{Max} - \text{Min}}{5} = \dfrac{14 - 4}{5} = \dfrac{10}{5} = 2$

Class	Midpoint, x	f	xf
4–5	4.5	10	40.5
6–7	6.5	6	39
8–9	8.5	3	25.5
10–11	10.5	7	73.5
12–14	13.0	6	78
		$N = 32$	$\sum xf = 261$

$\mu = \dfrac{\sum xf}{N} = \dfrac{261}{32} \approx 8.2$

© 2006 Pearson Education, Inc., Upper Saddle River, NJ. All rights reserved. This material is protected under all copyright laws as they currently exist. No portion of this material may be reproduced, in any form or by any means, without permission in writing from the publisher.

$x - \mu$	$(x - \mu)^2$	$(x - \mu)^2 f$
-3.7	13.69	136.90
-1.7	2.89	17.34
0.3	0.09	0.27
2.3	5.29	37.03
4.8	23.04	138.24
		$\sum(x - \mu)^2 f = 329.78$

$$\sigma = \sqrt{\frac{\Sigma(x - \mu)^2}{N}} = \sqrt{\frac{329.78}{32}} \approx 3.2$$

41.

x	f	xf
70.5	1	70.5
92.5	12	1110
114.5	25	2862.5
136.5	10	1365
158.5	2	317
	$n = 50$	$\Sigma xf = 5725$

$$\bar{x} = \frac{\Sigma xf}{n} = \frac{5725}{50} = 114.5$$

$x - \bar{x}$	$(x - \bar{x})^2$	$(x - \bar{x})^2 f$
-44	1936	1936
-22	484	5808
0	0	0
22	484	4840
44	1936	3872
		$\Sigma(x - \bar{x})^2 f = 16{,}456$

$$s = \sqrt{\frac{\Sigma(x - \bar{x})^2}{n - 1}} = \sqrt{\frac{16{,}456}{49}} = \sqrt{335.83} \approx 18.33$$

43.

Class	Midpoint, x	f	xf
0–4	2	19.9	39.8
5–13	9	35.2	316.8
14–17	15.5	16.9	261.95
18–24	21	29.8	625.8
25–34	29.5	38.3	1129.85
35–44	39.5	40.0	1580.00
45–64	54.5	78.3	4267.35
65+	70	39.0	2730
		$n = 297.4$	$\Sigma xf = 10{,}951.55$

$$\bar{x} = \frac{\Sigma xf}{n} = \frac{10{,}951.55}{297.4} \approx 36.82$$

© 2006 Pearson Education, Inc., Upper Saddle River, NJ. All rights reserved. This material is protected under all copyright laws as they currently exist. No portion of this material may be reproduced, in any form or by any means, without permission in writing from the publisher.

$x - \bar{x}$	$(x - \bar{x})^2$	$(x - \bar{x})^2 f$
-34.82	1212.43	24,127.36
-27.82	773.95	27,243.04
-21.32	454.54	7,681.73
-15.82	250.27	7,458.05
-7.32	53.58	2,052.11
2.68	7.18	287.20
17.68	312.58	24,475.01
33.18	1100.91	42,935.49
		$\sum(x - \bar{x})^2 f = 136,259.99$

$$s = \sqrt{\frac{\sum(x - \bar{x})^2}{n - 1}} = \sqrt{\frac{136,259.99}{296.4}} = \sqrt{459.72} \approx 21.44$$

45. $CV_{\text{heights}} = \dfrac{\sigma}{\mu} \cdot 100\% = \dfrac{3.44}{72.75} \cdot 100 \approx 4.73$

$CV_{\text{weights}} = \dfrac{\sigma}{\mu} \cdot 100\% = \dfrac{18.47}{187.83} \cdot 100 \approx 9.83$

It appears that weight is more variable than height.

47. (a) $\bar{x} = 550$ $s \approx 302.8$

(b) $\bar{x} = 5500$ $s \approx 3028$

(c) $\bar{x} = 55$ $s \approx 30.28$

(d) By multiplying each entry by a constant k, the new sample mean is $k \cdot \bar{x}$ and the new sample standard deviation is $k \cdot s$.

49. $1 - \dfrac{1}{k^2} = 0.99 \Rightarrow 1 - 0.99 = \dfrac{1}{k^2} \Rightarrow k^2 = \dfrac{1}{0.01} \Rightarrow k = \sqrt{\dfrac{1}{0.01}} = 10$

At least 99% of the data in any data set lie within 10 standard deviations of the mean.

2.5   MEASURES OF POSITION

2.5 Try It Yourself Solutions

1a. 0, 0, 1, 1, 1, 2, 3, 3, 3, 4, 5, 5, 5, 7, 9, 10, 12, 12, 13, 13, 13, 13, 13, 15, 16, 16, 17, 17, 18, 18, 18, 19, 19, 19, 20, 20, 21, 22, 23, 23, 24, 24, 25, 25, 26, 26, 26, 29, 33, 36, 37, 39, 39, 39, 40, 40, 41, 41, 41, 42, 44, 44, 45, 47, 48, 49, 49, 49, 51, 53, 56, 58, 58, 59, 60, 67, 68, 68, 72

b. $Q_2 = 23.5$

c. $Q_1 = 13$ $Q_3 = 41.5$

2a. (Enter the data)

b. $Q_1 = 17$ $Q_2 = 23$ $Q_3 = 28.5$

c. One quarter of the tuition costs is $17,000 or less, one half is $23,000 or less, and three quarters is $28,500 or less.

3a. $Q_1 = 13$ $Q_3 = 41.5$

b. $IQR = Q_3 - Q_1 = 41.5 - 13 = 28.5$

c. The ages in the middle half of the data set vary by 28.5 years.

© 2006 Pearson Education, Inc., Upper Saddle River, NJ. All rights reserved. This material is protected under all copyright laws as they currently exist. No portion of this material may be reproduced, in any form or by any means, without permission in writing from the publisher.

4a. Min = 0 $Q_1 = 13$ $Q_2 = 23.5$

$Q_3 = 41.5$ Max = 72

bc.   **Ages of Akhiok Residents**

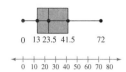

0   13 23.5 41.5   72

0 10 20 30 40 50 60 70 80

d. It appears that half of the ages are between 13 and 41.5 years.

5a. 80th percentile

b. 80% of the ages are 45 years or younger.

6a. $\mu = 70$, $\sigma = 8$

b. $x = 60$: $z = \dfrac{x - \mu}{\sigma} = \dfrac{60 - 70}{8} = -1.25$

$x = 71$: $z = \dfrac{x - \mu}{\sigma} = \dfrac{71 - 70}{8} = 0.125$

$x = 92$: $z = \dfrac{x - \mu}{\sigma} = \dfrac{92 - 70}{8} = 2.75$

c. From the z-score, the utility bill of $60 is 1.25 standard deviations below the mean, the bill of $71 is 0.125 standard deviations above the mean, and the bill of $92 is 2.75 standard deviations above the mean.

7a. NFL: $\mu = 23.6$, $\alpha = 6.0$

AFL: $\mu = 11.7$, $\sigma = 4.6$

b. Kansas City (NFL): $x = 16 \Rightarrow z = \dfrac{x - \mu}{\sigma} = \dfrac{16 - 23.6}{6.0} = -1.27$

Tampa Bay (AFL): $x = 12 \Rightarrow z = \dfrac{x - \mu}{\sigma} = \dfrac{12 - 11.7}{4.6} = 0.07$

c. The number of field goals scored by Kansas City is 1.27 standard deviations below the mean and the number of field goals scored by Tampa Bay is 0.07 standard deviations above the mean. Comparing the two measures of position indicates Tampa Bay has a higher position within the AFL than Kansas City in the NFL.

2.5 EXERCISE SOLUTIONS

1. (a)

lower half   upper half

1 2 2 4 4 5 5 5 6 6 6 7 7 7 7 8 8 8 9 9

↑   ↑   ↑

Q_1 Q_2 Q_3

$Q_1 = 4.5$ $Q_2 = 6$ $Q_3 = 7.5$

© 2006 Pearson Education, Inc., Upper Saddle River, NJ. All rights reserved. This material is protected under all copyright laws as they currently exist.
No portion of this material may be reproduced, in any form or by any means, without permission in writing from the publisher.

(b)

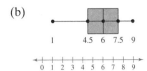

1   4.5 6 7.5 9

0 1 2 3 4 5 6 7 8 9

3. The basketball team scored more points per game than 75% of the teams in the league.

5. The student scored above 63% of the students who took the ACT placement test.

7. True

9. False. The 50th percentile is equivalent to Q_2.

11. (a) Min = 10   (b) Max = 20

     (c) $Q_1 = 13$ (d) $Q_2 = 15$

     (e) $Q_3 = 17$ (f) IQR = $Q_3 - Q_1 = 17 - 13 = 4$

13. (a) Min = 900   (b) Max = 2100

     (c) $Q_1 = 1250$ (d) $Q_2 = 1500$

     (e) $Q_3 = 1950$ (f) IQR = $Q_3 - Q_1 = 1950 - 1250 = 700$

15. (a) Min = -1.9 (b) Max = 2.1

     (c) $Q_1 = -0.5$ (d) $Q_2 = 0.1$

     (e) $Q_3 = 0.7$ (f) IQR = $Q_3 - Q_1 = 0.7 - (-0.5) = 1.2$

17. $Q_1 = B$, $Q_2 = A$, $Q_3 = C$

     25% of the entries are below B, 50% are below A, and 75% are below C.

19. (a) $Q_1 = 2$, $Q_2 = 4$, $Q_3 = 5$

     (b)   **Watching Television**

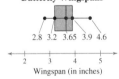

0   2   4 5   9

0 1 2 3 4 5 6 7 8 9

Hours

21. (a) $Q_1 = 3.2$, $Q_2 = 3.65$, $Q_3 = 3.9$

     (b)   **Butterfly Wingspans**

2.8 3.2 3.65 3.9 4.6

2   3   4   5

Wingspan (in inches)

23. (a) 5   (b) 50%   (c) 25%

25. $A \Rightarrow z = -1.43$

     $B \Rightarrow z = 0$

     $C \Rightarrow z = 2.14$

     The score 2.14 is unusual because it is so large.

© 2006 Pearson Education, Inc., Upper Saddle River, NJ. All rights reserved. This material is protected under all copyright laws as they currently exist. No portion of this material may be reproduced, in any form or by any means, without permission in writing from the publisher.

27. (a) Statistics:

$$x = 73 \Rightarrow z = \frac{x - \mu}{\sigma} = \frac{73 - 63}{7} \approx 1.43$$

(b) Biology:

$$x = 26 \Rightarrow z = \frac{x - \mu}{\sigma} = \frac{26 - 23}{3.9} \approx 0.77$$

(c) The student had a better score on the statistics test.

29. (a) Statistics:

$$x = 78 \Rightarrow z = \frac{x - \mu}{\sigma} = \frac{78 - 63}{7} \approx 2.14$$

(b) Biology:

$$x = 29 \Rightarrow z = \frac{x - \mu}{\sigma} = \frac{29 - 23}{3.9} \approx 1.54$$

(c) The student had a better score on the statistics test.

31. (a) $x = 34{,}000 \Rightarrow z = \frac{x - \mu}{\sigma} = \frac{34{,}000 - 35{,}000}{2{,}250} \approx -0.44$

$x = 37{,}000 \Rightarrow z = \frac{x - \mu}{\sigma} = \frac{37{,}000 - 35{,}000}{2{,}250} \approx 0.89$

$x = 31{,}000 \Rightarrow z = \frac{x - \mu}{\sigma} = \frac{31{,}000 - 35{,}000}{2{,}250} \approx -1.78$

None of the selected tires have unusual life spans.

(b) $x = 30{,}500 \Rightarrow z = \frac{x - \mu}{\sigma} = \frac{30{,}500 - 35{,}000}{2{,}250} = -2 \Rightarrow 2.5\text{th percentile}$

$x = 37{,}250 \Rightarrow z = \frac{x - \mu}{\sigma} = \frac{37{,}250 - 35{,}000}{2{,}250} = 1 \Rightarrow 84\text{th percentile}$

$x = 35{,}000 \Rightarrow z = \frac{x - \mu}{\sigma} = \frac{35{,}000 - 35{,}000}{2{,}250} = 0 \Rightarrow 50\text{th percentile}$

33. 67 inches

20% of the heights are below 67 inches.

35. $x = 74$: $z = \frac{x - \mu}{\sigma} = \frac{74 - 69.2}{2.9} \approx 1.66$

$x = 62$: $z = \frac{x - \mu}{\sigma} = \frac{62 - 69.2}{2.9} \approx -2.48$

$x = 80$: $z = \frac{x - \mu}{\sigma} = \frac{80 - 69.2}{2.9} \approx 3.72$

The height of 62 inches is unusual due to a rather small z-score. The height of 80 inches is very unusual due to a rather large z-score.

37. $x = 71.1$: $z = \frac{x - \mu}{\sigma} = \frac{71.1 - 69.2}{2.9} \approx 0.66$

Approximately the 70th percentile.

© 2006 Pearson Education, Inc., Upper Saddle River, NJ. All rights reserved. This material is protected under all copyright laws as they currently exist. No portion of this material may be reproduced, in any form or by any means, without permission in writing from the publisher.

39. (a)
```
27  28  31  32  32  33  35  36  36  36  36  37  38  39  39  40  40  40  41  41
   41  42  42  42  42  42  42  43  43  43  44  44  45  45  46  47  47  47  47  47
   48  48  48  48  48 |49  49  49  49  49  49  50  50  51  51  51  51  51  51  52
   52  52  53  53  54 |54  54  54  54  54 |54  54  55  56  56  56  57  57  57  59
   59  59  60  60  60 |61  61  61  62  62 |63  63  63  63  64 |65  67  68  74  82
              $Q_1$              $Q_2$              $Q_3$
```

$Q_1 = 42, \qquad Q_2 = 49, \qquad Q_3 = 56$

(b)   **Ages of Executives**

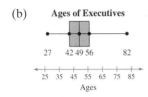

(c) Half of the ages are between 42 and 56 years.

(d) About 49 years old ($x = 49.62$ and $Q_2 = 49.00$), since half of the executives are older and half are younger.

41. 22   23   24   32   33   34   36   38   39   40   41   47

$Q_1 = 28 \qquad Q_2 \qquad Q_3 = 39.5$

$\text{Midquartile} = \dfrac{Q_1 + Q_3}{2} = \dfrac{28 + 39.5}{2} = 33.75$

43. 13.4 15.2 15.6 16.7 17.2 18.7 19.7 19.8 19.8 20.8 21.4 22.9 28.7 30.1 31.9

$Q_1 \qquad\qquad Q_2 \qquad\qquad Q_3$

$\text{Midquartile} = \dfrac{Q_1 + Q_3}{2} = \dfrac{16.7 + 22.9}{2} = 19.8$

CHAPTER 2 REVIEW EXERCISE SOLUTIONS

1.

Class	Midpoint	Boundaries	Frequency	Relative frequency	Cumulative frequency
20–23	21.5	19.5–23.5	1	0.05	1
24–27	25.5	23.5–27.5	2	0.10	3
28–31	29.5	27.5–31.5	6	0.30	9
32–35	33.5	31.5–35.5	7	0.35	16
36–39	37.5	35.5–39.5	4	0.20	20
			$\Sigma f = 20$	$\Sigma \dfrac{f}{n} = 1$	

© 2006 Pearson Education, Inc., Upper Saddle River, NJ. All rights reserved. This material is protected under all copyright laws as they currently exist. No portion of this material may be reproduced, in any form or by any means, without permission in writing from the publisher.

3.

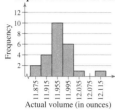

Liquid Volume 12-oz Cans

5.

Class	Midpoint, x	Frequency	Cumulative frequency
79–93	86	9	9
94–108	101	12	21
109–123	116	5	26
124–138	131	3	29
139–153	146	2	31
154–168	161	1	32
		$\Sigma f = 32$	

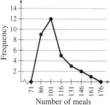

Meals Purchased

7.
```
1 | 3 7 8 9
2 | 0 1 2 3 3 3 4 4 5 5 5 7 8 8 9
3 | 1 1 2 3 4 5 7 8
4 | 3 4 7
5 | 1
```

9.

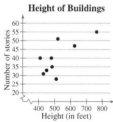

Height of Buildings

It appears as height increases, the number of stories increases.

11.

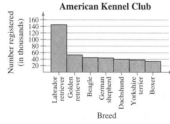

American Kennel Club

13. $\bar{x} = 8.6$

median $= 9$

mode $= 9$

© 2006 Pearson Education, Inc., Upper Saddle River, NJ. All rights reserved. This material is protected under all copyright laws as they currently exist. No portion of this material may be reproduced, in any form or by any means, without permission in writing from the publisher.

15.

Midpoint, x	Frequency, f	xf
21.5	1	21.5
25.5	2	51.0
29.5	6	177.0
33.5	7	234.5
37.5	4	150.0
	$n = 20$	$\Sigma xf = 634$

$$\bar{x} = \frac{\Sigma xf}{n} = \frac{634}{20} = 31.7$$

17. $\bar{x} = \dfrac{\Sigma xw}{w} = \dfrac{(65)(0.15) + (72)(0.15) + (84)(0.15) + (89)(0.15) + (70)(0.15) + (90)(0.25)}{0.15 + 0.15 + 0.15 + 0.15 + 0.15 + 0.25}$

$$= \frac{79.5}{1} = 79.5$$

19. Skewed　　**21.** Skewed left　　**23.** Median

25. Range = max − min = 8.26 − 5.46 = 2.8

27. $\mu = \dfrac{\Sigma x}{N} = \dfrac{108}{12} = 9$

$$\sigma = \sqrt{\frac{\Sigma(x - \mu)^2}{N}} = \sqrt{\frac{(6 - 9)^2 + (14 - 9)^2 + \cdots + (12 - 9)^2 + (10 - 9)^2}{12}}$$

$$= \sqrt{\frac{122}{12}} \approx \sqrt{10.17} \approx 3.2$$

29. $\bar{x} = \dfrac{\Sigma x}{n} = \dfrac{36,801}{15} = 2453.4$

$$s = \sqrt{\frac{\Sigma(x - \bar{x})^2}{n - 1}} = \sqrt{\frac{(2445 - 2453.4)^2 + \cdots + (2.377 - 2453.4)^2}{14}}$$

$$= \sqrt{\frac{1,311,783.6}{14}} \approx \sqrt{93,698.8} \approx 306.1$$

31. 99.7% of the distribution lies within 3 standard deviations of the mean.

$\mu + 3\sigma = 29 + (3)(2.50) = 36.5$

$\mu - 3\sigma = 29 - (3)(2.50) = 21.5$

99.7% of the distribution lies between $21.50 and $36.50.

33. $n = 40$　　　$\mu = 23$　　　$\sigma = 6$

$(11, 35) \rightarrow (23 - 2(6), 23 + 2(6)) \Rightarrow (\mu - 2\sigma, \mu + 2\sigma) \Rightarrow k = 2$

$1 = \dfrac{1}{k^2} = 1 - \dfrac{1}{(2)^2} = 1 - \dfrac{1}{4} = 0.75$

At least $(40)(0.75) = 30$ customers have a mean sale between $11 and $35.

© 2006 Pearson Education, Inc., Upper Saddle River, NJ. All rights reserved. This material is protected under all copyright laws as they currently exist. No portion of this material may be reproduced, in any form or by any means, without permission in writing from the publisher.

35. $\bar{x} = \dfrac{\Sigma xf}{n} = \dfrac{99}{40} \approx 2.5$

$s = \sqrt{\dfrac{\Sigma (x - \bar{x})^2 f}{n - 1}} = \sqrt{\dfrac{(0 - 1.24)^2(1) + (1 - 1.24)^2(8) + \cdots + (5 - 1.24)^2(3)}{39}}$

$\quad = \sqrt{\dfrac{59.975}{39}} \approx 1.2$

37. $Q_1 = 56$

39. $\text{IQR} = Q_3 - Q_1 = 70 - 56 = 14$

41. $\text{IQR} = Q_3 - Q_1 = 33 - 29 = 4$

43. 23% of the students scored higher than 68.

45. $x = 248 \Longrightarrow z = \dfrac{x - \mu}{\sigma} = \dfrac{248 - 192}{24} \approx 2.33$

This is an unusually heavy player.

47. $x = 222 \Longrightarrow z = \dfrac{x - \mu}{\sigma} = \dfrac{222 - 192}{24} = 1.25$

This player is not unusual.

CHAPTER 2 QUIZ SOLUTIONS

1. (a)

Class limits	Midpoint	Class boundaries	Frequency	Relative frequency	Cumulative frequency
101–112	106.5	100.5–112.5	3	0.12	3
113–124	118.5	112.5–124.5	11	0.44	14
125–136	130.5	124.5–136.5	7	0.28	21
137–148	142.5	136.5–148.5	2	0.08	23
149–160	154.5	148.5–160.5	2	0.08	25

(b) Frequency Histogram and Polygon   (c) Relative Frequency Histogram

(d) Skewed

(e)

(f)

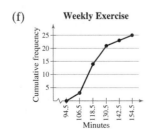

© 2006 Pearson Education, Inc., Upper Saddle River, NJ. All rights reserved. This material is protected under all copyright laws as they currently exist. No portion of this material may be reproduced, in any form or by any means, without permission in writing from the publisher.

2. $\bar{x} = \dfrac{\Sigma xf}{n} = \dfrac{3130.5}{25} \approx 125.22$

$s = \sqrt{\dfrac{\Sigma(x - \bar{x})^2 f}{n - 1}} = \sqrt{\dfrac{4055.04}{24}} \approx 13.00$

3. (a)

U.S. Sporting Goods

Footwear 18%

Recreational transport 41%

Clothing 13%

Equipment 28%

(b)

U.S. Sporting Goods

4. (a) $\bar{x} = \dfrac{\Sigma x}{n} = 751.6$

median = 784.5

mode = (none)

The mean best describes a typical salary because there are no outliers.

(b) range = max − min = 575

$s^2 = \dfrac{\Sigma(x - \bar{x})^2}{n - 1} = 48{,}135.1$

$s = \sqrt{\dfrac{\Sigma(x - \bar{x})^2}{n - 1}} = 219.4$

5. $\bar{x} - 2s = 155{,}000 - 2 \cdot 15{,}000 = \$125{,}000$

$\bar{x} + 2s = 155{,}000 + 2 \cdot 15{,}000 = \$185{,}000$

95% of the new home prices fall between $125,000 and $185,000.

6. (a) $x = 200{,}000 \qquad z = \dfrac{x - \mu}{\sigma} = \dfrac{200{,}000 - 155{,}000}{15{,}000} = 3 \Longrightarrow$ unusual price

(b) $x = 55{,}000 \qquad z = \dfrac{x - \mu}{\sigma} = \dfrac{55{,}000 - 155{,}000}{15{,}000} \approx -6.67 \Longrightarrow$ very unusual price

(c) $x = 175{,}000 \qquad z = \dfrac{x - \mu}{\sigma} = \dfrac{175{,}000 - 155{,}000}{15{,}000} \approx 1.33 \Longrightarrow$ not unusual

(d) $x = 122{,}000 \qquad z = \dfrac{x - \mu}{\sigma} = \dfrac{122{,}000 - 155{,}000}{15{,}000} = -2.2 \Longrightarrow$ unusual price

7. (a) $Q_1 = 71 \qquad Q_2 = 84.5 \qquad Q_3 = 90$

(b) IQR $= Q_3 - Q_1 = 90 - 71 = 19$

(c)   **Wins for Each Team**

43   71 84.5 90 101

40 50 60 70 80 90 100
Number of wins

© 2006 Pearson Education, Inc., Upper Saddle River, NJ. All rights reserved. This material is protected under all copyright laws as they currently exist.
No portion of this material may be reproduced, in any form or by any means, without permission in writing from the publisher.

Probability

3.1 BASIC CONCEPTS OF PROBABILITY

3.1 Try It Yourself Solutions

1ab. (1) 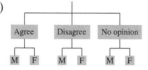 (2)

  c. (1) 6 outcomes   (2) 9 outcomes

  d. (1) Let A = Agree, D = Disagree, N = No Opinion, M = Male and F = Female
        Sample space = {AM, AF, DM, DF, NM, NF}

     (2) Let A = Agree, D = Disagree, N = No Opinion, R = Republican, De = Democrat,
        O = Other
        Sample space = {AR, ADe, AO, DR, DDe, DO, NR, NDe, NO}

2a. (1) 6 outcomes   (2) 1 outcome

  b. (1) Not a simple event   (2) Simple event

3a. (1) 52   (2) 1   (3) $P(\text{7 of diamonds}) = \dfrac{1}{52} \approx 0.0192$

  b. (1) 52   (2) 13   (3) $P(\text{diamond}) = \dfrac{13}{52} = 0.25$

  c. (1) 52   (2) 52   (3) $P(\text{diamond, heart, club, or spade}) = \dfrac{52}{52} = 1$

4a. Event = the next claim processed is fraudulent (Freq = 4)

  b. Total Frequency = 100

  c. $P(\text{fraudulent claim}) = \dfrac{4}{100} = 0.04$

5a. Frequency = 54

  b. Total of the Frequencies = 1000

  c. $P(\text{age 15 to 24}) = \dfrac{54}{1000} = 0.054$

6a. Event = salmon successfully passing through a dam on the Columbia River.

  b. Estimated from the results of an experiment.

  c. Empirical probability

7a. $P(\text{red gill}) = \dfrac{17}{40} = 0.425$

  b. $P(\text{not red gill}) = 1 - \dfrac{17}{40} = \dfrac{23}{40} = 0.575$

  c. $\dfrac{23}{40}$ or 0.575

© 2006 Pearson Education, Inc., Upper Saddle River, NJ. All rights reserved. This material is protected under all copyright laws as they currently exist.
No portion of this material may be reproduced, in any form or by any means, without permission in writing from the publisher.

3.1 EXERCISE SOLUTIONS

1. (a) Yes, the probability of an event occurring must be contained in the interval $[0, 1]$ or $[0\%, 100\%]$.

   (b) No, the probability of an event occurring cannot be greater than 1.

   (c) No, the probability of an event occurring cannot be less than 0.

   (d) Yes, the probability of an event occurring must be contained in the interval $[0, 1]$ or $[0\%, 100\%]$.

   (e) Yes, the probability of an event occurring must be contained in the interval $[0, 1]$ or $[0\%, 100\%]$.

3. $\{0, 1, 2, 3, 4, 5, 6, 7, 8, 9\}$

5. $\{(P, A), (P, B), (P, AB), (P, O), (N, A), (N, B), (N, AB), (N, O)\}$ where (P, A) represents positive Rh-factor with A- blood type and (N, A) represents negative Rh-factor with A- blood type.

7. Simple event because it is an event that consists of a single outcome.

9. Not a simple event because it is an event that consists of more than a single outcome.

   king = {king of hearts, king of spades, king of clubs, king of diamonds}

11. Empirical probability since company records were probably used to calculate the frequency of a washing machine breaking down.

13. $P(\text{less than } 1000) = \dfrac{999}{6296} \approx 0.159$

15. $P(\text{number divisible by } 1000) = \dfrac{6}{6296} \approx 0.000953$

17. $P(\text{voted in 2002 Gubernatorial election}) = \dfrac{3,219,864}{6,797,293} \approx 0.474$

19. $P(\text{between 21 and 24}) = \dfrac{7.3}{129.5} \approx 0.056$

21. $P(\text{not between 18 and 20}) = 1 - \dfrac{4.8}{129.5} \approx 1 - 0.037 \approx 0.963$

23. $P(\text{Phd}) = \dfrac{8}{89} \approx 0.090$

25. $P(\text{master's}) = \dfrac{21}{89} \approx 0.236$

27. (a) $P(\text{pink}) = \dfrac{2}{4} = 0.5$ (b) $P(\text{red}) = \dfrac{1}{4} = 0.25$ (c) $P(\text{white}) = \dfrac{1}{4} = 0.25$

29. $P(\text{service industry}) = \dfrac{102,811}{135,073} \approx 0.761$

31. $P(\text{not in service industry}) = 1 - P(\text{service industry}) = 1 - 0.761 = 0.239$

© 2006 Pearson Education, Inc., Upper Saddle River, NJ. All rights reserved. This material is protected under all copyright laws as they currently exist.
No portion of this material may be reproduced, in any form or by any means, without permission in writing from the publisher.

33. The probability of choosing a tea drinker who does not have a college degree.

35. (a) $P(\text{at least } 21) = \frac{44}{80} \approx 0.55$ (b) $P(\text{between 40 and 50 inclusive}) = \frac{14}{80} \approx 0.175$

(c) $P(\text{older than } 65) = \frac{4}{80} = 0.05$

37. (a)

Sum	P(sum)	Probability
2	1/36	0.028
3	2/36	0.056
4	3/36	0.083
5	4/36	0.111
6	5/36	0.139
7	6/36	0.167
8	5/36	0.139
9	4/36	0.111
10	3/36	0.083
11	2/36	0.056
12	1/36	0.028

(b) Answers will vary.

(c) The answers in part (a) and (b) will be similar.

39. Let S = Sunny Day and R = Rainy Day

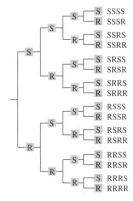

41. No, the odds of winning a prize are 1:6. (One winning cap and 6 losing caps) Thus, the statement should read, "one in seven game pieces win a prize."

43. $13:39 = 1:3$

3.2 CONDITIONAL PROBABILITY AND THE MULTIPLICATION RULE

3.2 Try It Yourself Solutions

1a. (1) 30 and 102   (2) 11 and 50

b. (1) $P(\text{not have gene}) = \frac{30}{102} \approx 0.294$ (2) $P(\text{not have gene}|\text{normal IQ}) = \frac{11}{50} = 0.22$

2a. (1) No   (2) Yes

b. (1) Independent   (2) Dependent

© 2006 Pearson Education, Inc., Upper Saddle River, NJ. All rights reserved. This material is protected under all copyright laws as they currently exist. No portion of this material may be reproduced, in any form or by any means, without permission in writing from the publisher.

3a. (1) Independent   (2) Dependent

b. (1) Let A = {swimming through 1st dam}

   B = {swimming through 2nd dam}

   $P(A \text{ and } B) = P(A) \cdot P(B|A) = (0.85) \cdot (0.85) = 0.723$

   (2) Let A = {selecting a heart}

   B = {selecting a second heart}

   $P(A \text{ and } B) = P(A) \cdot P(B|A) = \left(\dfrac{13}{52}\right) \cdot \left(\dfrac{12}{51}\right) \approx 0.059$

4a. (1) Find probability of the event   (2) Find probability of the complement of the event

b. (1) $P(3 \text{ salmon successful}) = (0.90) \cdot (0.90) \cdot (0.90) = 0.729$

   (2) $P(\text{at least one salmon successful}) = 1 - P(\text{none are successful})$

   $$= 1 - (0.10) \cdot (0.10) \cdot (0.10) = 0.999$$

3.2 EXERCISE SOLUTIONS

1. Two events are independent if the occurrence of one of the events does not affect the probability of the occurrence of the other event.

   If $P(B|A) = P(B)$ or $P(A|B) = P(A)$, then Events A and B are independent.

3. False. If two events are independent, $P(A|B) = P(A)$.

5. These events are independent since the outcome of the 1st card drawn does not affect the outcome of the 2nd card drawn.

7. These events are dependent since the outcome of the 1st ball drawn affects the outcome of the 2nd ball drawn.

9. Let A = {have mutated BRCA gene} and B = {develop breast cancer}. Thus

   $P(B) = \dfrac{1}{8}$, $P(A) = \dfrac{1}{250}$, and $P(B|A) = \dfrac{8}{10}$.

   (a) $P(B|A) = \dfrac{8}{10} = 0.8$

   (b) $P(A \text{ and } B) = P(A) \cdot P(B|A) = \left(\dfrac{1}{250}\right) \cdot \left(\dfrac{8}{10}\right) = 0.0032$

   (c) Dependent since $P(B|A) \neq P(B)$.

11. Let A = {own a computer} and B = {summer vacation this year}.

   (a) $P(B|A) = \dfrac{46}{57} \approx 0.807$ (b) $P(A \text{ and } B) = P(A)P(B|A) = \left(\dfrac{57}{146}\right)\left(\dfrac{46}{57}\right) = 0.315$

   (c) Dependent, since $P(B|A) \neq P(B)$. The probability that the family takes a summer vacation depends on whether or not they own a computer.

© 2006 Pearson Education, Inc., Upper Saddle River, NJ. All rights reserved. This material is protected under all copyright laws as they currently exist.
No portion of this material may be reproduced, in any form or by any means, without permission in writing from the publisher.

13. Let A = {pregnant} and B = {multiple births}. Thus $P(A) = 0.24$ and $P(B|A) = 0.07$.

    (a) $P(A \text{ and } B) = P(A) \cdot P(B|A) = (0.24) \cdot (0.07) = 0.0168$

    (b) $P(B'|A) = 1 - P(B|A) = 1 - 0.07 = 0.93$

    (c) It is not unusual since the probability of a pregnancy and multiple births is 0.0168.

15. Let A = {household in U.S. has a computer} and B = {has Internet access}

    $P(A \text{ and } B) = P(A)P(B|A) = (0.57)(0.51) = 0.291$

17. Let A = {1st part drawn is defective} and B = {2nd part drawn is defective}

    (a) $P(A \text{ and } B) = P(A) \cdot P(A|B) = \left(\dfrac{4}{11}\right) \cdot \left(\dfrac{3}{10}\right) \approx 0.109$

    (b) $P(A' \text{ and } B') = P(A') \cdot P(B'|A') = \left(\dfrac{7}{11}\right) \cdot \left(\dfrac{6}{10}\right) \approx 0.382$

    (c) $P(\text{at least one part defective})$

19. Let A = {have one month's income or more} and B = {man}

    (a) $P(A) = \dfrac{138}{287} \approx 0.481$

    (b) $P(A'|B) = \dfrac{66}{142} \approx 0.465$

    (c) $P(B'|A) = \dfrac{62}{138} \approx 0.449$

    (d) Dependent since $P(A') \approx 0.519 \neq 0.465 \approx P(A'|B)$ Whether a person has at least one month's income saved depends on whether or not the person is male.

21. (a) $P(\text{all five have AB+}) = (0.03) \cdot (0.03) \cdot (0.03) \cdot (0.03) \cdot (0.03) = 0.0000000243$

    (b) $P(\text{none have AB+}) = (0.97) \cdot (0.97) \cdot (0.97) \cdot (0.97) \cdot (0.97) \approx 0.859$

    (c) $P(\text{at least one has AB+}) = 1 - P(\text{none have AB+}) = 1 - 0.859 = 0.141$

23. (a) $P(\text{first question correct}) = 0.2$

    (b) $P(\text{first two questions correct}) = (0.2) \cdot (0.2) = 0.04$

    (c) $P(\text{first three questions correct}) = (0.2)^3 = 0.008$

    (d) $P(\text{none correct}) = (0.8)^3 = 0.512$

    (e) $P(\text{at least one correct}) = 1 - P(\text{none correct}) = 1 - 0.512 = 0.488$

25. $P\,(\text{all three products came from the third factory}) = \dfrac{25}{110} \cdot \dfrac{24}{109} \cdot \dfrac{23}{108} \approx 0.011$

27. $P(A|B) = \dfrac{P(A) \cdot P(B|A)}{P(A) \cdot P(B|A) + P(A') \cdot P(B|A')} = \dfrac{\left(\dfrac{2}{3}\right) \cdot \left(\dfrac{1}{5}\right)}{\left(\dfrac{2}{3}\right) \cdot \left(\dfrac{1}{5}\right) + \left(\dfrac{1}{3}\right) \cdot \left(\dfrac{1}{2}\right)}$

    $= \dfrac{0.133}{0.133 + 0.167} = 0.444$

© 2006 Pearson Education, Inc., Upper Saddle River, NJ. All rights reserved. This material is protected under all copyright laws as they currently exist.
No portion of this material may be reproduced, in any form or by any means, without permission in writing from the publisher.

29. $P(A|B) = \dfrac{P(A)P(B|A)}{(A)P(B|A) + P(A')P(B|A')}$

$= \dfrac{(0.25)(0.3)}{(0.25)(0.3) + (0.75)(0.5)} = \dfrac{0.075}{0.075 + 0.375} = 0.167$

31. $P(A) = \dfrac{1}{200} = 0.005$

$P(B|A) = 0.80$

$P(B|A') = 0.05$

(a) $P(A|B) = \dfrac{P(A) \cdot P(B|A)}{P(A) \cdot P(B|A) + P(A') \cdot P(B|A')}$

$= \dfrac{(0.005) \cdot (0.8)}{(0.005) \cdot (0.8) + (0.995) \cdot (0.05)} = \dfrac{0.004}{0.004 + 0.04975} \approx 0.074$

(b) $P(A'|B') = \dfrac{P(A') \cdot P(B'|A')}{P(A') \cdot P(B'|A') + P(A) \cdot P(B'|A)}$

$= \dfrac{(0.995) \cdot (0.95)}{(0.995) \cdot (0.95) + (0.005) \cdot (0.2)} = \dfrac{0.94525}{0.94525 + 0.001} \approx 0.999$

33. Let $A = \{\text{flight departs on time}\}$ and $B = \{\text{flight arrives on time}\}$

$P(A|B) = \dfrac{P(A \text{ and } B)}{P(B)} = \dfrac{(0.83)}{(0.87)} \approx 0.954$

3.3 THE ADDITION RULE

3.3 Try It Yourself Solutions

1a. (1) None of the statements are true.

(2) None of the statements are true.

(3) Events A and B cannot occur at the same time.

b. (1) A and B are not mutually exclusive.

(2) A and B are not mutually exclusive.

(3) A and B are mutually exclusive.

2a. (1) Mutually exclusive   (2) Not mutually exclusive

b. (1) Let $A = \{6\}$ and $B = \{\text{odd}\}$

$P(A) = \dfrac{1}{6}$ and $P(B) = \dfrac{3}{6} = \dfrac{1}{2}$

(2) Let $A = \{\text{face card}\}$ and $B = \{\text{heart}\}$

$P(A) = \dfrac{12}{52}, P(B) = \dfrac{13}{52}, \text{and } P(A \text{ and } B) = \dfrac{3}{52}$

© 2006 Pearson Education, Inc., Upper Saddle River, NJ. All rights reserved. This material is protected under all copyright laws as they currently exist. No portion of this material may be reproduced, in any form or by any means, without permission in writing from the publisher.

c. (1) $P(A \text{ or } B) = P(A) + P(B) = \dfrac{1}{6} + \dfrac{1}{2} \approx 0.667$

(2) $P(A \text{ or } B) = P(A) + P(B) - P(A \text{ and } B) = \dfrac{12}{52} + \dfrac{13}{52} - \dfrac{3}{52} \approx 0.423$

3a. $A = \{\text{sales between \$0 and \$24,999}\}$

$B = \{\text{sales between \$25,000 and \$49,000}\}$

b. A and B cannot occur at the same time $\rightarrow A$ and B are mutually exclusive

c. $P(A) = \dfrac{3}{36}$ and $P(B) = \dfrac{5}{36}$

d. $P(A \text{ or } B) = P(A) + P(B) = \dfrac{3}{36} + \dfrac{5}{36} \approx 0.222$

4a. (1) Mutually exclusive   (2) Not mutually exclusive

b. (1) $P(B \text{ or } AB) = P(B) + P(AB) = \dfrac{45}{409} + \dfrac{16}{409} \approx 0.149$

(2) $P(O \text{ or } Rh+) = P(O) + P(Rh+) - P(O \text{ and } Rh+) = \dfrac{184}{409} + \dfrac{344}{409} - \dfrac{156}{409} \approx 0.910$

5a. Let $A = \{\text{linebacker}\}$ and $B = \{\text{quarterback}\}$

$P(A \text{ or } B) = P(A) + P(B) = \dfrac{31}{255} + \dfrac{17}{255} \approx 0.188$

b. $P(\text{not a linebacker or quarterback}) = 1 - P(A \text{ or } B) \approx 1 - 0.188 \approx 0.812$

3.3 EXERCISE SOLUTIONS

1. $P(A \text{ and } B) = 0$ because A and B cannot occur at the same time.

3. True

5. False, $P(A \text{ or } B) = P(A) + P(B) - P(A \text{ and } B)$

7. Not mutually exclusive since the two events can occur at the same time.

9. Not mutually exclusive since the two events can occur at the same time. The worker can be female and have a college degree.

11. Mutually exclusive since the two events cannot occur at the same time. The person cannot be in both age classes.

13. (a) No, it is possible for the events {overtime} and {temporary help} to occur at the same time.

(b) $P(\text{OT or temp}) = P(\text{OT}) + P(\text{temp}) - P(\text{OT and temp}) = \dfrac{18}{52} + \dfrac{9}{52} - \dfrac{5}{52} \approx 0.423$

15. (a) Not mutually exclusive since the two events can occur at the same time. A carton can have a puncture and a smashed corner.

(b) $P(\text{puncture or corner}) = P(\text{puncture}) + P(\text{corner}) - P(\text{puncture and corner})$
$$= 0.05 + 0.08 - 0.004 = 0.126$$

© 2006 Pearson Education, Inc., Upper Saddle River, NJ. All rights reserved. This material is protected under all copyright laws as they currently exist.
No portion of this material may be reproduced, in any form or by any means, without permission in writing from the publisher.

17. (a) $P(\text{heart or } 3) = P(\text{heart}) + P(3) \cdot P(\text{heart and } 3)$

$$= \frac{13}{52} + \frac{4}{52} - \frac{1}{52} \approx 0.308$$

(b) $P(\text{black or king}) = P(\text{black}) + P(\text{king}) - P(\text{black and king})$

$$= \frac{26}{52} + \frac{4}{52} - \frac{2}{52} \approx 0.538$$

(c) $P(5 \text{ or face card}) = P(5) + P(\text{face card}) - P(5 \text{ and face card})$

$$= \frac{4}{52} + \frac{12}{52} - 0 \approx 0.307$$

19. (a) $P(\text{under } 5) = 0.067$

(b) $P(\text{not } 65+) = 1 - P(65+) = 1 - 0.132 = 0.868$

(c) $P(\text{between } 18 \text{ and } 34) = P(\text{between } 18 \text{ and } 24 \text{ or between } 25 \text{ and } 34) = P(\text{between } 18 \text{ and } 24) + P(\text{between } 25 \text{ and } 34) = 0.101 + 0.130 = 0.231$

21. (a) $P(\text{not confident}) = \dfrac{112}{1018} \approx 0.11$

(b) $P(\text{somewhat confident or very confident}) = P(\text{somewhat confident}) + P(\text{very confident})$

$$= \frac{397}{1018} + \frac{336}{1018} = \frac{733}{1018} \approx 0.72$$

23. (a) $P(\text{1st LH and 2nd LH}) = \left(\dfrac{120}{1000}\right) \cdot \left(\dfrac{119}{999}\right) \approx 0.014$

(b) $P(\text{neither are LH}) = \left(\dfrac{880}{1000}\right) \cdot \left(\dfrac{879}{999}\right) \approx 0.774$

(c) $P(\text{at least one is LH}) = 1 - P(\text{neither are LH}) = 1 - \left(\dfrac{880}{1000}\right) \cdot \left(\dfrac{879}{999}\right) \approx 0.226$

25. Answers will vary.

Conclusion: If two events, $\{A\}$ and $\{B\}$, are independent, $P(A \text{ and } B) = P(A) \cdot P(B)$. If two events are mutually exclusive, $P(A \text{ and } B) = 0$. The only scenario when two events can be independent and mutually exclusive is if $P(A) = 0$ or $P(B) = 0$.

27. $P(A \text{ or } B \text{ or } C) = P(A) + P(B) + P(C) - P(A \text{ and } B) - P(A \text{ and } C) - P(B \text{ and } C)$

$$+ P(A \text{ and } B \text{ and } C)$$

$$= 0.35 + 0.35 + 0.30 - 0.15 - 0.25 - 0.19 + 0.13$$

$$= 0.54$$

3.4 COUNTING PRINCIPLES

3.4 Try It Yourself Solutions

1a. Manufacturer: 4
    Size: 3
    Color: 6

b. $4 \cdot 3 \cdot 6 = 72$ ways

© 2006 Pearson Education, Inc., Upper Saddle River, NJ. All rights reserved. This material is protected under all copyright laws as they currently exist.
No portion of this material may be reproduced, in any form or by any means, without permission in writing from the publisher.

2a. (1) Each letter is an event (26 choices)

(2) Each letter is an event (26, 25, 24, 23, 22, and 21 choices)

b. (1) $26 \cdot 26 \cdot 26 \cdot 26 \cdot 26 \cdot 26 = 26^6 = 308{,}915{,}776$

(2) $26 \cdot 25 \cdot 24 \cdot 23 \cdot 22 \cdot 21 = 165{,}765{,}600$

3a. $n = 6$ teams   **b.** $6! = 720$

4a. $_8P_3 = \dfrac{8!}{(8-3)!} = \dfrac{8!}{5!} = \dfrac{8 \cdot 7 \cdot 6 \cdot 5 \cdot 4 \cdot 3 \cdot 2 \cdot 1}{5 \cdot 4 \cdot 3 \cdot 2 \cdot 1} = 8 \cdot 7 \cdot 6 = 336$

b. There are 336 possible ways that three horses can finish in first, second, and third place.

5a. $n = 12, r = 4$ **b.** $_{12}P_4 = \dfrac{12!}{(12-4)!} = \dfrac{12!}{8!} = 12 \cdot 11 \cdot 10 \cdot 9 = 11{,}880$

6a. $n = 20, n_1 = 6, n_2 = 9, n_3 = 5$ **b.** $\dfrac{n!}{n_1! \cdot n_2! \cdot n_3!} = \dfrac{20!}{6! \cdot 9! \cdot 5!} = 77{,}597{,}520$

7a. $n = 16, r = 3$

b. $_{16}C_3 = 560$

c. There are 560 different possible 3 person committees that can be selected from 16 employees.

8a. 1 favorable outcome and $\dfrac{6!}{1! \cdot 2! \cdot 2! \cdot 1!} = 180$ distinguishable permutations.

b. $P(\text{Letter}) = \dfrac{1}{180} \approx 0.0056$

9a. $(_5C_3) \cdot (_7C_0) = 10 \cdot 1 = 10$ **b.** $_{12}C_3 = 220$ **c.** $\dfrac{10}{220} \approx 0.045$

3.4 EXERCISE SOLUTIONS

1. You are counting the number of ways two or more events can occur in sequence.

3. False, a permutation is an ordered arrangement of objects.

5. $7! = (7)(6)(5)(4)(3)(2)(1) = 5040$

7. $_7C_4 = \dfrac{7!}{4!(7-4)!} = \dfrac{(7)(6)(5)(4)(3)(2)(1)}{[(4)(3)(2)(1)][(3)(2)(1)]} = \dfrac{540}{(24)(6)} = 35$

9. Permutation, since order of the fifteen people in line matters.

11. $10 \cdot 8 \cdot {}_{13}C_2 = 6240$

13. $9 \cdot 10 \cdot 10 \cdot 5 = 4500$

15. $8! = 40{,}320$

17. $10! = 3{,}628{,}800$

19. $_{12}P_3 = 1320$

21. $_{14}P_4 = 24{,}024$

23. $\dfrac{18!}{4! \cdot 8! \cdot 6!} = 9{,}189{,}180$

© 2006 Pearson Education, Inc., Upper Saddle River, NJ. All rights reserved. This material is protected under all copyright laws as they currently exist. No portion of this material may be reproduced, in any form or by any means, without permission in writing from the publisher.

25. $_{40}C_{12} = 5{,}586{,}853{,}480$

27. $_9C_3 = 84$

29. (a) $_8C_4 = 70$ (b) $2 \cdot 2 \cdot 2 \cdot 2 = 16$ (c) $_4C_2\left[\dfrac{(_2C_0) \cdot (_2C_0) \cdot (_2C_2) \cdot (_2C_2)}{_8C_4}\right] \approx 0.086$

31. (a) $(26)(26)(10)(10)(10)(10)(10) = 67{,}600{,}000$

   (b) $(26)(25)(10)(9)(8)(7)(6) = 19{,}656{,}000$

   (c) $\dfrac{1}{67{,}600{,}000}$

33. (a) $5! = 120$ (b) $2! \cdot 3! = 12$ (c) $3! \cdot 2! = 12$ (d) 0.4

35. $(6\%)(1200) = (0.06)(1200) = 72$ of the 1200 rate financial shape as excellent.

   $P(\text{all four rate excellent}) = \dfrac{_{72}C_4}{_{1200}C_4} = \dfrac{1{,}028{,}790}{85{,}968{,}659{,}700} \approx 0.0000120$

37. $(39\%)(500) = (0.39)(500) = 195$ of the 1500 rate financial shape as fair $\Rightarrow 500 - 195 = 305$ rate shape as not fair.

   $P(\text{none of 80 selected rate fair}) = \dfrac{_{305}C_{80}}{_{500}C_{80}} \approx 6.00 \times 10^{-20}$

39. (a) $_{40}C_5 = 658{,}008$ (b) $P(\text{win}) = \dfrac{1}{658{,}008} \approx 0.00000152$

41. $_{14}C_4 = 1001$ possible 4 digit arrangements if order is not important.

   Assign 1000 of the 4 digit arrangements to the 13 teams since 1 arrangement is excluded.

43. $P(\text{1st}) = \dfrac{250}{1000} = 0.250$ $P(\text{8th}) = \dfrac{29}{1000} = 0.029$

   $P(\text{2nd}) = \dfrac{200}{1000} = 0.200$ $P(\text{9th}) = \dfrac{18}{1000} = 0.018$

   $P(\text{3rd}) = \dfrac{157}{1000} = 0.157$ $P(\text{10th}) = \dfrac{11}{1000} = 0.011$

   $P(\text{4th}) = \dfrac{120}{1000} = 0.120$ $P(\text{11th}) = \dfrac{7}{1000} = 0.007$

   $P(\text{5th}) = \dfrac{89}{1000} = 0.089$ $P(\text{12th}) = \dfrac{6}{1000} = 0.006$

   $P(\text{6th}) = \dfrac{64}{1000} = 0.064$ $P(\text{13th}) = \dfrac{5}{1000} = 0.005$

   $P(\text{7th}) = \dfrac{44}{1000} = 0.044$

45. Let $A = \{$team with the worst record wins third pick$\}$ and

   $B = \{$team with the best record, ranked 13th, wins first pick$\}$ and

   $C = \{$team ranked 2nd wins the second pick$\}$.

   $P(A|B \text{ and } C) = \dfrac{250}{995} + \dfrac{250}{(1000 - (200 + 5))} = \dfrac{250}{995} + \dfrac{250}{795} \approx 0.2513 + 0.3144 \approx 0.566$

© 2006 Pearson Education, Inc., Upper Saddle River, NJ. All rights reserved. This material is protected under all copyright laws as they currently exist.
No portion of this material may be reproduced, in any form or by any means, without permission in writing from the publisher.

CHAPTER 3 REVIEW EXERCISE SOLUTIONS

1. Sample space:

   {HHHH, HHHT, HHTH, HHTT, HTHH, HTHT, HTTH, HTTT, THHH, THHT, THTH, THTT, TTHH, TTHT, TTTH, TTTT}

   Event: Getting three heads
   {HHHT, HHTH, HTHH, THHH}

3. Sample space: {0, 1, 2, 3, 4, 5, 6, 7, 8, 9}

   Event: Choosing a number less than 2
   {0, 1}

5. Empirical probability

7. Subjective probability

9. Classical probability

11. $P(\text{at least 20}) = 1 - P(\text{less than 19}) = 1 - 0.28 = 0.72$

13. $P(\text{undergrad} \mid +) = 0.92$

15. Independent, the first event does not affect the outcome of the second event.

17. $P(\text{correct toothpaste and correct dental rinse}) = P(\text{correct toothpaste}) \cdot P(\text{correct dental rinse})$
$$= \left(\frac{1}{8}\right) \cdot \left(\frac{1}{5}\right) \approx 0.025$$

19. Mutually exclusive since both events cannot occur at the same time.

21. $P(\text{home or work}) = P(\text{home}) + P(\text{work}) - P(\text{home and work}) = 0.44 + 0.37 - 0.21 = 0.60$

23. $P(\text{4–8 or club}) = P(\text{4–8}) + P(\text{club}) - P(\text{4–8 and club}) = \frac{20}{52} + \frac{13}{52} - \frac{5}{52} \approx 0.538$

25. $P(\text{odd or less than 4}) = P(\text{odd}) + P(\text{less than 4}) - P(\text{odd and less than 4})$
$$= \frac{6}{12} + \frac{3}{12} - \frac{2}{12} \approx 0.583$$

27. $P(\text{600 or more}) = P(600 - 999) + P(\text{1000 or more})$
$$= 0.192 + 0.271 = 0.463$$

29. $P(\text{poor taste or hard to find}) = P(\text{poor taste}) + P(\text{hard to find})$
$$= \frac{60}{500} + \frac{55}{500} = \frac{115}{500} = 0.23$$

31. $8 \cdot 2 \cdot 9 = 144$

33. Order is important: $_{15}P_3 = 2730$

35. Order is not important: $_{17}C_4 = 2380$

37. $P(\text{3 kings and 2 queens}) = \frac{_4C_3 \cdot _4C_2}{_{52}C_5} = \frac{4 \cdot 6}{2{,}598{,}960} \approx 0.00000923$

39. (a) $P(\text{no defectives}) = \frac{_{197}C_3}{_{200}C_3} = \frac{1{,}254{,}890}{1{,}313{,}400} \approx 0.955$

© 2006 Pearson Education, Inc., Upper Saddle River, NJ. All rights reserved. This material is protected under all copyright laws as they currently exist. No portion of this material may be reproduced, in any form or by any means, without permission in writing from the publisher.

(b) $P(\text{all defective}) = \dfrac{_3C_3}{_{200}C_3} = \dfrac{1}{1,313,400} = \approx 0.000000761$

(c) $P(\text{at least one defective}) = 1 - P(\text{no defective}) = 1 - 0.955 = 0.045$

(d) $P(\text{at least one non-defective}) = 1 - P(\text{all defective}) = 1 - 0.000000761 \approx 0.999999239$

CHAPTER 3 QUIZ SOLUTIONS

1. (a) $P(\text{bachelor}) = \dfrac{1322}{2466} \approx 0.536$

(b) $P(\text{bachelor}|\text{F}) = \dfrac{769}{1460} \approx 0.527$

(c) $P(\text{bachelor}|\text{M}) = \dfrac{553}{1006} \approx 0.550$

(d) $P(\text{associate or bachelor}) = P(\text{associate}) + P(\text{bachelor})$

$$= \dfrac{632}{2466} + \dfrac{1322}{2466} \approx 0.792$$

(e) $P(\text{doctorate}|\text{M}) = \dfrac{25}{1006} \approx 0.025$

(f) $P(\text{master or female}) = P(\text{master}) + P(\text{female}) - P(\text{master and female})$

$$= \dfrac{467}{2466} + \dfrac{1460}{2466} - \dfrac{270}{2466} = 0.672$$

(g) $P(\text{associate and male}) = P(\text{associate}) \cdot P(\text{male}|\text{associate})$

$$= \dfrac{632}{2466} \cdot \dfrac{231}{632} = \dfrac{145,992}{1,558,512} \approx 0.094$$

(h) $P(\text{F}|\text{bachelor}) = \dfrac{769}{1322} \approx 0.582$

2. Not mutually exclusive since both events can occur at the same time.

Dependent since one event can affect the occurrence of the second event.

3. (a) $_{147}C_3 = 518,665$ (b) $_3C_3 = 1$ (c) $_{150}C_3 - _3C_3 = 551,300 - 1 = 551,299$

4. (a) $\dfrac{_{147}C_3}{_{150}C_3} = \dfrac{518,665}{551,300} \approx 0.94$

(b) $\dfrac{_3C_3}{_{150}C_3} = \dfrac{1}{551,300} \approx 0.00000181$

(c) $\dfrac{_{150}C_3 - _3C_3}{_{150}C_3} = \dfrac{551,299}{551,300} \approx 0.999998$

5. $9 \cdot 10 \cdot 10 \cdot 5 = 4500$

6. $_{25}P_4 = 303,600$

© 2006 Pearson Education, Inc., Upper Saddle River, NJ. All rights reserved. This material is protected under all copyright laws as they currently exist. No portion of this material may be reproduced, in any form or by any means, without permission in writing from the publisher.

Discrete Probability Distributions

4.1 Try It Yourself Solutions

1a. (1) measured   (2) counted

b. (1) Random variable is continuous since x can be any amount of time needed to complete a test.

   (2) Random variable is discrete since x can be counted.

2ab.

x	f	$P(x)$
0	16	0.16
1	19	0.19
2	15	0.15
3	21	0.21
4	9	0.09
5	10	0.10
6	8	0.08
7	2	0.02
	$n = 100$	$\sum P(x) = 1$

New Employee Sales

3a. Each $P(x)$ is between 0 and 1.

b. $\sum P(x) = 1$

c. Since both conditions are met, the distribution is a probability distribution.

4a. (1) Yes, each outcome is between 0 and 1.   (2) Yes, each outcome is between 0 and 1.

b. (1) No, $\sum P(x) = \dfrac{18}{16} \neq 1$.   (2) Yes, $\sum P(x) = 1$.

c. (1) Not a probability distribution   (2) Is a probability distribution

5ab.

x	$P(x)$	$xP(x)$
0	0.16	$(0)(0.16) = 0.00$
1	0.19	$(1)(0.19) = 0.19$
2	0.15	$(2)(0.15) = 0.30$
3	0.21	$(3)(0.21) = 0.63$
4	0.09	$(4)(0.09) = 0.36$
5	0.10	$(5)(0.10) = 0.50$
6	0.08	$(6)(0.08) = 0.48$
7	0.02	$(7)(0.02) = 0.14$
	$\sum P(x) = 1$	$\sum xP(x) = 2.60$

c. $\mu = \sum xP(x) = 2.6$

On average, 2.6 sales are made per day.

© 2006 Pearson Education, Inc., Upper Saddle River, NJ. All rights reserved. This material is protected under all copyright laws as they currently exist. No portion of this material may be reproduced, in any form or by any means, without permission in writing from the publisher.

6ab.

x	$P(x)$	$x - \mu$	$(x - \mu)^2$	$P(x)(x - \mu)^2$
0	0.16	−2.6	6.76	$(0.16)(6.76) = 1.0816$
1	0.19	−1.6	2.56	$(0.19)(2.56) = 0.4864$
2	0.15	−0.6	0.36	$(0.15)(0.36) = 0.054$
3	0.21	0.4	0.16	$(0.21)(0.16) = 0.0336$
4	0.09	1.4	1.96	$(0.09)(1.96) = 0.1764$
5	0.10	2.4	5.76	$(0.10)(5.76) = 0.576$
6	0.08	3.4	11.56	$(0.08)(11.56) = 0.9248$
7	0.02	4.4	19.36	$(0.02)(19.36) = 0.3872$
	$\Sigma P(x) = 1$			$\Sigma P(x)(x - \mu)^2 = 3.72$

c. $\sigma = \sqrt{\sigma^2} = \sqrt{3.720} \approx 1.9$

d. A typical distance or deviation of the random variable from the mean is 1.9 sales per day.

7ab.

x	f	$P(x)$	$xP(x)$
0	25	0.111	$(0)(0.111) = 0.000$
1	48	0.213	$(1)(0.213) = 0.213$
2	60	0.267	$(2)(0.267) = 0.533$
3	45	0.200	$(3)(0.200) = 0.600$
4	20	0.089	$(4)(0.089) = 0.356$
5	10	0.044	$(5)(0.044) = 0.222$
6	8	0.036	$(6)(0.036) = 0.213$
7	5	0.022	$(7)(0.022) = 0.156$
8	3	0.013	$(8)(0.013) = 0.107$
9	1	0.004	$(9)(0.004) = 0.040$
	$n = 225$	$\sum P(x) \approx 1$	$\sum xP(x) = 2.440$

c. $E(x) = \Sigma xP(x) = 2.4$

d. You can expect an average of 2.4 sales per day.

4.1 EXERCISE SOLUTIONS

1. A random variable represents a numerical value assigned to an outcome of a probability experiment.

Examples: Answers will vary.

3. False. In most applications, discrete random variables represent counted data, while continuous random variables represent measured data.

5. True

7. Discrete, because home attendance is a random variable that is countable.

9. Continuous, because annual vehicle-miles driven is a random variable that cannot be counted.

11. Discrete, because the random variable is countable.

13. Continuous, because the random variable has an infinite number of possible outcomes and cannot be counted.

15. Discrete, because the random variable is countable.

17. Continuous, because the random variable has an infinite number of possible outcomes and cannot be counted.

19. (a) $P(x > 2) = 0.25 + 0.10 = 0.35$

   (b) $P(x < 4) = 1 - P(4) = 1 - 0.10 = 0.90$

© 2006 Pearson Education, Inc., Upper Saddle River, NJ. All rights reserved. This material is protected under all copyright laws as they currently exist. No portion of this material may be reproduced, in any form or by any means, without permission in writing from the publisher.

21. $\Sigma P(x) = 1 \rightarrow P(3) = 0.22$

23. Yes

25. No, $\Sigma P(x) = 0.95$ and $P(5) < 0$.

27. (a)

x	f	$P(x)$	$xP(x)$	$(x - \mu)$	$(x - \mu)^2$	$(x - \mu)^2 P(x)$
0	1491	0.686	$(0)(0.686) = 0$	-0.501	0.251	$(0.251)(0.686) = 0.169$
1	425	0.195	$(1)(0.195) = 0.195$	0.499	0.249	$(0.249)(0.195) = 0.049$
2	168	0.077	$(2)(0.077) = 0.155$	1.499	2.246	$(2.246)(0.077) = 0.173$
3	48	0.022	$(3)(0.022) = 0.066$	2.499	6.244	$(6.244)(0.022) = 0.138$
4	29	0.013	$(4)(0.013) = 0.053$	3.499	12.241	$(12.241)(0.013) = 0.160$
5	14	0.006	$(5)(0.006) = 0.030$	4.499	20.238	$(20.238)(0.006) = 0.122$
	$n = 2175$	$\sum P(x) \approx 1$	$\sum xP(x) = 0.497$			$\sum (x - \mu)^2 P(x) = 0.811$

(b) $\mu = \Sigma xP(x) \approx 0.5$

(c) $\sigma^2 = \Sigma(x - \mu)^2 P(x) \approx 0.8$

(d) $\sigma = \sqrt{\sigma^2} \approx \sqrt{0.8246} \approx 0.9$

(e) A household on average has 0.5 dogs with a standard deviation of 0.9.

29. (a)

x	f	$P(x)$	$xP(x)$	$(x - \mu)$	$(x - \mu)^2$	$(x - \mu)^2 P(x)$
0	300	0.432	0.000	-0.764	0.584	$(0.584)(0.432) = 0.252$
1	280	0.403	0.403	0.236	0.056	$(0.056)(0.403) = 0.022$
2	95	0.137	0.274	1.236	1.528	$(1.528)(0.137) = 0.209$
3	20	0.029	0.087	2.236	5.000	$(5.000)(0.029) = 0.145$
	$n = 695$	$\sum P(x) \approx 1$	$\sum xP(x) = 0.764$			$\sum (x - \mu)^2 P(x) = 0.629$

(b) $\mu = \Sigma xP(x) \approx 0.8$

(c) $\sigma^2 = \Sigma(x - \mu)^2 P(x) \approx 0.6$

(d) $\sigma = \sqrt{\sigma^2} \approx 0.8$

(e) A household on average has 0.8 computers with a standard deviation of 0.8 computers.

31. (a)

x	f	$P(x)$	$xP(x)$	$(x - \mu)$	$(x - \mu)^2$	$(x - \mu)^2 P(x)$
0	6	0.031	0.000	-3.411	11.638	$(11.638)(0.031) = 0.360$
1	12	0.063	0.063	-2.411	5.815	$(5.815)(0.063) = 0.366$
2	29	0.151	0.302	-1.411	1.992	$(1.992)(0.151) = 0.300$
3	57	0.297	0.891	-0.411	0.169	$(0.169)(0.297) = 0.050$
4	42	0.219	0.876	0.589	0.346	$(0.346)(0.219) = 0.076$
5	30	0.156	0.780	1.589	2.523	$(2.523)(0.156) = 0.394$
6	16	0.083	0.498	2.589	6.701	$(6.701)(0.083) = 0.557$
	$n = 192$	$\sum P(x) = 1$	$\sum xP(x) = 3.410$			$\sum (x - \mu)^2 P(x) = 2.103$

(b) $\mu = \Sigma xP(x) = 3.4$

(c) $\sigma^2 = \Sigma(x - \mu)^2 P(x) = 2.1$

(d) $\sigma = \sqrt{\sigma^2} = 1.4$

(e) An employee works an average of 3.4 overtime hours per week with a standard deviation of 1.4 hours.

© 2006 Pearson Education, Inc., Upper Saddle River, NJ. All rights reserved. This material is protected under all copyright laws as they currently exist. No portion of this material may be reproduced, in any form or by any means, without permission in writing from the publisher.

33.

x	$P(x)$	$xP(x)$	$(x - \mu)$	$(x - \mu)^2$	$(x - \mu)^2 P(x)$
0	0.02	0.00	-5.30	28.09	0.562
1	0.02	0.02	-4.30	18.49	0.372
2	0.06	0.12	-3.30	10.89	0.653
3	0.06	0.18	-2.30	5.29	0.317
4	0.08	0.32	-1.30	1.69	0.135
5	0.22	1.10	-0.30	0.09	0.020
6	0.30	1.80	0.70	0.49	0.147
7	0.16	1.12	1.70	2.89	0.462
8	0.08	0.64	2.70	7.29	0.583
	$\sum P(x) = 1$	$\sum xP(x) = 5.30$			$\sum (x - \mu)^2 P(x) = 3.250$

(a) $\mu = \Sigma xP(x) = 5.3$

(b) $\sigma^2 = \Sigma(x - \mu)^2 P(x) = 3.3$

(c) $\sigma = \sqrt{\sigma^2} = 1.8$

(d) $E[x] = \mu = \Sigma xP(x) = 5.3$

(e) The expected number of correctly answered questions is 5.3 with a standard deviation of 1.8.

35. (a) $\mu = \Sigma xP(x) = 2.150$

(b) $\sigma^2 = \Sigma(x - \mu)^2 P(x) \approx 1.142$

(c) $\sigma = \sqrt{\sigma^2} \approx 1.069$

(d) $E[x] = \mu = \Sigma xP(x) = 2.150$

(e) The average number of hurricanes that hit the U.S. is 2.150 with a standard deviation of 1.069.

37. (a) $\mu = \Sigma xP(x) = 2.55$

(b) $\sigma^2 = \Sigma(x - \mu)^2 P(x) \approx 1.90$

(c) $\sigma = \sqrt{\sigma^2} \approx 1.38$

(d) $E[x] = \mu = \Sigma xP(x) = 2.55$

(e) The average household size is 2.55 with a standard deviation of 1.38.

39. (a) $P(x < 2) = 0.6855 + 0.1954 = 0.8809$

(b) $P(x \geq 2) = 1 - P(x < 2) = 1 - 0.8809 - 0.1191$

(c) $P(2 \leq x \leq 4) = 0.0772 + 0.0221 + 0.0133 = 0.1126$

41. A household with three dogs is unusual since the probability is only 0.0221.

43. $E(x) = \mu = \Sigma xP(x) = (-1) \cdot \left(\dfrac{37}{38}\right) + (35) \cdot \left(\dfrac{1}{38}\right) \approx -\$0.05$

© 2006 Pearson Education, Inc., Upper Saddle River, NJ. All rights reserved. This material is protected under all copyright laws as they currently exist.
No portion of this material may be reproduced, in any form or by any means, without permission in writing from the publisher.

4.2 BINOMIAL DISTRIBUTIONS

4.2 Try It Yourself Solutions

1a. Trial: answering a question (10 trials)
Success: question answered correctly

b. Yes, the experiment satisfies the four conditions of a binomial experiment.

c. $n = 10, p = 0.25, q = 0.75, x = 0, 1, 2, \ldots, 9, 10$

2a. Trial: drawing a card with replacement (5 trials)
Success: card drawn is a club
Failure: card drawn is not a club

b. $n = 5, p = 0.25, q = 0.75, x = 3$

c. $P(3) = \dfrac{5!}{2!3!}(0.25)^3(0.75)^2 \approx 0.088$

3a. Trial: selecting a worker and asking a question (7 trials)
Success: Selecting a worker who will rely on pension
Failure: Selecting a worker who will not rely on pension

b. $n = 7, p = 0.34, q = 0.66, x = 0, 1, 2, \ldots, 6, 7$

c. $P(0) = {}_7C_0(0.34)^0(0.66)^7 = 0.0546$
$P(1) = {}_7C_1(0.34)^1(0.66)^6 = 0.197$
$P(2) = {}_7C_2(0.34)^2(0.66)^5 = 0.304$
$P(3) = {}_7C_3(0.34)^3(0.66)^4 = 0.261$
$P(4) = {}_7C_4(0.34)^4(0.66)^3 = 0.134$
$P(5) = {}_7C_5(0.34)^5(0.66)^2 = 0.0416$
$P(6) = {}_7C_6(0.34)^6(0.66)^1 = 0.00714$
$P(7) = {}_7C_7(0.34)^7(0.66)^0 = 0.000525$

d.

x	$P(x)$
0	0.0546
1	0.197
2	0.304
3	0.261
4	0.134
5	0.0416
6	0.00714
7	0.000525

4a. $n = 250, p = 0.71, x = 178$ **b.** $P(178) \approx 0.056$

c. The probability that exactly 178 people in the United States will use more than one topping on their hot dog is about 0.056.

5a. (1) $x = 2$ (2) $x = 2, 3, 4,$ or 5   (3) $x = 0$ or 1

b. (1) $P(2) \approx 0.217$

(2) $P(x \geq 2) = 1 - P(0) - P(1) = 1 - 0.308 - 0.409 = 0.283$

or

$P(x \geq 2) = P(2) + P(3) + P(4) + P(5)$

$= 0.217 + 0.058 + 0.008 + 0.0004$

$= 0.283$

(3) $P(x < 2) = P(0) + P(1) = 0.308 + 0.409 = 0.717$

c. (1) The probability that exactly two men consider fishing their favorite leisure-time activity is about 0.217.

(2) The probability that at least two men consider fishing their favorite leisure-time activity is about 0.283.

(3) The probability that fewer than two men consider fishing their favorite leisure-time activity is about 0.717.

© 2006 Pearson Education, Inc., Upper Saddle River, NJ. All rights reserved. This material is protected under all copyright laws as they currently exist. No portion of this material may be reproduced, in any form or by any means, without permission in writing from the publisher.

6a. Trial: selecting a business and asking a question (10 trials)

Success: Selecting a business with a Web site

Failure: Selecting a business without a site

b. $n = 10, p = 0.30, x = 4$ **c.** $P(4) \approx 0.200$

d. The probability of randomly selecting 10 small businesses and finding exactly four that have a website is 0.200.

7a. $P(0) = {}_6C_0(0.57)^0(0.43)^6 = 1(0.57)^0(0.43)^6 = 0.006$

$P(1) = {}_6C_1(0.57)^1(0.43)^5 = 6(0.57)^1(0.43)^5 = 0.050$

$P(2) = {}_6C_2(0.57)^2(0.43)^4 = 15(0.57)^2(0.43)^4 = 0.167$

$P(3) = {}_6C_3(0.57)^3(0.43)^3 = 20(0.57)^3(0.43)^3 = 0.294$

$P(4) = {}_6C_4(0.57)^4(0.43)^2 = 15(0.57)^4(0.43)^2 = 0.293$

$P(5) = {}_6C_5(0.57)^5(0.43)^1 = 6(0.57)^5(0.43)^1 = 0.155$

$P(6) = {}_6C_6(0.57)^6(0.43)^0 = 1(0.57)^6(0.43)^0 = 0.034$

b.

x	$P(x)$
0	0.006
1	0.050
2	0.167
3	0.294
4	0.293
5	0.155
6	0.340

c.

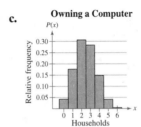

Owning a Computer

8a. Success: Selecting a clear day

$n = 31, p = 0.44, q = 0.56$

b. $\mu = np = (31)(0.44) = 13.6$

c. $\sigma^2 = npq = (31)(0.44)(0.56) = 7.6$

d. $\sigma = \sqrt{\sigma^2} = 2.8$

e. On average, there are about 14 clear days during the year. The standard deviation is about 3 days.

4.2 EXERCISE SOLUTIONS

1. (a) $p = 0.50$ (graph is symmetric)

(b) $p = 0.20$ (graph is skewed right $\rightarrow p < 0.5$)

(c) $p = 0.80$ (graph is skewed left $\rightarrow p > 0.5$)

3. (a) $n = 12, (x = 0, 1, 2, \ldots, 12)$

(b) $n = 4, (x = 0, 1, 2, 3, 4)$

(c) $n = 8, (x = 0, 1, 2, \ldots, 8)$

As n increases, the probability distribution becomes more symmetric.

5. Is a binomial experiment.

Success: baby recovers

$n = 5, p = 0.80, q = 0.20, x = 0, 1, 2, \ldots, 5$

7. Is not a binomial experiment because there are more than 2 possible outcomes for each trial.

© 2006 Pearson Education, Inc., Upper Saddle River, NJ. All rights reserved. This material is protected under all copyright laws as they currently exist. No portion of this material may be reproduced, in any form or by any means, without permission in writing from the publisher.

9. $\mu = np = (100)(0.4) = 40$

$\sigma^2 = npq = (100)(0.4)(0.6) = 24$

$\sigma = \sqrt{\sigma^2} = 4.9$

11. $\mu = np = (138)(0.16) = 22.08$

$\sigma^2 = npq = (138)(0.16)(0.84) = 18.547$

$\sigma = \sqrt{\sigma^2} = 4.307$

13. $n = 5, p = .25$

(a) $P(3) \approx 0.088$

(b) $P(x \geq 3) = P(3) + P(4) + P(5) = 0.088 + 0.015 + .001 = 0.104$

(c) $P(x < 3) = 1 - P(x \geq 3) = 1 - 0.104 = 0.896$

15. $n = 10, p = 0.54$ (using binomial formula)

(a) $P(8) = 0.069$

(b) $P(x \geq 8) = P(8) + P(9) + P(10) = 0.069 + 0.018 + 0.002 = 0.089$

(c) $P(x < 8) = 1 - P(x \geq 8) = 1 - 0.089 = 0.911$

17. $n = 10, p = 0.21$ (using binomial formula)

(a) $P(3) \approx 0.213$

(b) $P(x > 3) = 1 - P(0) - P(1) - P(2) - P(3)$

$= 1 - 0.095 - 0.252 - 3.01 - 0.213 = 0.139$

(c) $P(x \leq 3) = 1 - P(x > 3) = 1 - 0.139 = 0.861$

19. (a) $n = 6, p = 0.36$ (b)   (c) Symmetric

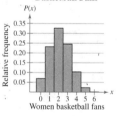

Basketball Fans

x	P(x)
0	0.069
1	0.232
2	0.326
3	0.245
4	0.103
5	0.023
6	0.002

(d) $\mu = np = (6)(0.36) = 2.2$

(e) $\sigma^2 = npq = (6)(0.36)(0.64) \approx 1.4$

(f) $\sigma = \sqrt{\sigma^2} \approx 1.2$

(g) On average 2.2, out of 6, women would consider themselves basketball fans. The standard deviation is 1.2 women.

$x = 0, 5,$ or 6 would be uncommon due to their low probabilities.

© 2006 Pearson Education, Inc., Upper Saddle River, NJ. All rights reserved. This material is protected under all copyright laws as they currently exist. No portion of this material may be reproduced, in any form or by any means, without permission in writing from the publisher.

21. (a) $n = 4, p = 0.05$ (b)   **Donating Blood**   (c) Skewed right

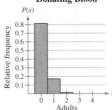

x	P(x)
0	0.814506
1	0.171475
2	0.013537
3	0.000475
4	0.000006

(d) $\mu = np = (4)(0.05) = 0.2$

(e) $\sigma^2 = npq = (4)(0.05)(0.95) = 0.2$

(f) $\sigma = \sqrt{\sigma^2} \approx 0.4$

(g) On average 0.2 eligible adults, out of every 4, give blood. The standard deviation is 0.4 adults.

$x = 2, 3,$ or 4 would be uncommon due to their low probabilities.

23. (a) $n = 6, p = 0.61$ (b) $P(2) = 0.129$

(c) $P(\text{at least } 5) = P(5) + P(6) = 0.197 + 0.052 = 0.249$

x	P(x)
0	0.004
1	0.033
2	0.129
3	0.269
4	0.316
5	0.198
6	0.052

25. $\mu = np = (6)(0.61) = 3.7$

$\sigma^2 = npq = (16)(0.61)(0.39) = 1.4$

$\sigma = \sqrt{\sigma^2} = 1.2$

If six drivers are randomly selected on average 3.7 drivers will name talking on cell phones as the most annoying habit of other drivers.

None of six randomly selected drivers naming talking on cell phones as the most annoying habit of other drivers is rare since $P(0) = 0.004$.

27. $P(5, 2, 2, 1) = \dfrac{10!}{5!2!2!1!}\left(\dfrac{9}{16}\right)^5\left(\dfrac{3}{16}\right)^2\left(\dfrac{3}{16}\right)^2\left(\dfrac{1}{16}\right)^1 \approx 0.033$

4.3 MORE DISCRETE PROBABILITY DISTRIBUTIONS

4.3 Try It Yourself Solutions

1a. $P(1) = (0.23)(0.77)^0 = 0.23$

$P(2) = (0.23)(0.77)^1 = 0.177$

$P(3) = (0.23)(0.77)^2 = 0.136$

b. $P(x < 4) = P(1) + P(2) + P(3) = 0.543$

c. The probability that your first sale will occur before your fourth sales call is 0.543.

© 2006 Pearson Education, Inc., Upper Saddle River, NJ. All rights reserved. This material is protected under all copyright laws as they currently exist. No portion of this material may be reproduced, in any form or by any means, without permission in writing from the publisher.

2a. $P(0) = \dfrac{3^0(2.71828)^{-3}}{0!} \approx 0.050$

$P(1) = \dfrac{3^1(2.71828)^{-3}}{1!} \approx 0.149$

$P(2) = \dfrac{3^2(2.71828)^{-3}}{2!} \approx 0.224$

$P(3) = \dfrac{3^3(2.71828)^{-3}}{3!} \approx 0.224$

$P(4) = \dfrac{3^4(2.71828)^{-3}}{4!} \approx 0.168$

b. $P(0) + P(1) + P(2) + P(3) + P(4) \approx 0.050 + 0.149 + 0.224 + 0.224 + 0.168 \approx 0.815$

c. $1 - 0.815 \approx 0.185$

d. The probability that more than four accidents will occur in any given month at the intersection is 0.185.

3a. $\mu = \dfrac{2000}{20{,}000} = 0.10$

b. $\mu = 0.10,\ x = 3$

c. $P(3) = 0.0002$

d. The probability of finding three brown trout in any given cubic meter of the lake is 0.0002.

4.3 EXERCISE SOLUTIONS

1. $P(3) = (0.8)(0.2)^2 = 0.032$

3. $P(6) = (0.09)(0.91)^5 = 0.056$

5. $P(4) = \dfrac{(2)^4(e^{-2})}{4!} = 0.090$

7. $P(2) = \dfrac{(1.5)^2(e^{-1.5})}{2!} = 0.251$

9. Geometric. We are interested in counting the number of trials until the first success.

11. Poisson. We are interested in counting the number of occurrences that take place within a given unit of space.

13. Binomial. We are interested in counting the number of successes out of n trials.

15. $p = 0.19$

(a) $P(5) = (0.19)(0.81)^4 \approx 0.082$

(b) $P(\text{sale on 1st, 2nd, or 3rd call})$

$= P(1) + P(2) + P(3) = (0.19)(0.81)^0 + (0.19)(0.81)^1 + (0.19)(0.81)^2 \approx 0.469$

(c) $P(x > 3) = 1 - P(x \le 3) = 1 - 0.469 = 0.531$

© 2006 Pearson Education, Inc., Upper Saddle River, NJ. All rights reserved. This material is protected under all copyright laws as they currently exist. No portion of this material may be reproduced, in any form or by any means, without permission in writing from the publisher.

17. $p = 0.01$

(a) $P(10) = (0.01)(0.99)^9 \approx 0.009$

(b) $P(\text{1st, 2nd, or 3rd part is defective}) = P(1) + P(2) + P(3)$

$$= (0.01)(0.99)^0 + (0.01)(0.99)^1 + (0.01)(0.99)^2 \approx 0.030$$

(c) $P(x > 10) = 1 - P(x \le 10) = 1 - [P(1) + P(2) + \cdots + P(10)] = 1 - [0.096] \approx 0.904$

19. $\mu = 8$

(a) $P(4) = \dfrac{8^4 e^{-8}}{4!} \approx 0.057$

(b) $P(x \ge 4) = 1 - (P(0) + P(1) + P(2) + P(3))$

$$\approx 1 - (0.0003 + 0.0027 + 0.0107 + 0.0286)$$

$$= 0.958$$

(c) $P(x > 4) = 1 - (P(0) + P(1) + P(2) + P(3) + P(4))$

$$\approx 1 - (0.0003 + 0.0027 + 0.0107 + 0.0286 + 0.0573)$$

$$= 0.900$$

21. $\mu = 0.7$

(a) $P(1) = 0.348$

(b) $P(X \le 1) = P(0) + P(1) = 0.4966 + 0.3476 = 0.8442$

(c) $P(X > 1) = 1 - P(X \le 1) = 1 - 0.8442 = 0.156$

23. (a) $n = 6500$, $p = 0.001$

$$P(5) = \frac{6500!}{6495!5!}(0.001)^5(0.999)^{6495} \approx 0.1453996179$$

(b) $\mu = \dfrac{6500}{1000} = 6.5$ warped glass items per 6500.

$P(5) = 0.1453688667$

The results are approximately the same.

25. $p = 0.001$

(a) $\mu = \dfrac{1}{p} = \dfrac{1}{0.001} = 1000$

$\sigma^2 = \dfrac{q}{p^2} = \dfrac{0.999}{(0.001)^2} = 999{,}000$

$\sigma = \sqrt{\sigma^2} \approx 999.5$

On average you would have to play 1000 times until you won the lottery. The standard deviation is 999.5.

(b) 1000 times

Lose money. On average you would win $500 every 1000 times you play the lottery. Hence, the net gain would be $-\$500$.

© 2006 Pearson Education, Inc., Upper Saddle River, NJ. All rights reserved. This material is protected under all copyright laws as they currently exist. No portion of this material may be reproduced, in any form or by any means, without permission in writing from the publisher.

27. $\mu = 3.9$

    (a) $\sigma^2 = 3.9$

      $\sigma = \sqrt{\sigma^2} \approx 2.0$

    The standard deviation is 2.0 strokes.

    (b) $P(X > 4) = 1 - P(X \le 4) = 1 - 0.648 = 0.352$

CHAPTER 4 REVIEW EXERCISE SOLUTIONS

1. Discrete

3. Continuous

5. No, $\Sigma P(x) \ne 1$.

7. Yes

9. Yes

11. (a)

x	Frequency	$P(x)$	$xP(x)$	$x - \mu$	$(x - \mu)^2$	$(x - \mu)^2 P(x)$
2	3	0.005	0.009	-4.371	19.104	0.088
3	12	0.018	0.055	-3.371	11.362	0.210
4	72	0.111	0.443	-2.371	5.621	0.623
5	115	0.177	0.885	-1.371	1.879	0.332
6	169	0.260	1.560	-0.371	0.137	0.036
7	120	0.185	1.292	0.629	0.396	0.073
8	83	0.128	1.022	1.629	2.654	0.339
9	48	0.074	0.665	2.629	6.913	0.510
10	22	0.034	0.338	3.629	13.171	0.446
11	6	0.009	0.102	4.629	21.430	0.198
	$n = 650$	$\sum P(x) = 1$	$\sum xP(x) = 6.371$			$\sum (x - \mu)^2 P(x) = 2.855$

(b)

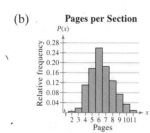

Pages per Section

(c) $\mu = \Sigma xP(x) \approx 6.4$

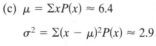

$\sigma^2 = \Sigma(x - \mu)^2 P(x) \approx 2.9$

$\sigma = \sqrt{\sigma^2} \approx 1.7$

13. (a)

x	Frequency	$P(x)$	$xP(x)$	$x - \mu$	$(x - \mu)^2$	$(x - \mu)^2 P(x)$
0	3	0.015	0.000	-2.315	5.359	0.080
1	38	0.190	0.190	-1.315	1.729	0.329
2	83	0.415	0.830	-0.315	0.099	0.041
3	52	0.260	0.780	0.685	0.469	0.122
4	18	0.090	0.360	1.685	2.839	0.256
5	5	0.025	0.125	2.685	7.209	0.180
6	1	0.005	0.030	3.685	13.579	0.068
	$n = 200$	$\sum P(x) = 1$	$\sum xP(x) = 2.315$			$\sum (x - \mu)^2 P(x) = 1.076$

© 2006 Pearson Education, Inc., Upper Saddle River, NJ. All rights reserved. This material is protected under all copyright laws as they currently exist. No portion of this material may be reproduced, in any form or by any means, without permission in writing from the publisher.

(b)

Televisions per Household

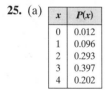

(c) $\mu = \Sigma x P(x) \approx 2.3$

$\sigma^2 = \Sigma(x - \mu)^2 P(x) \approx 1.1$

$\sigma = \sqrt{\sigma^2} \approx 1.0$

15. $E(x) = \mu = \Sigma x P(x) = 3.4$

17. Yes, $n = 12, p = 0.24, q = 0.76, x = 0, 1, \ldots, 12.$

19. $n = 8, p = 0.25$

   (a) $P(3) = 0.208$

   (b) $P(x \geq 3) = 1 - P(x < 3) = 1 - [P(0) + P(1) + P(2)] \approx 1 - [0.100 + 0.267 + 0.311] = 0.322$

   (c) $P(x > 3) = 1 - P(x \leq 3) = 1 - [P(0) + P(1) + P(2) + P(3)]$

$= 1 - [0.100 + 0.267 + 0.311 + 0.208] = 0.114$

21. $n = 7, p = 0.43$ (use binomial formula)

   (a) $P(3) = 0.294$

   (b) $P(x \geq 3) = 1 - P(x < 3) = 1 - [P(0) + P(1) + P(2)] \approx 1 - [0.020 + 0.103 + 0.234] = 0.643$

   (c) $P(x > 3) = 1 - P(x \leq 3) \approx 1 - [P(0) + P(1) + P(2) + P(3)]$

$\approx 1 - (0.020 + 0.103 + 0.234 + 0.294) = 0.349$

23. (a)

x	$P(x)$
0	0.007
1	0.059
2	0.201
3	0.342
4	0.291
5	0.099

(b)

Renting Movies

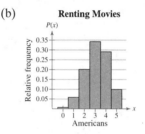

   (c) $\mu = np = (5)(0.63) \approx 3.2$

$\sigma^2 = npq = (5)(0.63)(0.37) = 1.2$

$\sigma = \sqrt{\sigma^2} \approx 1.1$

25. (a)

x	$P(x)$
0	0.012
1	0.096
2	0.293
3	0.397
4	0.202

(b)

Went to a Movie

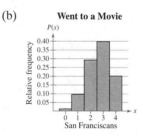

   (c) $\mu = np = (4)(0.67) \approx 2.7$

$\sigma^2 = npq = (4)(0.67)(0.33) = 0.9$

$\sigma = \sqrt{\sigma^2} \approx 0.9$

© 2006 Pearson Education, Inc., Upper Saddle River, NJ. All rights reserved. This material is protected under all copyright laws as they currently exist. No portion of this material may be reproduced, in any form or by any means, without permission in writing from the publisher.

27. $p = 0.167$

    (a) $P(4) \approx 0.096$

    (b) $P(x \leq 4) = P(1) + P(2) + P(3) + P(4) \approx 0.518$

    (c) $P(x > 3) = 1 - P(x \leq 3) = 1 - [P(1) + P(2) + P(3)] \approx 0.579$

29. $\mu = \dfrac{2768}{36} \approx 76.89$ lightning deaths/year $\rightarrow \mu = \dfrac{76.89}{365} \approx 0.211$ deaths/day

    (a) $P(0) = \dfrac{0.211^0 e^{-0.211}}{0!} \approx 0.810$

    (b) $P(1) = \dfrac{0.211^1 e^{-0.211}}{1!} \approx 0.171$

    (c) $P(x > 1) = 1 - [P(0) + P(1)] = 1 - [0.810 + 0.171] = 0.019$

CHAPTER 4 QUIZ SOLUTIONS

1. (a) Discrete because the random variable is countable.

    (b) Continuous because the random variable has an infinite number of possible outcomes and cannot be counted.

2. (a)

x	Frequency	$P(x)$	$xP(x)$	$x - \mu$	$(x - \mu)^2$	$(x - \mu)^2 P(x)$
1	61	0.370	0.370	-1.145	1.312	0.485
2	39	0.236	0.473	-0.145	0.021	0.005
3	48	0.291	0.873	0.855	0.730	0.212
4	14	0.085	0.339	1.855	3.439	0.292
5	3	0.018	0.091	2.855	8.148	0.148
	$n = 165$	$\sum P(x) = 1$	$\sum xP(x) = 2.145$			$\sum(x - \mu)^2 P(x) = 1.142$

    (b)

Hurricane Intensity

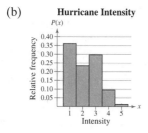

    (c) $\mu = \Sigma xP(x) \approx 2.1$

        $\sigma^2 = \Sigma(x - \mu)^2 P(x) \approx 1.1$

        $\sigma = \sqrt{\sigma^2} \approx 1.1$

    On average the intensity of a hurricane will be 2.1. The standard deviation is 1.1.

    (d) $P(x \geq 4) = P(4) + P(5) = 0.085 + 0.018 = 0.103$

© 2006 Pearson Education, Inc., Upper Saddle River, NJ. All rights reserved. This material is protected under all copyright laws as they currently exist. No portion of this material may be reproduced, in any form or by any means, without permission in writing from the publisher.

3. $n = 8, p = 0.80$

(a)

x	$P(x)$
0	0.000003
1	0.000082
2	0.001147
3	0.009175
4	0.045875
5	0.146801
6	0.293601
7	0.335544
8	0.167772

(b)

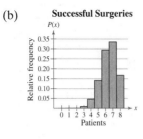

Successful Surgeries

(c) $\mu = np = (8)(0.80) = 6.4$

$\sigma^2 = npq = (8)(0.80)(0.20) = 1.3$

$\sigma = \sqrt{\sigma^2} \approx 1.1$

(d) $P(2) = 0.001$

(e) $P(x < 2) = P(0) + P(1) = 0.000003 + 0.000082 = 0.000085$

4. $\mu = 5$

(a) $P(5) = 0.1755$

(b) $P(x < 5) = P(0) + P(1) + P(2) + P(3) + P(4)$

$= 0.0067 + 0.0337 + 0.0842 + 0.1404 + 0.1755 = 0.4405$

(c) $P(0) = 0.0067$

© 2006 Pearson Education, Inc., Upper Saddle River, NJ. All rights reserved. This material is protected under all copyright laws as they currently exist.
No portion of this material may be reproduced, in any form or by any means, without permission in writing from the publisher.

Normal Probability Distributions

5.1 INTRODUCTION TO NORMAL DISTRIBUTIONS AND THE STANDARD NORMAL DISTRIBUTION

5.1 Try It Yourself Solutions

1a. A: 45, B: 60, C: 45 (B has the greatest mean)

b. Curve C is more spread out, so curve C has the greatest standard deviation.

2a. Mean = 3.5 feet

b. Inflection points: 3.3 and 3.7
Standard deviation = 0.2 feet

3a. (1) 0.0143   (2) 0.985

4a.

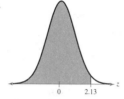

5a.

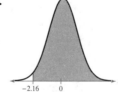

b. 0.9834

b. 0.0154

c. Area = $1 - 0.0154 = 0.9846$

6a. 0.0885   **b.** 0.0154

c. Area = $0.0885 - 0.0154 = 0.0731$

5.1 EXERCISE SOLUTIONS

1. Answers will vary.

3. Answers will vary.
Similarities: Both curves will have the same line of symmetry.
Differences: One curve will be more spread out than the other.

5. $\mu = 0$, $\sigma = 1$

7. "The" standard normal distribution is used to describe one specific normal distribution ($\mu = 0$, $\sigma = 1$). "A" normal distribution is used to describe a normal distribution with any mean and standard deviation.

9. No, the graph crosses the x-axis.

11. Yes, the graph fulfills the properties of the normal distribution.

13. No, the graph is skewed to the right.

15. The histogram represents data from a normal distribution since it's bell-shaped.

17. (Area left of $z = 1.2$) − (Area left of $z = 0$) = $0.8849 - 0.5 = 0.3849$

65

© 2006 Pearson Education, Inc., Upper Saddle River, NJ. All rights reserved. This material is protected under all copyright laws as they currently exist. No portion of this material may be reproduced, in any form or by any means, without permission in writing from the publisher.

19. (Area left of $z = 1.5$) − (Area left of $z = -0.5$) = $0.9332 - 0.3085 = 0.6247$

21. 0.9382

23. 0.975

25. $1 - 0.1711 = 0.8289$

27. $1 - 0.8997 = 0.1003$

29. 0.005

31. $1 - 0.95 = 0.05$

33. $0.975 - 0.5 = 0.475$

35. $0.5 - 0.0630 = 0.437$

37. $0.9750 - 0.0250 = 0.95$

39. $0.1003 + 0.1003 = 0.2006$

41. (a)

Light Bulb Life Spans

It is reasonable to assume that the life span is normally distributed since the histogram is nearly symmetric and bell-shaped.

(b) $\bar{x} = 1941.35$ $s \approx 432.385$

(c) The sample mean of 1941.35 hours is less than the claimed mean, so on the average the bulbs in the sample lasted for a shorter time. The sample standard deviation of 432 hours is greater than the claimed standard deviation, so the bulbs in the sample had a greater variation in life span than the manufacturer's claim.

43. (a) A = 2.97   B = 2.98   C = 3.01   D = 3.05

(b) $x = 3.01 \Longrightarrow z = \dfrac{x - \mu}{\sigma} = \dfrac{3.01 - 3}{0.02} = 0.5$

$x = 2.97 \Longrightarrow z = \dfrac{x - \mu}{\sigma} = \dfrac{2.97 - 3}{0.02} = -1.5$

$x = 2.98 \Longrightarrow z = \dfrac{x - \mu}{\sigma} = \dfrac{2.98 - 3}{0.02} = -1.0$

$x = 3.05 \Longrightarrow z = \dfrac{x - \mu}{\sigma} = \dfrac{3.05 - 3}{0.02} = 2.5$

(c) $x = 3.05$ is unusual due to a relatively large z-score (2, 5).

45. (a) A = 801   B = 950   C = 1250   D = 1467

(b) $x = 950 \Longrightarrow z = \dfrac{x - \mu}{\sigma} = \dfrac{950 - 1026}{209} = -0.36$

$x = 1250 \Longrightarrow z = \dfrac{x - \mu}{\sigma} = \dfrac{1250 - 1026}{209} = 1.07$

$x = 1467 \Longrightarrow z = \dfrac{x - \mu}{\sigma} = \dfrac{1467 - 1026}{209} = 2.11$

$x = 801 \Longrightarrow z = \dfrac{x - \mu}{\sigma} = \dfrac{801 - 1026}{209} = -1.08$

(c) $x = 1467$ is unusual due to a relatively large z-score (2.11).

47. 0.6915

49. $1 - 0.95 = 0.05$

51. $0.8413 - 0.3085 = 0.5328$

53. $P(z < 1.45) = 0.9265$

© 2006 Pearson Education, Inc., Upper Saddle River, NJ. All rights reserved. This material is protected under all copyright laws as they currently exist. No portion of this material may be reproduced, in any form or by any means, without permission in writing from the publisher.

55. $P(z > -1.95) = 1 - P(z < -1.95) = 1 - 0.0256 = 0.9744$

57. $P(-0.89 < z < 0) = 0.5 - 0.1867 = 0.3133$

59. $P(-1.65 < z < 1.65) = 0.9505 - .0495 = 0.901$

61. $P(z < -2.58$ or $z > 2.58) = 2(0.0049) = 0.0098$

63.

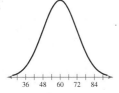

The normal distribution curve is centered at its mean (60) and has 2 points of inflection (48 and 72) representing $\mu \pm \sigma$.

65. (a) Area under curve = area of rectangle = (base)(height) = (1)(1) = 1

(b) $P(0.25 < x < 0.5) = $ (base)(height) = (0.25)(1) = 0.25

(c) $P(0.3 < x < 0.7) = $ (base)(height) = (0.4)(1) = 0.4

5.2 NORMAL DISTRIBUTIONS: FINDIING PROBABILITIES

5.2 Try It Yourself Solutions

1a.

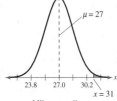

Miles per gallon

b. $z = \dfrac{x - \mu}{\sigma} = \dfrac{31 - 27}{1.6} = 2.50$

c. $P(z < 2.50) = 0.9938$

$P(z > 2.50) = 1 - 0.9938 = 0.0062$

d. The probability that a randomly selected manual transmission Focus will get more than 31 mpg in city driving is 0.0062.

2a.

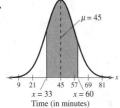

Time (in minutes)

© 2006 Pearson Education, Inc., Upper Saddle River, NJ. All rights reserved. This material is protected under all copyright laws as they currently exist. No portion of this material may be reproduced, in any form or by any means, without permission in writing from the publisher.

b. $z = \dfrac{x - \mu}{\sigma} = \dfrac{33 - 45}{12} = -1$

$z = \dfrac{x - \mu}{\sigma} = \dfrac{60 - 45}{12} = 1.25$

c. $P(z < -1) = 0.1587$

$P(z > 1.25) = 0.8944$

d. $P(-1 < z < 1.25) = 0.8944 - 0.1587 = 0.7357$

3a. Read user's guide for the technology tool.

b. Enter the data.

c. $P(190 < x < 225) = P(-1 < z < 0.4) = 0.4968$

The probability that a randomly selected U.S. man's cholesterol is between 190 and 225 is about 0.4968.

5.2 EXERCISE SOLUTIONS

1. $P(x < 80) = P(z < -1.2) = 0.1151$

3. $P(x > 92) = P(z > 1.2) = 1 - 0.8849 = 0.1151$

5. $P(70 < x < 80) = P(-3.2 < z < -1.2) = 0.1151 - 0.0007 = 0.1144$

7. $P(200 < x < 450) = P(-2.77 < z < -0.51) = 0.3050 - 0.0028 = 0.3022$

9. $P(200 < x < 239) = P(0.38 < z < 1.42) = 0.9222 - 0.6480 = 0.2742$

11. $P(167 < x < 174) = P(1.57 < z < 2.94) = 0.9984 - 0.9418 = 0.0566$

13. (a) $P(x < 66) = P(z < -1.10) = 0.1357$

(b) $P(66 < x < 72) = P(-1.10 < z < 0.97) = 0.8340 - 0.1357 = 0.6983$

(c) $P(x > 72) = P(z > 0.97) = 1 - P(z < 0.97) = 1 - 0.8340 = 0.1660$

15. (a) $P(x < 20) = P(z < -0.95) = 0.1711$

(b) $P(20 < x < 29) = P(-0.95 < z < 1.14) = 0.8729 - 0.1711 = 0.7018$

(c) $P(x > 29) = P(z > 1.14) = 1 - P(z < 1.14) = 1 - 0.8729 = 0.1271$

17. (a) $P(x < 4.5) = P(z < -2.5) = 0.0062$

(b) $P(4.5 < x < 9.5) = P(-2.5 < z < 2.5) = 0.9938 - 0.0062 = 0.9876$

(c) $P(x > 9.5) = P(z > 2.5) = 1 - P(z < 2.5) = 1 - 0.9938 = 0.0062$

19. (a) $P(x < 4) = (z < -2.44) = 0.0073$

(b) $P(4 < x < 7) = P(-2.44 < z < 0.89) = 0.8133 - 0.0073 = 0.8060$

(c) $P(x > 7) = P(z > 0.89) = 1 - 0.8133 = 0.1867$

21. (a) $P(x < 600) = P(z < 0.84) = 0.7995 \Rightarrow 79.95\%$

(b) $P(x > 550) = P(z > 0.39) = 1 - P(z < 0.39) = 1 - 0.6517 = 0.3483$

$(1000)(0.3483) = 348.3 \Rightarrow 348$

© 2006 Pearson Education, Inc., Upper Saddle River, NJ. All rights reserved. This material is protected under all copyright laws as they currently exist. No portion of this material may be reproduced, in any form or by any means, without permission in writing from the publisher.

23. (a) $P(x < 200) = P(z < 0.38) = 0.6480 \Rightarrow 64.80\%$

(b) $P(x > 240) = P(z > 1.45) = 1 - P(z < 1.45) = 1 - 0.9265 = 0.0735$

$(250)(0.0735) = 18.375 \Rightarrow 18$

25. (a) $P(x > 11) = P(z > 0.5) = 1 - P(z < 0.5) = 1 - 0.6915 = 0.3085 \Rightarrow 30.85\%$

(b) $P(x < 8) = P(z < -1) = 0.1587$

$(200)(0.1587) = 31.74 \Rightarrow 31$

27. (a) $P(x > 4) = P(z > -3) = 1 - P(z < -3) = 1 - 0.0013 = 0.9987 \Rightarrow 99.87\%$

(b) $P(x < 5) = P(z < -2) = 0.0228$

$(35)(0.0228) = 0.798$

29. $P(x > 2065) = P(z > 2.17) = 1 - P(z < 2.17) = 1 - 0.9850 = 0.0150 \Rightarrow 1.5\%$

It is unusual for a battery to have a life span that is more than 2065 hours because of the relatively large z-score (2.17).

31. Out of control, since the 10th observation plotted beyond 3 standard deviations.

33. Out of control, since the first nine observations lie below the mean and since two out of three consecutive points lie more than 2 standard deviations from the mean.

5.3 NORMAL DISTRIBUTIONS: FINDING VALUES

5.3 Try It Yourself Solutions

1ab. (1)   (2)

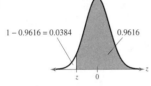
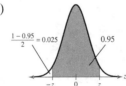

  c. (1) $z = -1.77$ (2) $z = \pm 1.96$

2a. (1)   (2)   (3)

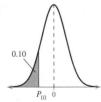
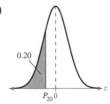
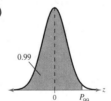

  b. (1) use area = 0.1003   (2) use area = 0.2005   (3) use area = 0.9901

  c. (1) $z = -1.28$ (2) $z = -0.84$ (3) $z = 2.33$

3a. $\mu = 70$, $\sigma = 8$

  b. $z = -0.75 \Rightarrow x = \mu + z\sigma = 70 + (-0.75)(8) = 64$

$z = 4.29 \Rightarrow x = \mu + z\sigma = 70 + (4.29)(8) = 104.32$

$z = -1.82 \Rightarrow x = \mu + z\sigma = 70 + (-1.82)(8) = 55.44$

  c. 64 and 55.44 are below the mean. 104.32 is above the mean.

© 2006 Pearson Education, Inc., Upper Saddle River, NJ. All rights reserved. This material is protected under all copyright laws as they currently exist. No portion of this material may be reproduced, in any form or by any means, without permission in writing from the publisher.

4a.

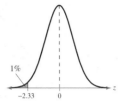

b. $z = -2.33$

c. $x = \mu + z\sigma = 158 + (-2.33)(6.51) \approx 142.83$

d. So, the longest braking distance a Ford F-150 could have and still be in the top 1% is 143 feet.

5a.

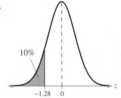

b. $z = -1.28$

c. $x = \mu + z\sigma = 11.2 + (-1.28)(2.1) = 8.512$

d. So, the maximum length of time an employee could have worked and still be laid off is 8 years.

5.3 EXERCISE SOLUTIONS

1. $z = -2.05$ **3.** $z = 0.85$ **5.** $z = -0.16$

7. $z = 2.39$ **9.** $z = -1.645$ **11.** $z = 0.99$

13. $z = -2.325$ **15.** $z = -0.25$ **17.** $z = 1.175$

19. $z = -0.675$ **21.** $z = 0.675$ **23.** $z = -0.385$

25. $z = -0.38$ **27.** $z = -0.58$ **29.** $z = \pm 1.645$

31.

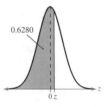

$\Rightarrow z = 0.325$

33.

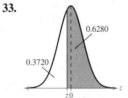

$\Rightarrow z = -0.33$

35.

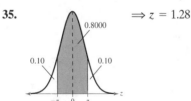

$\Rightarrow z = 1.28$

37.

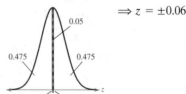

$\Rightarrow z = \pm 0.06$

© 2006 Pearson Education, Inc., Upper Saddle River, NJ. All rights reserved. This material is protected under all copyright laws as they currently exist. No portion of this material may be reproduced, in any form or by any means, without permission in writing from the publisher.

39. (a) 95th percentile $\Rightarrow$ Area $= 0.95 \Rightarrow z = 1.645$

$x = \mu + z\sigma = 64 + (1.645)(2.75) = 68.52$

(b) 1st quartile $\Rightarrow$ Area $= 0.25 \Rightarrow z = -0.675$

$x = \mu + z\sigma = 64 + (-0.675)(2.75) = 62.14$

41. (a) 10th percentile $\Rightarrow$ Area $= 0.10 \Rightarrow z = -1.28$

$x = \mu + z\sigma = 17.4 + (-1.28)(4) = 12.28$

(b) 3rd quartile $\Rightarrow$ Area $= 0.75 \Rightarrow z = 0.67$

$x = \mu + z\sigma = 17.4 + (0.67)(4) = 20.08$

43. (a) Top 30% $\Rightarrow$ Area $= 0.70 \Rightarrow z = 0.52$

$x = \mu + z\sigma = 127 + (0.52)(23.5) = 139.22$

(b) Bottom 10% $\Rightarrow$ Area $= 0.10 \Rightarrow z = -1.28$

$x = \mu + z\sigma = 127 + (-1.28)(23.5) = 96.92$

45. Lower 5% $\Rightarrow$ Area $= 0.05 \Rightarrow z = -1.645$

$x = \mu + z\sigma = 20 + (-1.645)(0.07) = 19.89$

47. Bottom 10% $\Rightarrow$ Area $= 0.10 \Rightarrow z = -1.28$

$x = \mu + z\sigma = 30,000 + (-1.28)(2500) = 26,800$

Tires which wear out by 26,800 miles will be replaced free of charge.

49. Top 1% $\Rightarrow$ Area $= 0.99 \Rightarrow z = 2.33$

$x = \mu + z\sigma \Rightarrow 8 = \mu + (2.33)(0.03) \Rightarrow \mu = 7.930$

5.4 SAMPLING DISTRIBUTIONS AND THE CENTRAL LIMIT THEOREM

5.4 Try It Yourself Solutions

1a.

Sample	Mean	Sample	Mean	Sample	Mean	Sample	Mean
1, 1, 1	1	3, 1, 1	1.67	5, 1, 1	2.33	7, 1, 1	3
1, 1, 3	1.67	3, 1, 3	2.33	5, 1, 3	3	7, 1, 3	3.67
1, 1, 5	2.33	3, 1, 5	3	5, 1, 5	3.67	7, 1, 5	4.33
1, 1, 7	3	3, 1, 7	3.67	5, 1, 7	4.33	7, 1, 7	5
1, 3, 1	1.67	3, 3, 1	2.33	5, 3, 1	3	7, 3, 1	3.67
1, 3, 3	2.33	3, 3, 3	3	5, 3, 3	3.67	7, 3, 3	4.33
1, 3, 5	3	3, 3, 5	3.67	5, 3, 5	4.33	7, 3, 5	5
1, 3, 7	3.67	3, 3, 7	4.33	5, 3, 7	5	7, 3, 7	5.67
1, 5, 1	2.33	3, 5, 1	3	5, 5, 1	3.67	7, 5, 1	4.33
1, 5, 3	3	3, 5, 3	3.67	5, 5, 3	4.33	7, 5, 3	5
1, 5, 5	3.67	3, 5, 5	4.33	5, 5, 5	5	7, 5, 5	5.67
1, 5, 7	4.33	3, 5, 7	5	5, 5, 7	5.67	7, 5, 7	6.33
1, 7, 1	3	3, 7, 1	3.67	5, 7, 1	4.33	7, 7, 1	5
1, 7, 3	3.67	3, 7, 3	4.33	5, 7, 3	5	7, 7, 3	5.67
1, 7, 5	4.33	3, 7, 5	5	5, 7, 5	5.67	7, 7, 5	6.33
1, 7, 7	5	3, 7, 7	5.67	5, 7, 7	6.33	7, 7, 7	7

© 2006 Pearson Education, Inc., Upper Saddle River, NJ. All rights reserved. This material is protected under all copyright laws as they currently exist. No portion of this material may be reproduced, in any form or by any means, without permission in writing from the publisher.

b.

$\bar{x}$	f	Probability
1	1	0.0156
1.67	3	0.0469
2.33	6	0.0938
3	10	0.1563
3.67	12	0.1875
4.33	12	0.1875
5	10	0.1563
5.67	6	0.0938
6.33	3	0.0469
7	1	0.0156

$\mu_{\bar{x}} = 4, \sigma_{\bar{x}}^2 \approx 1.667, \sigma_{\bar{x}} \approx 1.291$

c. $\mu_{\bar{x}} = \mu = 4, \sigma_{\bar{x}}^2 = \dfrac{\sigma^2}{n} = \dfrac{5}{3} = 1.667, \sigma_{\bar{x}} = \dfrac{\sigma}{\sqrt{n}} = \dfrac{\sqrt{5}}{\sqrt{3}} = 1.291$

2a. $\mu_{\bar{x}} = \mu = 64, \sigma_{\bar{x}} = \dfrac{\sigma}{\sqrt{n}} = \dfrac{9}{\sqrt{100}} = 0.9$

b. $n = 100$

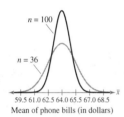

59.5 61.0 62.5 64.0 65.5 67.0 68.5
Mean of phone bills (in dollars)

c. With a larger sample size, the mean stays the same but the standard deviation decreases.

3a. $\mu_{\bar{x}} = \mu = 3.5, \sigma_{\bar{x}} = \dfrac{\sigma}{\sqrt{n}} = \dfrac{0.2}{\sqrt{16}} = 0.05$

b.

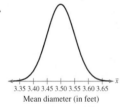

3.35 3.40 3.45 3.50 3.55 3.60 3.65
Mean diameter (in feet)

4a. $\mu_{\bar{x}} = \mu = 25, \sigma_{\bar{x}} = \dfrac{\sigma}{\sqrt{n}} = \dfrac{1.5}{\sqrt{100}} = 0.15$

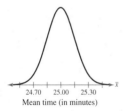

24.70   25.00   25.30
Mean time (in minutes)

© 2006 Pearson Education, Inc., Upper Saddle River, NJ. All rights reserved. This material is protected under all copyright laws as they currently exist. No portion of this material may be reproduced, in any form or by any means, without permission in writing from the publisher.

b. $\bar{x} = 24.7$: $z = \dfrac{\bar{x} - \mu}{\dfrac{\sigma}{\sqrt{n}}} = \dfrac{24.7 - 25}{\dfrac{1.5}{\sqrt{100}}} = -\dfrac{0.3}{0.15} = -2$

$\bar{x} = 25.5$: $z = \dfrac{\bar{x} - \mu}{\dfrac{\sigma}{\sqrt{n}}} = \dfrac{25.5 - 25}{\dfrac{1.5}{\sqrt{100}}} = \dfrac{0.5}{0.15} = 3.33$

c. $P(z < -2) \approx 0.0228$

$P(z < 3.33) = 0.9996$

$P(8.7 < \bar{x} < 9.5) = P(-2 < z < 3.33) = 0.9996 - 0.0228 = 0.9768$

5a. $\mu_{\bar{x}} = \mu = 243{,}756$, $\sigma_{\bar{x}} = \dfrac{\sigma}{\sqrt{n}} = \dfrac{44{,}000}{\sqrt{12}} \approx 12{,}701.7$

218,356 243,756 269,156
Mean sales price (in dollars)

b. $\bar{x} = 200{,}000$: $z = \dfrac{\bar{x} - \mu}{\dfrac{\sigma}{\sqrt{n}}} = \dfrac{200{,}000 - 243{,}756}{\dfrac{44{,}000}{\sqrt{12}}} = \dfrac{-43.756}{12{,}701.7} = -3.44$

c. $P(\bar{x} > 200{,}000) = P(z > -3.44) = 1 - P(z < -3.44) = 1 - 0.0003 = 0.9997$

6a. $x = 700$: $z = \dfrac{x - \mu}{\sigma} = \dfrac{700 - 625}{150} = 0.5$

$\bar{x} = 700$: $z = \dfrac{\bar{x} - \mu}{\dfrac{\sigma}{\sqrt{n}}} = \dfrac{700 - 625}{\dfrac{150}{\sqrt{10}}} = \dfrac{75}{47.43} = 1.58$

b. $P(z < 0.5) = 0.6915$

$P(z < 1.58) = 0.9429$

c. There is a 69% chance an *individual receiver* will cost less than $700. There is a 94% chance that the *mean of a sample of 10 receivers* is less than $700.

5.4 EXERCISE SOLUTIONS

1. $\mu_{\bar{x}} = \mu = 100$

$\sigma_{\bar{x}} = \dfrac{\sigma}{\sqrt{n}} = \dfrac{15}{\sqrt{50}} = 2.12$

3. $\mu_{\bar{x}} = \mu = 100$

$\sigma_{\bar{x}} = \dfrac{\sigma}{\sqrt{n}} = \dfrac{15}{\sqrt{250}} = 0.949$

5. False. As the size of the sample increases, the mean of the distribution of the sample mean does not change.

© 2006 Pearson Education, Inc., Upper Saddle River, NJ. All rights reserved. This material is protected under all copyright laws as they currently exist. No portion of this material may be reproduced, in any form or by any means, without permission in writing from the publisher.

7. False. The shape of the sampling distribution of sample means is normal for large sample sizes even if the shape of the population is non-normal.

9. $\mu_{\bar{x}} = 3.5$, $\sigma_{\bar{x}} = 1.708$

$\mu = 3.5$, $\sigma = 2.958$

Sample	Mean	Sample	Mean	Sample	Mean	Sample	Mean
0, 0, 0	0	2, 0, 0	0.67	4, 0, 0	1.33	8, 0, 0	2.67
0, 0, 2	0.67	2, 0, 2	1.33	4, 0, 2	2	8, 0, 2	3.33
0, 0, 4	1.33	2, 0, 4	2	4, 0, 4	2.67	8, 0, 4	4
0, 0, 8	2.67	2, 0, 8	3.33	4, 0, 8	4	8, 0, 8	5.33
0, 2, 0	0.67	2, 2, 0	1.33	4, 2, 0	2	8, 2, 0	3.33
0, 2, 2	1.33	2, 2, 2	2	4, 2, 2	2.67	8, 2, 2	4
0, 2, 4	2	2, 2, 4	2.67	4, 2, 4	3.33	8, 2, 4	4.67
0, 2, 8	3.33	2, 2, 8	4	4, 2, 8	4.67	8, 2, 8	6
0, 4, 0	1.33	2, 4, 0	2	4, 4, 0	2.67	8, 4, 0	4
0, 4, 2	2	2, 4, 2	2.67	4, 4, 2	3.33	8, 4, 2	4.67
0, 4, 4	2.67	2, 4, 4	3.33	4, 4, 4	4	8, 4, 4	5.33
0, 4, 8	4	2, 4, 8	4.67	4, 4, 8	5.33	8, 4, 8	6.67
0, 8, 0	2.67	2, 8, 0	3.33	4, 8, 0	4	8, 8, 0	5.33
0, 8, 2	3.33	2, 8, 2	4	4, 8, 2	4.67	8, 8, 2	6
0, 8, 4	4	2, 8, 4	4.67	4, 8, 4	5.33	8, 8, 4	6.67
0, 8, 8	5.33	2, 8, 8	6	4, 8, 8	6.67	8, 8, 8	8

11. (c) Since $\mu_{\bar{x}} = 16.5$, $\sigma_{\bar{x}} = \dfrac{\sigma}{\sqrt{n}} = \dfrac{11.9}{\sqrt{100}} = 1.19$ and the graph approximates a normal curve.

13. $\mu_{\bar{x}} = 87.5$

$\sigma_{\bar{x}} = \dfrac{\sigma}{\sqrt{n}} = \dfrac{6.25}{\sqrt{12}} \approx 1.804$

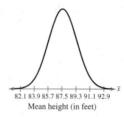

82.1 83.9 85.7 87.5 89.3 91.1 92.9
Mean height (in feet)

15. $\mu_{\bar{x}} = 349$

$\sigma_{\bar{x}} = \dfrac{\sigma}{\sqrt{n}} = \dfrac{8}{\sqrt{40}} = 1.26$

346.5   349   351.5
Mean price (in dollars)

17. $\mu_{\bar{x}} = 113.5$

$\sigma_{\bar{x}} = \dfrac{\sigma}{\sqrt{n}} = \dfrac{38.5}{\sqrt{20}} \approx 8.61$

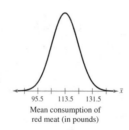

95.5   113.5   131.5
Mean consumption of
red meat (in pounds)

© 2006 Pearson Education, Inc., Upper Saddle River, NJ. All rights reserved. This material is protected under all copyright laws as they currently exist. No portion of this material may be reproduced, in any form or by any means, without permission in writing from the publisher.

19. $\mu_{\bar{x}} = 87.5, \sigma_{\bar{x}} = \dfrac{\sigma}{\sqrt{n}} = \dfrac{6.25}{\sqrt{24}} \approx 1.276$

$\mu_{\bar{x}} = 87.5, \sigma_{\bar{x}} = \dfrac{\sigma}{\sqrt{n}} = \dfrac{6.25}{\sqrt{36}} \approx 1.042$

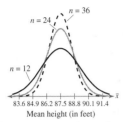

As the sample size increases, the standard error decreases, while the mean of the sample means remains constant.

21. $z = \dfrac{\bar{x} - \mu}{\dfrac{\sigma}{\sqrt{n}}} = \dfrac{38{,}000 - 40{,}500}{\dfrac{5600}{\sqrt{42}}} = \dfrac{-2500}{864.10} \approx -2.89$

$P(\bar{x} < 38{,}000) = P(z < -2.89) = 0.0019$

23. $z = \dfrac{\bar{x} - \mu}{\dfrac{\sigma}{\sqrt{n}}} = \dfrac{1.684 - 1.689}{\dfrac{0.045}{\sqrt{32}}} = \dfrac{-0.005}{0.00795} \approx -0.63$

$z = \dfrac{\bar{x} - \mu}{\dfrac{\sigma}{\sqrt{n}}} = \dfrac{1.699 - 1.689}{\dfrac{0.045}{\sqrt{32}}} = \dfrac{0.01}{0.00795} \approx 1.26$

$P(1.684 < \bar{x} < 1.699) = P(-0.63 < z < 1.26) = 0.8962 - 0.2643 = 0.6319$

25. $z = \dfrac{\bar{x} - \mu}{\dfrac{\sigma}{\sqrt{n}}} = \dfrac{66 - 64}{\dfrac{2.75}{\sqrt{60}}} = \dfrac{2}{0.355} \approx 5.63$

$P(\bar{x} > 68) = P(z > 5.63) \approx 0$

27. $z = \dfrac{\bar{x} - \mu}{\sigma} = \dfrac{70 - 64}{2.75} \approx 2.18$

$P(x < 70) = P(z < 2.18) = 0.9854$

$z = \dfrac{\bar{x} - \mu}{\dfrac{\sigma}{\sqrt{n}}} = \dfrac{70 - 64}{\dfrac{2.75}{\sqrt{20}}} = \dfrac{6}{0.615} \approx 9.76$

$P(\bar{x} < 70) = P(z < 9.76) \approx 1$

It is more likely to select a sample of 20 women with a mean height less than 70 inches, because the sample of 20 has a higher probability.

29. $z = \dfrac{\bar{x} - \mu}{\dfrac{\sigma}{\sqrt{n}}} = \dfrac{127.9 - 128}{\dfrac{0.20}{\sqrt{40}}} = \dfrac{-0.1}{0.032} \approx 3.16$

$P(\bar{x} < 127.9) = P(z < -3.16) = 0.0008$

Yes, it is very unlikely that we would have randomly sampled 40 cans with a mean equal to 127.9 ounces.

© 2006 Pearson Education, Inc., Upper Saddle River, NJ. All rights reserved. This material is protected under all copyright laws as they currently exist. No portion of this material may be reproduced, in any form or by any means, without permission in writing from the publisher.

31. (a) $\mu = 96$

$\sigma = 0.5$

$$z = \dfrac{\bar{x} - \mu}{\dfrac{\sigma}{\sqrt{\mu}}} = \dfrac{96.25 - 96}{\dfrac{0.5}{\sqrt{90}}} = \dfrac{0.25}{0.079} \approx 3.16$$

$P(\bar{x} \geq 96.25) = P(z > 3.16) = 1 - P(z < 3.16) = 1 - 0.9992 = 0.0008$

(b) Claim is inaccurate

(c) Assuming the distribution is normally distributed:

$$z = \dfrac{\bar{x} - \mu}{\sigma} = \dfrac{96.25 - 96}{0.5} = 0.5$$

$P(x > 96.25) = P(z > 0.5) = 1 - P(z < 0.5) = 1 - 0.6915 = 0.3085$

Assuming the manufacturer's claim is true, an individual board with a length of 96.25 would not be unusual. It is within 1 standard deviation of the mean for an individual board.

33. (a) $\mu = 50,000$

$\sigma = 800$

$$z = \dfrac{\bar{x} - \mu}{\dfrac{\sigma}{\sqrt{n}}} = \dfrac{49,721 - 50,000}{\dfrac{800}{\sqrt{100}}} = \dfrac{-279}{80} = -3.49$$

$P(\bar{x} \leq 49,721) = P(z \leq -3.49) = 0.0002$

(b) The manufacturer's claim is inaccurate.

(c) Assuming the distribution is normally distributed:

$$z = \dfrac{x - \mu}{\sigma} = \dfrac{49,721 - 50,000}{800} = -0.35$$

$P(x < 49,721) = P(z < -0.35) = 0.3669$

Assuming the manufacturer's claim is true, an individual tire with a life span of 49,721 miles is not unusual. It is within 1 standard deviation of the mean for an individual tire.

35. $\mu = 500$

$\sigma = 100$

$$z = \dfrac{\bar{x} - \mu}{\sigma/\sqrt{n}} = \dfrac{530 - 500}{100/\sqrt{50}} = \dfrac{30}{14.14} = 2.12$$

$P(\bar{x} \geq 530) = P(z \geq 2.12) = 1 - P(z \leq 2.12) = 1 - 0.9830 = 0.017$

The high school's claim is justified since it is rare to find a sample mean as large as 530.

37. Use the finite correction factor since $n = 55 > 40 = 0.05N$.

$$z = \dfrac{\bar{x} - \mu}{\dfrac{\sigma}{\sqrt{n}}\sqrt{\dfrac{N-n}{N-1}}} = \dfrac{1.683 - 1.688}{\dfrac{0.009}{\sqrt{55}}\sqrt{\dfrac{800-55}{800-1}}} = \dfrac{-0.005}{(0.00121)\sqrt{0.9324}} \approx -4.27$$

$P(\bar{x} < 1.683) = P(z < -4.27) \approx 0$

© 2006 Pearson Education, Inc., Upper Saddle River, NJ. All rights reserved. This material is protected under all copyright laws as they currently exist. No portion of this material may be reproduced, in any form or by any means, without permission in writing from the publisher.

5.5 NORMAL APPROXIMATIONS TO BINOMIAL DISTRIBUTIONS

5.5 Try It Yourself Solutions

1a. $n = 70, p = 0.61, q = 0.39$

b. $np = 42.7, nq = 27.3$

c. Since $np \geq 5$ and $nq \geq 5$, the normal distribution can be used.

d. $\mu = np = (0.70)(0.61) = 42.7$

$\sigma = \sqrt{npq} = \sqrt{(70)(0.61)(0.39)} \approx 4.08$

2a. (1) $57, 58, \ldots, 83$ (2) $\ldots, 52, 53, 54$

b. (1) $56.5 < x < 83.5$ (2) $x < 54.5$

3a. $n = 70, p = 0.61$

$np = 42.7 \geq 5$ and $nq = 27.3 \geq 5$

The normal distribution can be used.

b. $\mu = np = 42.7$

$\sigma = \sqrt{npq} \approx 4.08$

c. $x > 50.5$

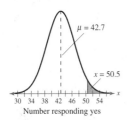

d. $z = \dfrac{x - \mu}{\sigma} = \dfrac{50.5 - 42.7}{4.08} \approx 1.91$

e. $P(z < 1.91) = 0.9719$

$P(x > 50.5) = P(z > 1.91) = 1 - P(z < 1.91) = 0.0281$

The probability that more than 50 respond yes is 0.0281.

4a. $n = 200, p = 0.38$

$np = 76 \geq 5$ and $nq = 124 \geq 5$

The normal distribution can be used.

b. $\mu = np = 76$

$\sigma = \sqrt{npq} \approx 6.86$

© 2006 Pearson Education, Inc., Upper Saddle River, NJ. All rights reserved. This material is protected under all copyright laws as they currently exist. No portion of this material may be reproduced, in any form or by any means, without permission in writing from the publisher.

  c. $P(x < 85.5)$

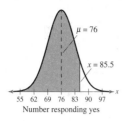

Number responding yes

  d. $z = \dfrac{x - \mu}{\sigma} = \dfrac{85.5 - 76}{6.86} \approx 1.38$

  e. $P(x < 65.5) = P(z < 1.38) = 0.9162$

    The probability that at most 65 people will say yes is 0.9162.

5a. $n = 200, p = 0.95$

  $np = 190 \geq 5$ and $nq = 10 \geq 5$

  The normal distribution can be used.

  b. $\mu = np = 190$

    $\sigma = \sqrt{npq} \approx 3.08$

  c. $P(190.5 < x < 191.5)$

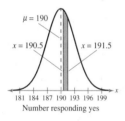

Number responding yes

  d. $z = \dfrac{x - \mu}{\sigma} = \dfrac{190.5 - 190}{3.08} \approx 0.16$

    $z = \dfrac{x - \mu}{\sigma} = \dfrac{191.5 - 190}{308.6} \approx 0.49$

  e. $P(z < 0.16) = 0.5636$

    $P(z < 0.49) = 0.6879$

    $P(0.16 < z < 0.49) = 0.6879 - 0.5636 = 0.1243$

    The probability that exactly 191 people will respond yes is 0.1243.

5.5 EXERCISE SOLUTIONS

1. $np = (20)(0.80) = 16 \geq 5$

  $nq = (20)(0.20) = 4 < 5$

  Cannot use normal distribution.

© 2006 Pearson Education, Inc., Upper Saddle River, NJ. All rights reserved. This material is protected under all copyright laws as they currently exist. No portion of this material may be reproduced, in any form or by any means, without permission in writing from the publisher.

3. $np = (15)(0.65) = 9.75 \geq 5$

$nq = (15)(0.35) = 5.25 \geq 5$

Use normal distribution.

5. $n = 10, p = 0.44, q = 0.56$

$np = 4.4 < 5, nq = 5.6 \geq 5$

Cannot use normal distribution.

7. $n = 10, p = 0.97, q = 0.03$

$np = 9.7 \geq 5, nq = 0.3 < 5$

Cannot use normal distribution.

9. d   **11.** a   **13.** a   **15.** c

17. Binomial: $P(5 \leq x \leq 7) = 0.162 + 0.198 + 0.189 = 0.549$

Normal: $P(4.5 \leq x \leq 7.5) = P(-0.97 < z < 0.56) = 0.7123 - 0.1660 = 0.5463$

19. $n = 30, p = 0.07 \rightarrow np = 2.1$ and $nq = 27.9$

Cannot use normal distribution.

(a) $P(x = 10) = {}_{30}C_{10}(0.07)^{10}(0.93)^{20} \approx 0.0000199$

(b) $P(x \geq 10) = 1 - P(x < 10)$

$$= 1 - \left[{}_{30}C_{0}(0.07)^{0}(0.93)^{30} + {}_{30}C_{1}(0.07)^{1}(0.93)^{29} + \cdots + {}_{30}C_{9}(0.07)^{9}(0.93)^{21} \right]$$

$$= 1 - .999977 \approx 0.000023$$

(c) $P(x < 10) \approx 0.999977$ (see part b)

(d) $n = 100, p = 0.07 \rightarrow np = 7$ and $nq = 93$

Use normal distribution.

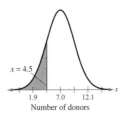

$z = \dfrac{x - \mu}{\sigma} = \dfrac{4.5 - 7}{2.55} \approx -0.98$

$P(x < 5) = P(x < 4.5) = P(z < -0.98) = 0.1635$

21. $n = 120, p = 0.05, q = 0.95$

$np = 6 \geq 5, nq = 114 \geq 5$

Use the normal distribution.

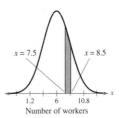

(a) $z = \dfrac{x - \mu}{\sigma} = \dfrac{7.5 - 6}{2.39} = 0.63$

$z = \dfrac{x - \mu}{\sigma} = \dfrac{8.5 - 6}{2.30} = 1.05$

$P(x = 8) \approx P(7.5 \leq x \leq 8.5) = P(0.63 \leq z \leq 1.05)$

$$= 0.8531 - 0.7357 = 0.1174$$

© 2006 Pearson Education, Inc., Upper Saddle River, NJ. All rights reserved. This material is protected under all copyright laws as they currently exist.
No portion of this material may be reproduced, in any form or by any means, without permission in writing from the publisher.

(b) $P(x \geq 8) \approx P(x \geq 7.5) = P(z \geq 0.63) = 1 - P(z \leq 0.63) = 1 - 0.7357 = 0.2643$

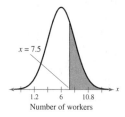

(c) $P(x < 8) \approx P(x \leq 7.5) = P(z \leq 0.63) = 0.7357$

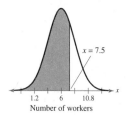

(d) $n = 250, p = 0.05, q = 0.95$

$np = 12.5 \geq 5, nq = 237.5 \geq 5$

Use normal distribution.

$z = \dfrac{x - \mu}{\sigma} = \dfrac{14.5 - 12.5}{3.45} = 0.58$

$P(x < 15) \approx P(x \leq 14.5) = P(z \leq 0.58) = 0.7190$

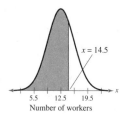

23. $n = 40, p = 0.52 \rightarrow np = 20.8$ and $nq = 19.2$

Use the normal distribution.

(a) $z = \dfrac{x - \mu}{\sigma} = \dfrac{15.5 - 20.8}{3.160} \approx -1.68$

$P(x \leq 15) = P(x < 15.5) = P(z < -1.68) = 0.0465$

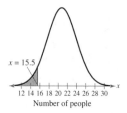

© 2006 Pearson Education, Inc., Upper Saddle River, NJ. All rights reserved. This material is protected under all copyright laws as they currently exist. No portion of this material may be reproduced, in any form or by any means, without permission in writing from the publisher.

(b) $z = \dfrac{x - \mu}{\sigma} = \dfrac{14.5 - 20.8}{3.160} \approx 1.99$

$P(x \geq 15) = P(x > 14.5) = P(z > -1.99) = 1 - P(z < 1.99) = 1 - 0.0233 = 0.9767$

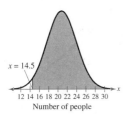

$x = 14.5$

12 14 16 18 20 22 24 26 28 30
Number of people

(c) $P(x > 15) = P(x > 15.5) = P(z > -1.68) = 1 - P(z < -1.68) = 1 - 0.0465 = 0.9535$

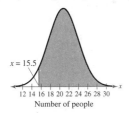

$x = 15.5$

12 14 16 18 20 22 24 26 28 30
Number of people

(d) $n = 650, p = 0.52 \rightarrow np = 338$ and $nq = 312$

Use normal distribution.

$z = \dfrac{x - \mu}{\sigma} = \dfrac{350.5 - 338}{12.74} \approx 0.98$

$P(x > 350) = P1(x > 350.5) = P(z > 0.98) = 1 - P(z < 0.98) = 1 - 0.8365 = 0.1635$

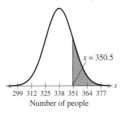

$x = 350.5$

299 312 325 338 351 364 377
Number of people

25. (a) $n = 25, p = 0.24, q = 0.76$

$np = 6 \geq 5, nq = 19 \geq 5$

Use normal distribution.

(b) $z = \dfrac{x - \mu}{\sigma} = \dfrac{8.5 - 6}{2.135} = 1.17$

$P(x > 8) \approx P(x \geq 8.5) = P(z \geq 1.17) = 1 - P(z \leq 1.17) = 1 - 0.8790 = 0.121$

(c) $z = \dfrac{x - \mu}{\sigma} = \dfrac{7.5 - 6}{2.135} = 0.70$

$z = \dfrac{x - \mu}{\sigma} = \dfrac{8.5 - 6}{2.135} = 1.17$

$P(x = 8) \approx P(7.5 \leq x \leq 8.5) = P(0.07 \leq z \leq 1.17) = 0.8790 - 0.7580 = 0.121$

It is not unusual for 8 out of 25 homeowners to say their home is too small.

© 2006 Pearson Education, Inc., Upper Saddle River, NJ. All rights reserved. This material is protected under all copyright laws as they currently exist. No portion of this material may be reproduced, in any form or by any means, without permission in writing from the publisher.

27. $n = 250, p = 0.70$

60% say no → $250(0.6) = 150$ say no while 100 say yes.

$$z = \frac{x - \mu}{\sigma} = \frac{99.5 - 175}{7.25} = -10.41$$

$P(\text{less than 100 yes}) = P(x < 100) = P(x < 99.5) = P(z < -10.41) \approx 0$

It is highly unlikely that 60% responded no. Answers will vary.

29. $n = 100, p = 0.75$

$$z = \frac{x - \mu}{\sigma} = \frac{69.5 - 75}{4.33} \approx 1.27$$

$P(\text{reject claim}) = P(x < 70) = P(x < 69.5) = P(z < -1.27) = 0.1020$

CHAPTER 5 REVIEW EXERCISE SOLUTIONS

1. $\mu = 15, \sigma = 3$

3. $x = 1.32$: $z = \dfrac{x - \mu}{\sigma} = \dfrac{1.32 - 1.5}{0.08} = -2.25$

$x = 1.54$: $z = \dfrac{x - \mu}{\sigma} = \dfrac{1.54 - 1.5}{0.08} = 0.5$

$x = 1.66$: $z = \dfrac{x - \mu}{\sigma} = \dfrac{1.66 - 1.5}{0.08} = 2$

$x = 1.78$: $z = \dfrac{x - \mu}{\sigma} = \dfrac{1.78 - 1.5}{0.08} = 3.5$

5. 0.2005

7. 0.3936

9. $1 - 0.9535 = 0.0465$

11. $0.5 - 0.0505 = 0.4495$

13. $0.9115 - 0.5596 = 0.3519$

15. $0.0668 + 0.0668 = 0.1336$

17. $P(z < 1.28) = 0.8997$

19. $P(-2.15 < x < 1.55) = 0.9394 - 0.0158 = 0.9236$

21. $P(z < -2.50 \text{ or } z > 2.50) = 2(0.0062) = 0.0124$

23. (a) $z = \dfrac{x - \mu}{\sigma} = \dfrac{1900 - 2200}{625} \approx -0.48$

$P(x < 1900) = P(z < -0.48) = 0.3156$

(b) $z = \dfrac{x - \mu}{\sigma} = \dfrac{2000 - 2200}{625} \approx -0.32$

$z = \dfrac{x - \mu}{\sigma} = \dfrac{25900 - 2200}{625} \approx 0.48$

$P(2000 < x < 2500) = P1(-0.32 < z < 0.48) = 0.6844 - 0.3745 = 0.3099$

© 2006 Pearson Education, Inc., Upper Saddle River, NJ. All rights reserved. This material is protected under all copyright laws as they currently exist. No portion of this material may be reproduced, in any form or by any means, without permission in writing from the publisher.

(c) $z = \dfrac{x - \mu}{\sigma} = \dfrac{2450 - 2200}{625} = -0.4$

$P(x > 2450) = P1(z > 0.4) = 0.3446$

25. $z = -0.07$

27. $z = 1.13$

29. $z = 1.04$

31. $x = \mu + z\sigma = 45.1 + (-2.4)(0.5) = 43.9$ meters

33. 95th percentile $\Rightarrow$ Area $= 0.95 \Rightarrow z = 1.645$

$x = \mu + z\sigma = 45.1 + (1.645)(0.5) = 45.9$ meters

35. Top 10% $\Rightarrow$ Area $= 0.90 \Rightarrow z = 1.28$

$x = \mu + z\sigma = 45.1 + (1.28)(0.5) = 45.74$ meters

37. {0 0 0, 0 0 200, 0 0 40, 0 0 600, 0 0 80, 0 200 0, 0 200 200, 0 200 40, 0 200 600, 0 200 80, 0 40 0, 0 40 200, 0 40 40, 0 40 600, 0 40 80, 0 600 0, 0 600 200, 0 600 40, 0 600 600, 0 600 80, 0 80 0, 0 80 200, 0 80 40, 0 80 600, 0 80 80, 200 0 0, 200 0 200, 200 0 40, 200 0 600, 200 0 80, 200 200 0, 200 200 200, 200 200 40, 200 200 600, 200 200 80, 200 40 0, 200 40 200, 200 40 40, 200 40 600, 200 40 80, 200 600 0, 200 600 200, 200 600 40, 200 600 600, 200 600 80, 200 80 0, 200 80 200, 200 80 40, 200 80 600, 200 80 80, 40 0 0, 40 0 200, 40 0 40, 40 0 600, 40 0 80, 40 200 0, 40 200 200, 40 200 40, 40 200 600, 40 200 80, 40 40 0, 40 40 200, 40 40 40, 40 40 600, 40 40 80, 40 600 0, 40 600 200, 40 600 40, 40 600 600, 40 600 80, 40 80 0, 40 80 200, 40 80 40, 40 80 600, 40 80 80, 600 0 0, 600 0 200, 600 0 40, 600 0 600, 600 0 80, 600 200 0, 600 200 200, 600 200 40, 600 200 600, 600 200 80, 600 40 0, 600 40 200, 600 40 40, 600 40 600, 600 40 80, 600 600 0, 600 600 200, 600 600 40, 600 600 600, 600 600 80, 600 80 0, 600 80 200, 600 80 40, 600 80 600, 600 80 80, 80 0 0, 80 0 200, 80 0 40, 80 0 600, 80 0 80, 80 200 0, 80 200 200, 80 200 40, 80 200 600, 80 200 80, 80 40 0, 80 40 200, 80 40 40, 80 40 600, 80 40 80, 80 600 0, 80 600 200, 80 600 40, 80 600 600, 80 600 80, 80 80 0, 80 80 200, 80 80 40, 80 80 600, 80 80 80}

$\mu = 184$, $\sigma \approx 218.504$

$\mu_{\bar{x}} = 184$, $\sigma_{\bar{x}} \approx 126.153$

39. $\mu_{\bar{x}} = 152.7$, $\sigma_{\bar{x}}\dfrac{\sigma}{\sqrt{n}} = \dfrac{51.6}{\sqrt{35}} \approx 8.72$

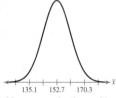

135.1   152.7   170.3 $\bar{x}$
Mean consumption (in pounds)

41. (a) $z = \dfrac{\bar{x} - \mu}{\dfrac{\sigma}{\sqrt{n}}} = \dfrac{1900 - 2200}{\dfrac{625}{\sqrt{12}}} = \dfrac{-300}{180.42} \approx -1.66$

$P(\bar{x} < 1900) = P(z < -1.66) = 0.0485$

© 2006 Pearson Education, Inc., Upper Saddle River, NJ. All rights reserved. This material is protected under all copyright laws as they currently exist. No portion of this material may be reproduced, in any form or by any means, without permission in writing from the publisher.

(b) $z = \dfrac{\bar{x} - \mu}{\dfrac{\sigma}{\sqrt{n}}} = \dfrac{2000 - 2200}{\dfrac{625}{\sqrt{12}}} = \dfrac{-200}{180.42} \approx -1.11$

$z = \dfrac{\bar{x} - \mu}{\dfrac{\sigma}{\sqrt{n}}} = \dfrac{2500 - 2200}{\dfrac{625}{\sqrt{12}}} = \dfrac{300}{180.42} \approx 1.66$

$P(2000 < \bar{x} < 2500) = P(-1.11 < z < 1.66) = 0.9515 - 0.1335 = 0.8180$

(c) $z = \dfrac{\bar{x} - \mu}{\dfrac{\sigma}{\sqrt{n}}} = \dfrac{2450 - 2200}{\dfrac{625}{\sqrt{12}}} = \dfrac{250}{180.42} \approx 1.39$

$P(\bar{x} > 2450) = P(z > 1.39) = 0.0823$

(a) and (c) are smaller, (b) is larger. This is to be expected because the standard error of the sample mean is smaller.

43. (a) $z = \dfrac{\bar{x} - \mu}{\dfrac{\sigma}{\sqrt{n}}} = \dfrac{23{,}700 - 24{,}700}{\dfrac{1500}{\sqrt{45}}} = \dfrac{-1000}{223.61} \approx -4.47$

$P(\bar{x} < 23{,}700) = P(z < -4.47) \approx 0$

(b) $z = \dfrac{\bar{x} - \mu}{\dfrac{\sigma}{\sqrt{n}}} = \dfrac{26{,}200 - 24{,}700}{\dfrac{1500}{\sqrt{45}}} = \dfrac{1500}{223.61} \approx 6.71$

$P(\bar{x} > 26{,}200) = P(z > 6.71) \approx 0$

45. Assuming the distribution is normally distributed:

$z = \dfrac{\bar{x} - \mu}{\dfrac{\sigma}{\sqrt{n}}} = \dfrac{1.125 - 1.5}{\dfrac{.5}{\sqrt{15}}} = \dfrac{-0.375}{0.129} \approx -2.90$

$P(\bar{x} < 1.125) = P(z < -2.90) = 0.0019$

47. $n = 12, p = 0.90, q = 0.10$

$np = 10.8 > 5$, but $nq = 1.2 < 5$

Cannot use the normal distribution.

49. $P(x \geq 25) = P(x > 24.5)$

51. $P(x = 45) = P(44.5 < x < 45.5)$

53. $n = 45, p = 0.65 \rightarrow np = 29.25, nq = 15.75$

Use normal distribution.

$\mu = np = 29.25, \sigma = \sqrt{npq} = \sqrt{45(0.65)(0.35)} \approx 3.200$

$z = \dfrac{x - \mu}{\sigma} = \dfrac{20.5 - 29.25}{3.200} \approx -2.73$

$P(x \leq 20) = P(x < 20.5) = P(z < -2.73) = 0.0032$

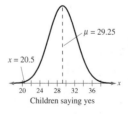

$\mu = 29.25$

$x = 20.5$

Children saying yes

© 2006 Pearson Education, Inc., Upper Saddle River, NJ. All rights reserved. This material is protected under all copyright laws as they currently exist. No portion of this material may be reproduced, in any form or by any means, without permission in writing from the publisher.

CHAPTER 5 QUIZ SOLUTIONS

1. (a) $P(z > -2.10) = 0.9821$

(b) $P(z < 3.22) = 0.9994$

(c) $P(-2.33 < z < 2.33) = 0.9901 - 0.0099 = 0.9802$

(d) $P(z < -1.75 \text{ or } z > -0.75) = 0.0401 + 0.7734 = 0.8135$

2. (a) $z = \dfrac{x - \mu}{\sigma} = \dfrac{5.36 - 5.5}{0.08} \approx -1.75$

$z = \dfrac{x - \mu}{\sigma} = \dfrac{5.64 - 5.5}{0.08} \approx 1.75$

$P(5.36 < x < 5.64) = P(-1.75 < z < 1.75) = 0.9599 - 0.0401 = 0.9198$

(b) $z = \dfrac{x - \mu}{\sigma} = \dfrac{-5.00 - (-8.2)}{7.84} \approx 0.41$

$z = \dfrac{x - \mu}{\sigma} = \dfrac{0 - (-8.2)}{7.84} \approx 1.05$

$P(-5.00 < x < 0) = P(0.41 < z < 1.05) = 0.8531 - 0.6591 = 0.1940$

(c) $z = \dfrac{x - \mu}{\sigma} = \dfrac{0 - 18.5}{9.25} = -2$

$z = \dfrac{x - \mu}{\sigma} = \dfrac{37 - 18.5}{9.25} = 2$

$P(x < 0 \text{ or } x > 37) = P(z < -2 \text{ or } z > 2) = 2(0.0228) = 0.0456$

3. $z = \dfrac{x - \mu}{\sigma} = \dfrac{315 - 281}{34.4} \approx 0.99$

$P(x > 315) = P(z > 0.99) = 0.1611$

4. $z = \dfrac{x - \mu}{\sigma} = \dfrac{250 - 281}{34.4} \approx -0.90$

$z = \dfrac{x - \mu}{\sigma} = \dfrac{305 - 281}{34.4} \approx 0.70$

$P(250 < x < 305) = P(-0.90 < z < 0.70) = 0.7580 - 0.1841 = 0.5739$

5. $P(x > 250) = P(z > -0.90) = 0.8159 \rightarrow 81.59\%$

6. $z = \dfrac{x - \mu}{\sigma} = \dfrac{300 - 281}{34.4} \approx 0.55$

$P(x < 300) = P(z < 0.55) = 0.7088$

$(2000)(0.7088) = 1417.6$

7. top $5\% \rightarrow z \approx 1.645$

$\mu + z\sigma = 281 + (1.645)(34.4) = 337.588$

8. bottom $25\% \rightarrow z \approx -0.67$

$\mu + z\sigma = 281 + (-0.67)(34.4) = 257.952$

© 2006 Pearson Education, Inc., Upper Saddle River, NJ. All rights reserved. This material is protected under all copyright laws as they currently exist. No portion of this material may be reproduced, in any form or by any means, without permission in writing from the publisher.

9. $z = \dfrac{\bar{x} - \mu}{\dfrac{\sigma}{\sqrt{n}}} = \dfrac{300 - 281}{\dfrac{34.4}{\sqrt{60}}} = \dfrac{19}{4.44} \approx 4.28$

$P(\bar{x} > 300) = P(z > 4.28) \approx 0$

10. $z = \dfrac{x - \mu}{\sigma} = \dfrac{300 - 281}{34.4} \approx 0.55$

$P(\bar{x} > 300) = P(z > 0.55) = 0.2912$

$z = \dfrac{\bar{x} - \mu}{\dfrac{\sigma}{\sqrt{n}}} = \dfrac{305 - 281}{\dfrac{34.4}{\sqrt{15}}} = \dfrac{24}{8.88} \approx 2.70$

$P(\bar{x} > 300) = P(z > 2.70) = 0.0035$

You are more likely to select one student with a test score greater than 300 because the standard error of the mean is less than the standard deviation.

11. $n = 24, p = 0.68 \rightarrow np = 16.32, nq = 7.68$

Use normal distribution.

$\mu = np = 16.32 \qquad \sigma = \sqrt{npq} \approx 2.285$

12. $z = \dfrac{x - \mu}{\sigma} = \dfrac{15.5 - 16.32}{2.285} \approx -0.36$

$P(x \leq 15) = P(x < 15.5) = P(z < -0.36) = 0.3594$

© 2006 Pearson Education, Inc., Upper Saddle River, NJ. All rights reserved. This material is protected under all copyright laws as they currently exist.
No portion of this material may be reproduced, in any form or by any means, without permission in writing from the publisher.

Confidence Intervals

6.1 CONFIDENCE INTERVALS FOR THE MEAN (LARGE SAMPLES)

6.1 Try It Yourself Solutions

1a. $\bar{x} \approx 14.767$

  b. The mean number of sentences per magazine advertisement is 14.767.

2a. $Z_c = 1.96, n = 30, s = 16.536$

  b. $E = Z_c \dfrac{s}{\sqrt{n}} = 1.96 \dfrac{16.536}{\sqrt{30}} \approx 5.917$

  c. You are 95% confident that the maximum error of the estimate is about 5.917 sentences per magazine advertisement.

3a. $\bar{x} \approx 14.767, E \approx 5.917$

  b. $\bar{x} - E = 14.767 - 5.917 = 8.850$
     $\bar{x} + E = 14.767 + 5.917 = 20.684$

  c. You are 95% confident that the mean number of sentences per magazine advertisements is between 8.850 and 20.684.

4b. 75% CI: (11.6, 13.2)
     85% CI: (11.4, 13.4)

  c. The width of the interval increases as the level of confidence increases.

5a. $n = 30, \bar{x} = 22.9, \sigma = 1.5, Z_c = 1.645$

  b. $E = Z_c \dfrac{\sigma}{\sqrt{n}} = 1.645 \dfrac{1.5}{\sqrt{30}} \approx 0.451$

     $\bar{x} - E = 22.9 - 0.451 \approx 22.4$
     $\bar{x} + E = 22.9 + 0.451 \approx 23.4$

  c. You are 90% confident that the mean age of the students is between 22.4 and 23.4 years.

6a. $Z_c = 1.96, E = 2, s \approx 5.0$

  b. $n = \left(\dfrac{Z_c s}{E}\right)^2 = \left(\dfrac{1.96 \cdot 5.0}{2}\right)^2 = 24.01 \rightarrow 25$

  c. You should have at least 25 magazine advertisements in your sample.

6.1 EXERCISE SOLUTIONS

1. You are more likely to be correct using an interval estimate since it is unlikely that a point estimate will equal the population mean exactly.

3. d; As the level of confidence increases, z_c increases therefore creating wider intervals.

5. 1.28   **7.** 1.15

© 2006 Pearson Education, Inc., Upper Saddle River, NJ. All rights reserved. This material is protected under all copyright laws as they currently exist.
No portion of this material may be reproduced, in any form or by any means, without permission in writing from the publisher.

9. $|\bar{x} - \mu| = |3.8 - 4.27| = 0.47$

11. $|\bar{x} - \mu| = |26.43 - 24.67| = 1.76$

13. $|\bar{x} - \mu| = |0.7 - 1.3| = 0.60$

15. $E = z_c \dfrac{s}{\sqrt{n}} = 1.645 \dfrac{2.5}{\sqrt{36}} \approx 0.685$

17. $E = z_c \dfrac{s}{\sqrt{n}} = 0.93 \dfrac{1.5}{\sqrt{50}} = 0.197$

19. $c = 0.88 \Longrightarrow z_c = 1.55$

$\bar{x} = 57.2, s = 7.1, n = 50$

$\bar{x} \pm z_c \dfrac{s}{\sqrt{n}} = 57.2 \pm 1.55 \dfrac{7.1}{\sqrt{50}} = 57.2 \pm 1.556 \approx (55.6, 58.8)$

Answer: (c)

21. $c = 0.95 \Longrightarrow z_c = 1.96$

$\bar{x} = 57.2, s = 7.1, n = 50$

$\bar{x} \pm z_c \dfrac{s}{\sqrt{n}} = 57.2 \pm 1.96 \dfrac{7.1}{\sqrt{50}} = 57.2 \pm 1.968 \approx (55.2, 59.2)$

Answer: (b)

23. $\bar{x} \pm z_c \dfrac{s}{\sqrt{n}} = 15.2 \pm 1.645 \dfrac{2.0}{\sqrt{60}} = 15.2 \pm 0.425 \approx (14.8, 15.6)$

25. $\bar{x} \pm z_c \dfrac{s}{\sqrt{n}} = 4.27 \pm 1.96 \dfrac{0.3}{\sqrt{42}} = 4.27 \pm 0.091 \approx (4.18, 4.36)$

27. $c = 0.90 \Longrightarrow z_c = 1.645$

$n = \left(\dfrac{z_c \sigma}{E}\right)^2 = \left(\dfrac{(1.645)(6.8)}{1}\right)^2 = 125.13 \Longrightarrow 126$

29. $c = 0.80 \Longrightarrow z_c = 1.28$

$n = \left(\dfrac{z_c \sigma}{E}\right)^2 = \left(\dfrac{(1.28)(4.1)}{2}\right)^2 = 6.89 \Longrightarrow 7$

31. $(2.1, 3.5) \Longrightarrow 2E = 3.5 - 2.1 = 1.4 \Longrightarrow E = 0.7$ and $\bar{x} = 2.1 + E$
$$= 2.1 + 0.7 = 2.8$$

33. 90% CI: $\bar{x} \pm z_c \dfrac{s}{\sqrt{n}} = 630.90 \pm 1.645 \dfrac{56.70}{\sqrt{32}} = 630.9 \pm 16.49 \approx (614.41, 647.39)$

95% CI: $\bar{x} \pm z_c \dfrac{s}{\sqrt{n}} = 630.90 \pm 1.96 \dfrac{56.70}{\sqrt{32}} = 630.9 \pm 19.65 \approx (611.25, 650.55)$

The 95% confidence interval is wider.

35. 90% CI: $\bar{x} \pm z_c \dfrac{s}{\sqrt{n}} = 26.8 \pm 1.645 \dfrac{8.0}{\sqrt{156}} = 26.8 \pm 1.054 \approx (25.7, 27.9)$

95% CI: $\bar{x} \pm z_c \dfrac{s}{\sqrt{n}} = 26.8 \pm 1.96 \dfrac{8.0}{\sqrt{156}} = 26.8 \pm 1.255 \approx (25.5, 28.1)$

The 95% confidence interval is wider.

37. $\bar{x} \pm z_c \dfrac{s}{\sqrt{n}} = 100 \pm 1.96 \dfrac{17.50}{\sqrt{40}} = 100 \pm 5.423 \approx (95.58, 105.42)$

© 2006 Pearson Education, Inc., Upper Saddle River, NJ. All rights reserved. This material is protected under all copyright laws as they currently exist.
No portion of this material may be reproduced, in any form or by any means, without permission in writing from the publisher.

39. $\bar{x} \pm z_c \dfrac{s}{\sqrt{n}} = 100 \pm 1.96 \dfrac{17.50}{\sqrt{80}} = 100 \pm 3.835 \approx (96.17, 104.84)$

$n = 40$ CI is wider because we have taken a smaller sample giving us less information about the population.

41. $\bar{x} \pm z_c \dfrac{s}{\sqrt{n}} = 10.452 \pm 2.575 \dfrac{2.130}{\sqrt{56}} = 10.452 \pm 0.733 \approx (9.719, 11.185)$

43. $\bar{x} \pm z_c \dfrac{s}{\sqrt{n}} = 10.452 \pm 2.575 \dfrac{5.130}{\sqrt{56}} = 10.452 \pm 1.765 \approx (8.687, 12.217)$

$s = 5.130$ CI is wider because of the increased variability within the population.

45. (a) An increase in the level of confidence will widen the confidence interval.

(b) An increase in the sample size will narrow the confidence interval.

(c) An increase in the standard deviation will widen the confidence interval.

47. $\bar{x} = \dfrac{\Sigma x}{n} = \dfrac{136}{15} \approx 9.1$

90% CI: $\bar{x} \pm z_c \dfrac{\sigma}{\sqrt{n}} = 9.1 \pm 1.645 \dfrac{1.5}{\sqrt{15}} = 9.1 \pm 0.637 \approx (8.4, 9.7)$

99% CI: $\bar{x} \pm z_c \dfrac{\sigma}{\sqrt{n}} = 9.1 \pm 2.575 \dfrac{1.5}{\sqrt{15}} = 9.1 \pm 0.997 \approx (8.1, 10.1)$

99% CI is wider.

49. $n = \left(\dfrac{z_c \sigma}{E}\right)^2 = \left(\dfrac{1.96 \cdot 4.8}{1}\right)^2 \approx 88.510 \rightarrow 89$

51. (a) $n = \left(\dfrac{z_c \sigma}{E}\right)^2 = \left(\dfrac{1.96 \cdot 2.8}{0.5}\right)^2 \approx 120.473 \rightarrow 121$

(b) $n = \left(\dfrac{z_c \sigma}{E}\right)^2 = \left(\dfrac{2.575 \cdot 2.8}{0.5}\right)^2 \approx 207.936 \rightarrow 208$

99% CI requires larger sample because more information is needed from the population to be 99% confident.

53. (a) $n = \left(\dfrac{z_c \sigma}{E}\right)^2 = \left(\dfrac{1.645 \cdot 0.85}{0.25}\right)^2 \approx 31.282 \rightarrow 32$

(b) $n = \left(\dfrac{z_c \sigma}{E}\right)^2 = \left(\dfrac{1.645 \cdot 0.85}{0.15}\right)^2 \approx 86.893 \rightarrow 87$

$E = 0.15$ requires a larger sample size. As the error size decreases, a larger sample must be taken to obtain enough information from the population to ensure desired accuracy.

55. $n = \left(\dfrac{z_c \sigma}{E}\right)^2 = \left(\dfrac{1.960 \cdot 0.25}{0.125}\right)^2 = 15.3664 \rightarrow 16$

$n = \left(\dfrac{z_c \sigma}{E}\right)^2 = \left(\dfrac{1.960 \cdot 0.25}{0.0625}\right)^2 = 61.4656 \rightarrow 62$

$E = 0.0625$ requires a larger sample size. As the error size decreases, a larger sample must be taken to obtain enough information from the population to ensure desired accuracy.

© 2006 Pearson Education, Inc., Upper Saddle River, NJ. All rights reserved. This material is protected under all copyright laws as they currently exist. No portion of this material may be reproduced, in any form or by any means, without permission in writing from the publisher.

57. (a) $n = \left(\dfrac{z_c \sigma}{E}\right)^2 = \left(\dfrac{2.575 \cdot 0.25}{0.1}\right)^2 \approx 41.441 \rightarrow 42$

(b) $n = \left(\dfrac{z_c \sigma}{E}\right)^2 = \left(\dfrac{2.575 \cdot 0.30}{0.1}\right)^2 \approx 59.676 \rightarrow 60$

$\sigma = 0.30$ requires a larger sample size. Due to the increased variability in the population, a larger sample size is needed to ensure the desired accuracy.

59. (a) An increase in the level of confidence will increase the minimum sample size required.

(b) An increase (larger E) in the error tolerance will decrease the minimum sample size required.

(c) An increase in the population standard deviation will increase the minimum sample size required.

61. $\bar{x} = 307.4,\, s \approx 11.190,\, n = 32$

$\bar{x} \pm z_c \dfrac{s}{\sqrt{n}} = 307.4 \pm 1.96 \dfrac{11.190}{\sqrt{32}} = 307.4 \pm 3.877 \approx (303.5, 311.3)$

63. $\bar{x} = 14.440,\, s \approx 2.124,\, n = 30$

$\bar{x} \pm z_c \dfrac{s}{\sqrt{n}} = 14.440 \pm 1.96 \dfrac{2.124}{\sqrt{30}} = 14.440 \pm 0.760 \approx (13.680, 15.200)$

65. (a) $\sqrt{\dfrac{N-n}{N-1}} = \sqrt{\dfrac{1000-500}{1000-1}} \approx 0.707$

(b) $\sqrt{\dfrac{N-n}{N-1}} = \sqrt{\dfrac{1000-100}{1000-1}} \approx 0.949$

(c) $\sqrt{\dfrac{N-n}{N-1}} = \sqrt{\dfrac{1000-75}{1000-1}} \approx 0.962$

(d) $\sqrt{\dfrac{N-n}{N-1}} = \sqrt{\dfrac{1000-50}{1000-1}} \approx 0.975$

(e) The finite population correction factor approaches 1 as the sample size decreases while the population size remains the same.

67. $n = \left(\dfrac{z_c \sigma}{E}\right)^2 \rightarrow \sqrt{n} = \dfrac{z_c \sigma}{E} \rightarrow E = \dfrac{z_c \sigma}{\sqrt{n}}$

6.2 CONFIDENCE INTERVALS FOR THE MEAN (SMALL SAMPLES)

6.2 Try It Yourself Solutions

1a. d.f. $= n - 1 = 22 - 1 = 21$ **b.** $c = 0.90$ **c.** 1.721

2a. 90% CI: $t_c = 1.753$

$E = t_c \dfrac{s}{\sqrt{n}} = 1.753 \dfrac{10}{\sqrt{16}} \approx 4.383$

99% CI: $t_c = 2.947$

$E = t_c \dfrac{s}{\sqrt{n}} = 2.947 \dfrac{10}{\sqrt{16}} \approx 7.368$

© 2006 Pearson Education, Inc., Upper Saddle River, NJ. All rights reserved. This material is protected under all copyright laws as they currently exist. No portion of this material may be reproduced, in any form or by any means, without permission in writing from the publisher.

b. 90% CI: $\bar{x} \pm E = 162 \pm 4.383 \approx (157.6, 166.4)$

  99% CI: $\bar{x} \pm E = 162 \pm 7.368 \approx (154.6, 169.4)$

c. You are 90% confident that the mean temperature of coffee sold is between 157.6° and 166.4°.

  You are 99% confident that the mean temperature of coffee sold is between 154.6° and 169.4°.

3a. 90% CI: $t_c = 1.729$

$$E = t_c \frac{s}{\sqrt{n}} = 1.729 \frac{0.42}{\sqrt{20}} \approx 0.162$$

  95% CI: $t_c = 2.093$

$$E = t_c \frac{s}{\sqrt{n}} = 2.093 \frac{0.42}{\sqrt{20}} \approx 0.197$$

b. 90% CI: $\bar{x} \pm E = 6.93 \pm 0.162 \approx (6.77, 7.09)$

  95% CI: $\bar{x} \pm E = 6.93 \pm 0.197 \approx (6.73, 7.13)$

c. You are 90% confident that the mean mortgage interest rate is contained between 6.77% and 7.10%.

  You are 95% confident that the mean mortgage interest rate is contained between 6.73% and 7.13%.

4a. Is $n \geq 30$? No

  Is the population normally distributed? Yes

  Is σ known? No

  Use the t-distribution to construct the 90% CI.

6.2 EXERCISE SOLUTIONS

1. 1.833   **3.** 2.947

5. (a) $E = z_c \frac{s}{\sqrt{n}} = 1.96 \frac{5}{\sqrt{16}} \approx 2.450$ (b) $E = t_c \frac{s}{\sqrt{n}} = 2.131 \frac{5}{\sqrt{16}} \approx 2.664$

7. (a) $\bar{x} \pm t_c \frac{s}{\sqrt{n}} = 12.5 \pm 2.015 \frac{2.0}{\sqrt{6}} = 12.5 \pm 1.645 \approx (10.9, 14.1)$

  (b) $\bar{x} \pm t_c \frac{s}{\sqrt{n}} = 12.5 \pm 1.645 \frac{2.0}{\sqrt{6}} = 12.5 \pm 1.343 \approx (11.2, 13.8)$

  t-CI is wider.

9. (a) $\bar{x} \pm t_c \frac{s}{\sqrt{n}} = 4.3 \pm 2.650 \frac{0.34}{\sqrt{14}} = 4.3 \pm 0.241 \approx (4.1, 4.5)$

  (b) $\bar{x} \pm z_c \frac{s}{\sqrt{n}} = 4.3 \pm 2.326 \frac{0.34}{\sqrt{14}} = 4.3 \pm 0.211 \approx (4.1, 4.5)$

  t-CI is wider.

11. $\bar{x} \pm t_c \frac{s}{\sqrt{n}} = 75 \pm 2.776 \frac{12.50}{\sqrt{5}} = 75 \pm 15.518 \approx (59.48, 90.52)$

$$E = t_c \frac{s}{\sqrt{n}} = 2.776 \frac{12.50}{\sqrt{5}} \approx 15.518$$

© 2006 Pearson Education, Inc., Upper Saddle River, NJ. All rights reserved. This material is protected under all copyright laws as they currently exist. No portion of this material may be reproduced, in any form or by any means, without permission in writing from the publisher.

13. $\bar{x} \pm z_c\frac{\sigma}{\sqrt{n}} = 75 \pm 1.96\frac{15}{\sqrt{5}} = 75 \pm 13.148 \approx (61.85, 88.15)$

$E = z_c\frac{\sigma}{\sqrt{n}} = 1.96\frac{15}{\sqrt{5}} \approx 13.148$

t-CI is wider.

15. (a) $\bar{x} \pm t_c\frac{s}{\sqrt{n}} = 4.5 \pm 1.833\frac{1.2}{\sqrt{10}} = 4.5 \pm 0.696 \approx (3.8, 5.2)$

(b) $\bar{x} \pm z_c\frac{s}{\sqrt{n}} = 4.5 \pm 1.645\frac{1.2}{\sqrt{500}} = 4.5 \pm 0.088 \approx (4.4, 4.6)$

t-CI is wider.

17. (a) $\bar{x} = 4174.75$ (b) $s \approx 100.341$

(c) $\bar{x} \pm t_c\frac{s}{\sqrt{n}} = 4174.75 \pm 3.250\frac{100.341}{\sqrt{10}} = 4174.75 \pm 103.124 \approx (4071.63, 4277.87)$

19. (a) $\bar{x} \approx 909.1$ (b) $s \approx 305.266$

(c) $\bar{x} \pm t_c\frac{s}{\sqrt{n}} = 909.1 \pm 3.106\frac{305.266}{\sqrt{12}} = 909.1 \pm 273.709 \approx (635.4, 1182.8)$

21. $n \geq 30 \rightarrow$ use normal distribution

$\bar{x} \pm z_c\frac{s}{\sqrt{n}} = 1.25 \pm 1.96\frac{0.01}{\sqrt{70}} = 1.25 \pm 0.002 \approx (1.248, 1.252)$

23. $\bar{x} = 24, s = 3, n < 30, \sigma$ known, and pop normally distributed $\rightarrow$ use t-distribution

$\bar{x} \pm t_c\frac{s}{\sqrt{n}} = 24 \pm 2.064\frac{3}{\sqrt{25}} = 24 \pm 1.238 \approx (23, 25)$

25. $n < 30, \sigma$ unknown, and pop *not* normally distributed $\rightarrow$ cannot use either the normal or t-distributions.

27. $n = 25, \bar{x} = 56.0, s = 0.25$

$\pm t_{0.99} \rightarrow 99\%$ t-CI

$\bar{x} \pm t_c\frac{s}{\sqrt{n}} = 56.0 \pm 2.797\frac{0.25}{\sqrt{25}} = 56.0 \pm 0.140 \approx (55.9, 56.1)$

They are not making good tennis balls since desired bounce height of 55.5 inches is not contained between 55.9 and 56.1 inches.

6.3 CONFIDENCE INTERVALS FOR POPULATION PROPORTIONS

6.3 Try It Yourself Solutions

1a. $x = 1177, n = 3859$

b. $\hat{p} = \frac{1177}{3859} \approx 0.305$

2a. $\hat{p} \approx 0.305, \hat{q} \approx 0.695$

b. $n\hat{p} = (3859)(0.305) = 1175.995 > 5$

$n\hat{q} = (3859)(0.695) = 2682.005 > 5$

© 2006 Pearson Education, Inc., Upper Saddle River, NJ. All rights reserved. This material is protected under all copyright laws as they currently exist. No portion of this material may be reproduced, in any form or by any means, without permission in writing from the publisher.

c. $z_c = 1.645$

$$E = z_c \sqrt{\frac{\hat{p}\hat{q}}{n}} = 1.645 \sqrt{\frac{0.305 \cdot 0.695}{3859}} \approx 0.011$$

d. $\hat{p} \pm E = 0.305 \pm 0.011 \approx (0.293, 0.317)$

e. You are 90% confident that the proportion of adults that admired Franklin D. Roosevelt the most is contained between 29.3% and 31.7%.

3a. $n = 900, \hat{p} \approx 0.33$

b. $\hat{q} = 1 - \hat{p} = 1 - 0.33 \approx 0.67$

c. $n\hat{p} = 900 \cdot 0.33 \approx 297 > 5$

$n\hat{q} = 900 \cdot 0.67 \approx 603 > 5$

Distribution of $\hat{p}$ is approximately normal.

d. $z_c = 2.575$

e. $\hat{p} \pm z_c \sqrt{\frac{\hat{p}\hat{q}}{n}} = 0.33 \pm 2.575 \sqrt{\frac{0.33 \cdot 0.67}{900}} = 0.33 \pm 0.04 \approx (0.290, 0.370)$

f. You are 99% confident that the proportion of adults who think that people over 75 are more dangerous drivers is contained between 29.0% and 37.0%.

4. (1) **a.** $\hat{p} = 0.50, \hat{q} = 0.50$

$z_c = 1.645, E = 0.02$

b. $n = \hat{p}\hat{q}\left(\frac{z_c}{E}\right)^2 = (0.50)(0.50)\left(\frac{1.645}{0.02}\right)^2 = 1691.266 \rightarrow 1692$

c. At least 1692 adults should be included in the sample.

(2) **a.** $\hat{p} = 0.04, \hat{q} = 0.96$

$z_c = 1.645, E = 0.02$

b. $n = \hat{p}\hat{q}\left(\frac{z_c}{E}\right)^2 = 0.04 \cdot 0.96\left(\frac{1.645}{0.02}\right)^2 \approx 259.778 \rightarrow 260$

c. At least 260 adults should be included in the sample.

6.3 EXERCISE SOLUTIONS

1. False. To estimate the value of p, the population proportion of successes, use the point estimate $\hat{p} = \frac{x}{n}$.

3. $\hat{p} = \frac{x}{n} = \frac{122}{1024} \approx 0.119$

$\hat{q} = 1 - \hat{p} \approx 0.881$

5. $\hat{p} = \frac{x}{n} = \frac{2634}{4115} \approx 0.640$

$\hat{q} = 1 - \hat{p} \approx 0.360$

7. $\hat{p} = \frac{x}{n} = \frac{102}{848} \approx 0.120$

$\hat{q} = 1 - \hat{p} \approx 0.880$

9. $\hat{p} = \frac{x}{n} = \frac{197}{284} \approx 0.694$

$\hat{q} = 1 - \hat{p} \approx 0.306$

11. $\hat{p} = \frac{x}{n} = \frac{264}{586} = 0.451$

$q = 1 - \hat{p} = 1 - 0.451 = 0.549$

© 2006 Pearson Education, Inc., Upper Saddle River, NJ. All rights reserved. This material is protected under all copyright laws as they currently exist. No portion of this material may be reproduced, in any form or by any means, without permission in writing from the publisher.

13. $\hat{p} = 0.48$, $E = 0.03$

$\hat{p} \pm E = 0.48 \pm 0.03 = (0.45, 0.51)$

15. 95% CI: $\hat{p} \pm z_c\sqrt{\dfrac{\hat{p}\hat{q}}{n}} = 0.119 \pm 1.96\sqrt{\dfrac{0.119 \cdot 0.881}{1024}} = 0.119 \pm 0.020 \approx (0.099, 0.139)$

99% CI: $\hat{p} \pm z_c\sqrt{\dfrac{\hat{p}\hat{q}}{n}} = 0.119 \pm 2.575\sqrt{\dfrac{0.119 \cdot 0.881}{1024}} = 0.119 \pm 0.026 \approx (0.093, 0.145)$

99% CI is wider.

17. 95% CI: $\hat{p} \pm z_c\sqrt{\dfrac{\hat{p}\hat{q}}{n}} = 0.640 \pm 1.96\sqrt{\dfrac{0.64 \cdot 0.36}{4115}} = 0.640 \pm 0.015 \approx (0.625, 0.655)$

99% CI: $\hat{p} \pm z_c\sqrt{\dfrac{\hat{p}\hat{q}}{n}} = 0.640 \pm 2.575\sqrt{\dfrac{0.64 \cdot 0.36}{4115}} = 0.640 \pm 0.019 \approx (0.621, 0.659)$

99% CI is wider.

19. 95% CI: $\hat{p} \pm z_c\sqrt{\dfrac{\hat{p}\hat{q}}{n}} = 0.120 \pm 1.96\sqrt{\dfrac{0.120 \cdot 0.880}{848}} = 0.120 \pm 0.022 \approx (0.098, 0.142)$

99% CI: $\hat{p} \pm z_c\sqrt{\dfrac{\hat{p}\hat{q}}{n}} = 0.120 \pm 2.575\sqrt{\dfrac{0.120 \cdot 0.880}{848}} = 0.120 \pm 0.029 \approx (0.091, 0.149)$

99% CI is wider.

21. (a) $n = \hat{p}\hat{q}\left(\dfrac{z_c}{E}\right)^2 = 0.5 \cdot 0.5\left(\dfrac{1.96}{0.03}\right)^2 \approx 1067.111 \rightarrow 1068$

(b) $n = \hat{p}\hat{q}\left(\dfrac{z_c}{E}\right)^2 = 0.26 \cdot 0.74\left(\dfrac{1.96}{0.03}\right)^2 \approx 821.249 \rightarrow 822$

(c) Having an estimate of the proportion reduces the minimum sample size needed.

23. (a) $n = \hat{p}\hat{q}\left(\dfrac{z_c}{E}\right)^2 = 0.5 \cdot 0.5\left(\dfrac{2.055}{0.025}\right)^2 = 1689.21 \rightarrow 1690$

(b) $n = \hat{p}\hat{q}\left(\dfrac{z_c}{E}\right)^2 = 0.25 \cdot 0.75\left(\dfrac{2.055}{0.025}\right)^2 \approx 1266.91 \rightarrow 1267$

(c) Having an estimate of the proportion reduces the minimum sample size needed.

25. (a) $\hat{p} = 0.61$, $n = 500$

$\hat{p} \pm z_c\sqrt{\dfrac{\hat{p}\hat{q}}{n}} = 0.61 \pm 2.575\sqrt{\dfrac{0.61 \cdot 0.39}{500}} = 0.61 \pm 0.056 \approx (0.554, 0.666)$

(b) $\hat{p} = 0.44$, $n = 500$

$\hat{p} \pm z_c\sqrt{\dfrac{\hat{p}\hat{q}}{n}} = 0.44 \pm 2.575\sqrt{\dfrac{0.44 \cdot 0.56}{500}} = 0.44 \pm 0.057 \approx (0.383, 0.497)$

It is unlikely that the two proportions are equal because the confidence intervals estimating the proportions do not overlap.

27. (a) $\hat{p} = 0.24$, $\hat{q} = 0.76$, $n = 600$

$\hat{p} \pm z_c\sqrt{\dfrac{\hat{p}\hat{q}}{n}} = 0.24 \pm 2.575\sqrt{\dfrac{(0.24)(0.76)}{600}} = 0.24 \pm 0.45 = (0.195, 0.285)$

© 2006 Pearson Education, Inc., Upper Saddle River, NJ. All rights reserved. This material is protected under all copyright laws as they currently exist. No portion of this material may be reproduced, in any form or by any means, without permission in writing from the publisher.

(b) $\hat{p} = 0.30$, $\hat{q} = 0.70$, $n = 600$

$$\hat{p} \pm z_c \sqrt{\frac{\hat{p}\hat{q}}{n}} = 0.30 \pm 2.575 \sqrt{\frac{(0.30)(0.70)}{600}} = 0.30 \pm 0.048 = (0.252, 0.348)$$

(c) $\hat{p} = 0.37$, $\hat{q} = 0.63$, $n = 429$

$$\hat{p} \pm z_c \sqrt{\frac{\hat{p}\hat{q}}{n}} = 0.37 \pm 2.575 \sqrt{\frac{(0.37)(0.63)}{429}} = 0.37 \pm 0.060 = (0.310, 0.430)$$

29. $31.4\% \pm 1\% \rightarrow (30.4\%, 32.4\%)$

$$E = z_c \sqrt{\frac{\hat{p}\hat{q}}{n}} \rightarrow z_c = E \sqrt{\frac{n}{\hat{p}\hat{q}}} = 0.01 \sqrt{\frac{8451}{0.314 \cdot 0.686}} \approx 1.981 \rightarrow z_c = 1.98 \rightarrow c = 0.952$$

$(30.4\%, 32.4\%)$ is approximately a 95.2% CI.

31. If $n\hat{p} < 5$ or $n\hat{q} < 5$, the sampling distribution of $\hat{p}$ may not be normally distributed; therefore preventing the use of z_c when calculating the confidence interval.

33.

p	$q = 1 - p$	pq	p	$q = 1 - p$	pq
0.0	1.0	0.00	0.45	0.55	0.2475
0.1	0.9	0.09	0.46	0.54	0.2484
0.2	0.8	0.16	0.47	0.53	0.2491
0.3	0.7	0.21	0.48	0.52	0.2496
0.4	0.6	0.24	0.49	0.51	0.2499
0.5	0.5	0.25	0.50	0.50	0.2500
0.6	0.4	0.24	0.51	0.49	0.2499
0.7	0.3	0.21	0.52	0.48	0.2496
0.8	0.2	0.16	0.53	0.47	0.2491
0.9	0.1	0.09	0.54	0.46	0.2484
1.0	0.0	0.00	0.55	0.45	0.2475

$\hat{p} = 0.5$ give the maximum value of $\hat{p}\hat{q}$.

6.4 CONFIDENCE INTERVALS FOR VARIANCE AND STANDARD DEVIATION

6.4 Try It Yourself Solutions

1a. d.f. $= n - 1 = 24$

level of confidence $= 0.95$

b. Area to the right of χ^2_R is 0.025.

Area to the left of χ^2_L is 0.975.

c. $\chi^2_R = 39.364$, $\chi^2_L = 12.401$

2a. 90% CI: $\chi^2_R = 42.557$, $\chi^2_L = 17.708$

95% CI: $\chi^2_R = 45.722$, $\chi^2_L = 16.047$

b. 90% CI for σ^2: $\left(\frac{(n-1)s^2}{\chi^2_R}, \frac{(n-1)s^2}{\chi^2_L} \right) = \left(\frac{29 \cdot (1.2)^2}{42.557}, \frac{29 \cdot (1.2)^2}{17.708} \right) \approx (0.98, 2.36)$

95% CI for σ^2: $\left(\frac{(n-1)s^2}{\chi^2_R}, \frac{(n-1)s^2}{\chi^2_L} \right) = \left(\frac{29 \cdot (1.2)^2}{45.722}, \frac{29 \cdot (1.2)^2}{16.047} \right) \approx (0.91, 2.60)$

© 2006 Pearson Education, Inc., Upper Saddle River, NJ. All rights reserved. This material is protected under all copyright laws as they currently exist. No portion of this material may be reproduced, in any form or by any means, without permission in writing from the publisher.

c. 90% CI for σ: $\left(\sqrt{0.981}, \sqrt{2.358}\right) = (0.99, 1.54)$

95% CI for σ: $\left(\sqrt{0.913}, \sqrt{2.602}\right) = (0.96, 1.61)$

d. You are 90% confident that the population variance is between 0.98 and 2.36, and that the population standard deviation is between 0.99 and 1.54. You are 95% confident that the population variance is between 0.91 and 2.60, and that the population standard deviation is between 0.96 and 1.61.

6.4 EXERCISE SOLUTIONS

1. $\chi_R^2 = 16.919$, $\chi_L^2 = 3.325$

3. $\chi_R^2 = 35.479$, $\chi_L^2 = 10.283$

5. $\chi_R^2 = 52.336$, $\chi_L^2 = 13.121$

7. (a) $s = 0.00843$

$$\left(\frac{(n-1)s^2}{\chi_R^2}, \frac{(n-1)s^2}{\chi_L^2}\right) = \left(\frac{13 \cdot (0.00843)^2}{22.362}, \frac{13 \cdot (0.00843)^2}{5.892}\right) \approx (0.0000413, 0.000157)$$

(b) $\left(\sqrt{0.0000413}, \sqrt{0.000157}\right) \approx (0.00643, 0.0125)$

9. (a) $s = 0.253$

$$\left(\frac{(n-1)s^2}{\chi_R^2}, \frac{(n-1)s^2}{\chi_L^2}\right) = \left(\frac{17 \cdot (0.253)^2}{35.718}, \frac{17 \cdot (0.253)^2}{5.697}\right) \approx (0.031, 0.191)$$

(b) $\left(\sqrt{0.0305}, \sqrt{0.191}\right) \approx (0.175, 0.437)$

11. (a) $\left(\frac{(n-1)s^2}{\chi_R^2}, \frac{(n-1)s^2}{\chi_L^2}\right) = \left(\frac{11 \cdot (3.25)^2}{26.757}, \frac{11 \cdot (3.25)^2}{2.603}\right) \approx (4.34, 44.64)$

(b) $\left(\sqrt{4.342}, \sqrt{44.636}\right) \approx (2.08, 6.68)$

13. (a) $\left(\frac{(n-1)s^2}{\chi_R^2}, \frac{(n-1)s^2}{\chi_L^2}\right) = \left(\frac{9 \cdot (26)^2}{16.919}, \frac{9 \cdot (26)^2}{3.325}\right) \approx (360, 1830)$

(b) $\left(\sqrt{359.596}, \sqrt{1829.774}\right) \approx (19, 43)$

15. (a) $\left(\frac{(n-1)s^2}{\chi_R^2}, \frac{(n-1)s^2}{\chi_L^2}\right) = \left(\frac{18 \cdot (15)^2}{31.526}, \frac{18 \cdot (15)^2}{8.231}\right) \approx (128, 492)$

(b) $\left(\sqrt{128.465}, \sqrt{492.042}\right) \approx (11, 22)$

17. (a) $\left(\frac{(n-1)s^2}{\chi_R^2}, \frac{(n-1)s^2}{\chi_L^2}\right) = \left(\frac{19 \cdot (107)^2}{32.852}, \frac{19 \cdot (107)^2}{8.907}\right) \approx (6622, 24{,}422)$

(b) $\left(\sqrt{6621.545}, \sqrt{24{,}422.477}\right) \approx (81, 156)$

19. (a) $\left(\frac{(n-1)s^2}{\chi_R^2}, \frac{(n-1)s^2}{\chi_L^2}\right) = \left(\frac{(14)(0.42)^2}{31.319}, \frac{(14)(0.42)^2}{4.075}\right) = (0.08, 0.61)$

(b) $\left(\sqrt{0.08}, \sqrt{0.61}\right) = (0.28, 0.78)$

21. 90% CI for σ: $(0.00643, 0.0125)$

Yes, because the confidence interval is below 0.015.

© 2006 Pearson Education, Inc., Upper Saddle River, NJ. All rights reserved. This material is protected under all copyright laws as they currently exist. No portion of this material may be reproduced, in any form or by any means, without permission in writing from the publisher.

CHAPTER 6 REVIEW EXERCISE SOLUTIONS

1. (a) $\bar{x} \approx 103.5$

   (b) $s \approx 34.663$

$$E = z_c \frac{s}{\sqrt{n}} = 1.645 \frac{34.663}{\sqrt{40}} \approx 9.016$$

3. $\bar{x} \pm z_c \frac{s}{\sqrt{n}} = 10.3 \pm 1.96 \frac{0.277}{\sqrt{100}} = 10.3 \pm 0.054 \approx (10.2, 10.4)$

5. $s = 34.663$

$$n = \left(\frac{z_c \sigma}{E}\right)^2 = \left(\frac{1.96 \cdot 34.663}{10}\right)^2 \approx 46.158 \Rightarrow 47$$

7. $n = \left(\frac{z_c \sigma}{E}\right)^2 = \left(\frac{(1.96)(7.098)}{2}\right)^2 = 48.39 \Rightarrow 49$

9. $t_c = 1.415$ **11.** $t_c = 2.624$

13. $E = t_c \frac{s}{\sqrt{n}} = 1.753 \frac{23.4}{\sqrt{16}} \approx 10.255$ **15.** $E = t_c \frac{s}{\sqrt{n}} = 2.718\left(\frac{0.9}{\sqrt{12}}\right) = 0.7$

17. $\bar{x} \pm z_c \frac{s}{\sqrt{n}} = 52.8 \pm 1.753 \frac{23.4}{\sqrt{16}} = 52.8 \pm 10.255 \approx (42.5, 63.1)$

19. $\bar{x} \pm t_c \frac{s}{\sqrt{n}} = 6.8 \pm 2.718\left(\frac{0.9}{\sqrt{12}}\right) = 6.8 \pm 0.706 = (6.1, 7.5)$

21. $\bar{x} \pm t_c \frac{s}{\sqrt{n}} = 80 \pm 1.761 \frac{14}{\sqrt{15}} = 80 \pm 6.366 \approx (74, 86)$

23. $\hat{p} = \frac{x}{n} = \frac{1378}{2120} = 0.65, \hat{q} = 0.35$ **25.** $\hat{p} = \frac{x}{n} = \frac{597}{1011} = 0.591, \hat{q} = 0.409$

27. $\hat{p} = \frac{x}{n} = \frac{116}{644} = 0.180, \hat{q} = 0.820$ **29.** $\hat{p} = \frac{x}{n} = \frac{548}{1371} = 0.400, \hat{q} = 0.600$

31. $\hat{p} \pm z_c \sqrt{\frac{\hat{p}\hat{q}}{n}} = 0.650 \pm 1.96 \sqrt{\frac{0.650 \cdot 0.350}{2120}} = 0.650 \pm 0.020 \approx (0.630, 0.670)$

33. $\hat{p} \pm z_c \sqrt{\frac{\hat{p}\hat{q}}{n}} = 0.591 \pm 1.645 \sqrt{\frac{0.591 \cdot 0.409}{1011}} = 0.591 \pm 0.025 \approx (0.566, 0.616)$

35. $\hat{p} \pm z_c \sqrt{\frac{\hat{p}\hat{q}}{n}} = 0.180 \pm 2.575 \sqrt{\frac{0.180 \cdot 0.820}{644}} = 0.180 \pm 0.039 = (0.141, 0.219)$

37. $\hat{p} \pm z_c \sqrt{\frac{\hat{p}\hat{q}}{n}} = 0.400 \pm 1.96 \sqrt{\frac{(0.400)(0.600)}{1371}} = 0.400 \pm 0.026 = (0.374, 0.426)$

39. $n = \hat{p}\hat{q}\left(\frac{z_c}{E}\right)^2 = 0.23 \cdot 0.77\left(\frac{1.96}{0.05}\right)^2 \approx 272.139 \rightarrow 273$

41. $\chi_R^2 = 23.337, \chi_L^2 = 4.404$ **43.** $\chi_R^2 = 14.067, \chi_L^2 = 2.167$

45. $s = 0.0727$

$$95\% \text{ CI for } \sigma^2: \left(\frac{(n-1)s^2}{\chi_R^2}, \frac{(n-1)s^2}{\chi_L^2}\right) = \left(\frac{15 \cdot (0.0727)^2}{27.488}, \frac{15 \cdot (0.0727)^2}{6.262}\right) \approx (0.0029, 0.0127)$$

$$95\% \text{ CI for } \sigma: \left(\sqrt{0.0029}, \sqrt{0.0127}\right) \approx (0.0539, 0.1127)$$

© 2006 Pearson Education, Inc., Upper Saddle River, NJ. All rights reserved. This material is protected under all copyright laws as they currently exist. No portion of this material may be reproduced, in any form or by any means, without permission in writing from the publisher.

47. $s = 1.12$

90% CI for σ^2: $\left(\dfrac{(n-1)s^2}{\chi_R^2}, \dfrac{(n-1)s^2}{\chi_L^2}\right) = \left(\dfrac{(23)(1.12)^2}{35.172}, \dfrac{(23)(1.12)^2}{13.091}\right) = (0.82, 2.20)$

90% CI for σ: $\left(\sqrt{0.82}, \sqrt{2.20}\right) \approx (0.91, 1.48)$

CHAPTER 6 QUIZ SOLUTIONS

1. (a) $\bar{x} \approx 98.110$

(b) $s \approx 24.722$

$$E = t_c \frac{s}{\sqrt{n}} = 1.960 \frac{24.722}{\sqrt{30}} \approx 8.847$$

(c) $\bar{x} \pm t_c \dfrac{s}{\sqrt{n}} = 98.110 \pm 1.960 \dfrac{24.722}{\sqrt{30}} = 98.110 \pm 8.847 \approx (89.263, 106.957)$

You are 95% confident that the population mean repair costs is contained between \$89.26 and \$106.96.

2. $n = \left(\dfrac{z_c \sigma}{E}\right)^2 = \left(\dfrac{2.575 \cdot 22.50}{10}\right) \approx 33.568 \rightarrow$ sample size must be 34

3. (a) $\bar{x} = 6.61$ (b) $s \approx 3.38$

(c) $\bar{x} \pm t_c \dfrac{s}{\sqrt{n}} = 6.61 \pm 1.833 \dfrac{3.38}{\sqrt{10}} = 6.61 \pm 1.957 \approx (4.65, 8.57)$

(d) $\bar{x} \pm z_c \dfrac{\sigma}{\sqrt{n}} = 6.61 \pm 1.645 \dfrac{3.5}{\sqrt{10}} = 6.61 \pm 1.821 \approx (4.79, 8.43)$

The t-CI is wider since less information is available.

4. $\bar{x} \pm t_c \dfrac{s}{\sqrt{n}} = 4744 \pm 2.365 \dfrac{580}{\sqrt{8}} = 4744 \pm 484.97 \approx (4259, 5229)$

5. (a) $\hat{p} = \dfrac{x}{n} = \dfrac{643}{1037} = 0.620$

(b) $\hat{p} \pm z_c \sqrt{\dfrac{\hat{p}\hat{q}}{n}} = 0.620 \pm 1.645 \sqrt{\dfrac{0.620 \cdot 0.38}{1037}} = 0.620 \pm 0.025 \approx (0.595, 0.645)$

(c) $n = \hat{p}\hat{q}\left(\dfrac{z_c}{E}\right)^2 = 0.620 \cdot 0.38\left(\dfrac{2.575}{0.04}\right)^2 \approx 976.36 \rightarrow 977$

6. (a) $\left(\dfrac{(n-1)s^2}{\chi_R^2}, \dfrac{(n-1)s^2}{\chi_L^2}\right) = \left(\dfrac{29 \cdot (24.722)^2}{45.722}, \dfrac{29 \cdot (24.722)^2}{16.047}\right) \approx (387.650, 1104.514)$

(b) $\left(\sqrt{387.650}, \sqrt{1104.514}\right) \approx (19.689, 33.234)$

© 2006 Pearson Education, Inc., Upper Saddle River, NJ. All rights reserved. This material is protected under all copyright laws as they currently exist. No portion of this material may be reproduced, in any form or by any means, without permission in writing from the publisher.

7.1 INTRODUCTION TO HYPOTHESIS TESTING

7.1 Try It Yourself Solutions

1a. (1) The mean ... is not 74 months.

$\mu \neq 74$

(2) The variance ... is less than or equal to 3.5.

$\sigma^2 \leq 3.5$

(3) The proportion ... is greater than 39%.

$p > 0.39$

b. (1) $\mu = 74$ (2) $\sigma^2 > 3.5$ (3) $p \leq 0.39$

c. (1) $H_0: \mu = 74$; $H_a: \mu \neq 74$; (claim)

(2) $H_0: \sigma^2 \leq 3.5$ (claim); $H_a: \sigma^2 > 3.5$

(3) $H_0: p \leq 0.39$; $H_a: p > 0.39$ (claim)

2a. $H_0: p \leq 0.01$; $H_a: p > 0.01$

b. Type I error will occur if the actual proportion is less than or equal to 0.01, but you decided to reject H_0.

Type II error will occur if the actual proportion is greater than 0.01, but you do not reject H_0.

c. Type II error is more serious since you would be misleading the consumer, possibly causing serious injury or death.

3a. (1) $H_0: \mu = 74$; $H_a: \mu \neq 74$
(2) $H_0: p \leq 0.39$; $H_a: p > 0.39$

b. (1) Two-tailed   (2) Right-tailed

c. (1)    (2)

4a. There is enough evidence to support the radio station's claim.

b. There is not enough evidence to support the radio station's claim.

5a. (No answer required)

b. (1) Support claim.   (2) Reject claim.

c. (1) $H_0: \mu \geq 650$; $H_a: \mu < 650$ (claim)

(2) $H_0: \mu = 98.6$ (claim); $H_a: \mu \neq 98.6$

© 2006 Pearson Education, Inc., Upper Saddle River, NJ. All rights reserved. This material is protected under all copyright laws as they currently exist.
No portion of this material may be reproduced, in any form or by any means, without permission in writing from the publisher.

7.1 EXERCISE SOLUTIONS

1. Null hypothesis (H_0) and alternative hypothesis (H_a). One represents the claim, the other, its complement.

3. False. In a hypothesis test, you assume the null hypothesis is true.

5. True

7. False. A small P-value in a test will favor a rejection of the null hypothesis.

9. $H_0: \mu \leq 645$; $H_a: \mu > 645$

11. $H_0: \sigma = 5$; $H_a: \sigma \neq 5$

13. $H_0: p \geq 0.45$: $H_a: p < 0.45$

15. c, $H_0: \mu \leq 3$

17. b, $H_0: \mu = 3$

19. Right-tailed

21. Two-tailed

23. $\mu > 750$
   $H_0: \mu \leq 750$; $H_a: \mu > 750$ (claim)

25. $\sigma \leq 1220$
   $H_0: \sigma \leq 1220$ (claim); $H_a: \sigma > 1220$

27. $p = 0.84$
   $H_0: p = 0.84$ (claim); $H_a: p \neq 0.84$

29. Type I: Rejecting $H_0: p \geq 0.24$ when actually $p \geq 0.24$.
   Type II: Not rejecting $H_0: p \geq 0.24$ when actually $p < 0.24$.

31. Type I: Rejecting $H_0: \sigma \leq 23$ when actually $\sigma \leq 23$.
   Type II: Not rejecting $H_0: \sigma \leq 23$ when actually $\sigma > 23$.

33. Type I: Rejecting $H_0: p = 0.88$ when actually $p = 0.88$.
   Type II: Not rejecting $H_0: p = 0.88$ when actually $p \neq 0.88$.

35. The null hypothesis is $H_0: p \geq 0.14$, the alternative hypothesis is $H_a: p < 0.14$. Therefore, because the alternative hypothesis contains <, the test is a left-tailed test.

37. The null hypothesis is $H_0: p = 0.90$, the alternative hypothesis is $H_a: p \neq 0.90$. Therefore, because the alternative hypothesis contains ≠, the test is a two-tailed test.

39. The null hypothesis is $H_0: p = 0.053$, the alternative hypothesis is $H_a: p \neq 0.053$. Therefore, because the alternative hypothesis contains ≠, the test is a two-tailed test.

41. (a) There is enough evidence to support the company's claim.

   (b) There is not enough evidence to support the company's claim.

43. (a) There is enough evidence to support the Dept of Labor's claim.

   (b) There is not enough evidence to decide that the Dept of Labor's claim is true.

45. (a) There is enough evidence to reject the manufacturer's claim.

   (b) There is not enough evidence to reject the manufacturer's claim.

47. $H_0: \mu = 10$; and $H_a: \mu \neq 10$

49. (a) $H_0: \mu \leq 15$ $H_a: \mu > 15$ (b) $H_0: \mu \geq 15$; $H_a: \mu < 15$

51. If you decrease, you are decreasing the probability that you reject H_0. Therefore, you are increasing the probability of failing to reject H_0. This could increase β, the probability of failing to reject H_0 when H_0 is false.

© 2006 Pearson Education, Inc., Upper Saddle River, NJ. All rights reserved. This material is protected under all copyright laws as they currently exist. No portion of this material may be reproduced, in any form or by any means, without permission in writing from the publisher.

53. (a) Reject H_0 since the CI is located below 70.

(b) Do not reject H_0 since the CI includes values larger than 70.

(c) Do not reject H_0 since the CI includes values larger than 70.

55. (a) Reject H_0 since the CI is located above 0.20.

(b) Do not reject H_0 since the CI includes values less than 0.20.

(c) Do not reject H_0 since the CI includes values less than 0.20.

7.2 HYPOTHESIS TESTING FOR THE MEAN (LARGE SAMPLES)

7.2 Try It Yourself Solutions

1a. (1) $P = 0.0347 > 0.01 = \alpha$ (2) $P = 0.0347 < 0.05 = \alpha$

b. (1) Fail to reject H_0 because $0.0347 > 0.01$.

(2) Reject H_0 because $0.0347 < 0.05$.

2a. 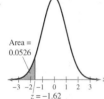   **b.** $P = 0.0526$

c. Fail to reject H_0 since $P = 0.0526 > 0.05 = \alpha$.

3a. Area that corresponds to $z = 2.31$ is 0.9896.

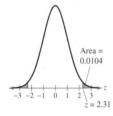

b. $P = 2 \,(\text{area}) = 2(0.0104) = 0.0208$

c. Fail to reject H_0 since $P = 0.0208 > 0.01 = \alpha$.

4a. The claim is "the mean speed is greater than 35 miles per hour."

$H_0: \mu \le 35; H_a: \mu > 35$ (claim)

b. $\alpha = 0.05$

c. $z = \dfrac{\bar{x} - \mu}{\frac{s}{\sqrt{n}}} = \dfrac{36 - 35}{\frac{4}{\sqrt{100}}} = \dfrac{1}{0.4} = 2.500$

d. P-value = Area right of $z = 2.50 = 0.0062$

e. Reject H_0 since P-value $= 0.0062 < 0.05 = \alpha$.

f. Because you reject H_0, there is enough evidence to claim the average speed limit is greater than 35 miles per hour.

© 2006 Pearson Education, Inc., Upper Saddle River, NJ. All rights reserved. This material is protected under all copyright laws as they currently exist. No portion of this material may be reproduced, in any form or by any means, without permission in writing from the publisher.

5a. $H_0: \mu = 150$ (claim); $H_a: \mu \neq 150$

b. $\alpha = 0.01$

c. $z = \dfrac{\bar{x} - \mu}{\frac{\sigma}{\sqrt{n}}} = \dfrac{143 - 150}{\frac{15}{\sqrt{35}}} = \dfrac{-7}{2.535} \approx -2.76$

d. P-value $= 0.0058$

e. Reject H_0 since P-value $= 0.0058 < 0.01 = \alpha$.

f. There is enough evidence to state the claim is false.

6a. $P = 0.0391 > 0.01 = \alpha$

b. Fail to reject H_0.

7a.

8a.
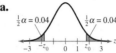

b. Area $= 0.1003$

b. 0.0401 and 0.9599

c. $z_0 = -1.28$

c. $z_0 = -1.75$ and 1.75

d. $z < -1.28$

d. $z < -1.75$, $z > 1.75$

e. Reject H_0.

9a. $H_0: \mu > 8.5$; $H_a: \mu < 8.5$ (claim)

b. $\alpha = 0.01$

c. $z_0 = -2.33$; Rejection region: $z < -2.33$

d. $z = \dfrac{x - \mu}{\frac{s}{\sqrt{n}}} = \dfrac{8.2 - 8.5}{\frac{0.5}{\sqrt{35}}} = \dfrac{-0.300}{0.0845} \approx -3.550$

e.
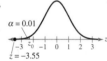

Reject H_0.

f. There is enough evidence to support the claim.

10a. $\alpha = 0.01$

b. $\pm z_0 = \pm2.575$; Rejection regions: $z < -2.575$, $z > 2.575$

c. Fail to reject H_0.

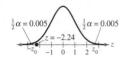

d. There is not enough evidence to support the claim that the mean cost is significantly different from \$9405 at the 1% level of significance.

© 2006 Pearson Education, Inc., Upper Saddle River, NJ. All rights reserved. This material is protected under all copyright laws as they currently exist. No portion of this material may be reproduced, in any form or by any means, without permission in writing from the publisher.

7.2 EXERCISE SOLUTIONS

1.

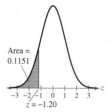

$P = 0.1151$; Fail to reject H_0 since $P = 0.1151 > 0.10 = \alpha$.

3.

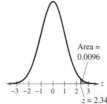

$P = 0.0096$; Reject H_0 since $P = 0.0096 < 0.01 = \alpha$.

5.

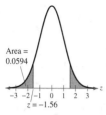

$P = 2(\text{Area}) = 2(0.0594) = 0.1188$; Fail to reject H_0 since $P = 0.1188 > 0.05 = \alpha$.

7. c   **9.** e   **11.** b

13. (a) Fail to reject H_0.

　　 (b) Reject $H_0 (P = 0.0461 < 0.05 = \alpha)$.

15. 1.645   **17.** -1.88 **19.** ± 2.33

21. Right-tailed ($\alpha = 0.01$)   **23.** Two-tailed ($\alpha = 0.10$)

25. (a) Fail to reject H_0 since $-1.645 < z < 1.645$.

　　 (b) Reject H_0 since $z > 1.645$.

　　 (c) Fail to reject H_0 since $-1.645 < z < 1.645$.

　　 (d) Reject H_0 since $z < -1.645$.

27. (a) Fail to reject H_0 since $z < 1.285$.

　　 (b) Fail to reject H_0 since $z < 1.285$.

　　 (c) Fail to reject H_0 since $z < 1.285$.

　　 (d) Reject H_0 since $z > 1.285$.

29. $H_0: \mu = 40$; $H_a: \mu \neq 40$

$\mu = 0.05 \rightarrow z_0 = \pm 1.96$

$$z = \frac{\bar{x} - \mu}{\frac{s}{\sqrt{n}}} = \frac{39.2 - 40}{\frac{3.23}{\sqrt{75}}} = \frac{-0.8}{0.373} \approx -2.145$$

Reject H_0. There is enough evidence to reject the claim.

© 2006 Pearson Education, Inc., Upper Saddle River, NJ. All rights reserved. This material is protected under all copyright laws as they currently exist. No portion of this material may be reproduced, in any form or by any means, without permission in writing from the publisher.

31. $H_0: \mu = 6000;$ $H_a: \mu \neq 6000$

$\alpha = 0.01 \rightarrow z_0 = \pm 2.575$

$z = \dfrac{\bar{x} - \mu}{\frac{s}{\sqrt{n}}} = \dfrac{5800 - 6000}{\frac{350}{\sqrt{35}}} = \dfrac{-200}{59.161} \approx -3.381$

Reject H_0. There is enough evidence to support the claim.

33. (a) $H_0: \mu \leq 260;$ $H_a: \mu > 260$ (claim)

(b) $z = \dfrac{\bar{x} - \mu}{\frac{s}{\sqrt{n}}} = \dfrac{265 - 260}{\frac{55}{\sqrt{85}}} = \dfrac{5}{5.966} \approx 0.838$ Area $= 0.7995$

(c) P-value $= \{$Area to right of $z = 0.84\} = 0.2005$

(d) Fail to reject H_0. There is insufficient evidence at the 4% level of significance to support the claim that the mean score for Illinois' eighth grades is more than 260.

35. (a) $H_0: \mu \leq 7;$ $H_a: \mu > 7$ (claim)

(b) $z = \dfrac{\bar{x} - \mu}{\frac{s}{\sqrt{n}}} = \dfrac{7.8 - 7}{\frac{2.67}{\sqrt{100}}} = \dfrac{0.8}{0.267} \approx 2.996$ Area $= 0.9987$

(c) P-value $= \{$Area to right of $z = 3.00\} = 0.0013$

(d) Reject H_0.

(e) There is sufficient evidence at the 7% level of significance to support the claim that the mean consumption of tea by a person in the U.S. is more than 7 gallons per year.

37. (a) $H_0: \mu = 15$ (claim); $H_a: \mu \neq 15$

(b) $\bar{x} \approx 14.834$ $s \approx 4.288$

$z = \dfrac{\bar{x} - \mu}{\frac{s}{\sqrt{n}}} = \dfrac{14.834 - 15}{\frac{4.288}{\sqrt{32}}} = \dfrac{-0.166}{0.758} \approx -0.219$ Area $= 0.4129$

(c) P-value $= 2\{$Area to left of $z = -0.22\} = 2\{0.4129\} = 0.8258$

(d) Fail to reject H_0.

(e) There is insufficient evidence at the 5% level of significance to reject the claim that the mean time it takes smokers to quit smoking permanently is 15 years.

39. (a) $H_0: \mu = 40$ (claim); $H_a: \mu \neq 40$

(b) $z_0 = \pm 2.575$; Rejection regions: $z < -2.575$ and $z > 2.575$

(c) $z = \dfrac{\bar{x} - \mu}{\frac{s}{\sqrt{n}}} = \dfrac{39.2 - 40}{\frac{7.5}{\sqrt{30}}} = \dfrac{-0.8}{1.369} \approx -0.584$

(d) Fail to reject H_0.

(e) There is insufficient evidence at the 1% level of significance to reject the claim that the mean caffeine content per one twelve-ounce bottle of cola is 40 milligrams.

© 2006 Pearson Education, Inc., Upper Saddle River, NJ. All rights reserved. This material is protected under all copyright laws as they currently exist. No portion of this material may be reproduced, in any form or by any means, without permission in writing from the publisher.

41. (a) H_0: $\mu \geq 750$ (claim); H_a: $\mu < 750$

(b) $z_0 = -2.05$; Rejection region: $z < -2.05$

(c) $z = \dfrac{\bar{x} - \mu}{\frac{s}{\sqrt{n}}} = \dfrac{745 - 750}{\frac{60}{\sqrt{36}}} = \dfrac{-5}{10} \approx -0.500$

(d) Fail to reject H_0.

(e) There is insufficient evidence at the 2% level of significance to reject the claim that the mean life of the bulb is at least 750 hours.

43. (a) H_0: $\mu \leq 28$; H_a: $\mu > 28$ (claim)

(b) $z_0 = 1.55$; Rejection region: $z > 1.55$

(c) $\bar{x} \approx 32.861$ $s \approx 22.128$

$z = \dfrac{\bar{x} - \mu}{\frac{s}{\sqrt{n}}} = \dfrac{32.861 - 28}{\frac{22.128}{\sqrt{36}}} = \dfrac{4.861}{3.688} \approx 1.318$

(d) Fail to reject H_0.

(e) There is insufficient evidence at the 6% level of significance to support the claim that the mean nitrogen dioxide level in West London is greater than 28 parts per billion.

45. (a) H_0: $\mu \geq 10$ (claim); H_a: $\mu < 10$

(b) $z_0 = 1.88$; Rejection region: $z < 1.88$

(c) $\bar{x} \approx 9.780$, $s \approx 2.362$

$x = \dfrac{\bar{x} - \mu}{\frac{s}{\sqrt{n}}} = \dfrac{9.780 - 10}{\frac{2.362}{\sqrt{30}}} = \dfrac{-0.22}{0.431} \approx -0.510$

(d) Fail to reject H_0.

(e) There is insufficient evidence at the 3% level to reject the claim that the mean weight loss after 1 month is at least 10 pounds.

47. $z = \dfrac{\bar{x} - \mu}{\frac{s}{\sqrt{n}}} = \dfrac{10,700 - 10,800}{\frac{280}{\sqrt{30}}} = \dfrac{-100}{51.121} \approx -1.956$

P-value = {Area left of $z = -1.96$} = 0.025

Fail to reject H_0 because the standardized test statistic $z = -1.96$ is greater than the critical value $z_0 = -2.33$.

49. (a) $\alpha = 0.02$; Fail to reject H_0.

(b) $\alpha = 0.03$; Reject H_0.

(c) $z = \dfrac{\bar{x} - \mu}{\frac{s}{\sqrt{n}}} = \dfrac{9900 - 10,000}{\frac{280}{\sqrt{50}}} = \dfrac{-100}{39.598} \approx -2.525$

P-value = {Area left of $z = -2.53$} = 0.0057 $\rightarrow$ Reject H_0.

© 2006 Pearson Education, Inc., Upper Saddle River, NJ. All rights reserved. This material is protected under all copyright laws as they currently exist. No portion of this material may be reproduced, in any form or by any means, without permission in writing from the publisher.

(d) $z = \dfrac{\bar{x} - \mu}{\dfrac{s}{\sqrt{n}}} = \dfrac{9900 - 10{,}000}{\dfrac{280}{\sqrt{100}}} = \dfrac{-100}{28} \approx -3.571$

P-value = {Area left of $z = -3.57$} < 0.0001 → Reject H_0.

51. Using the classical z-test, the test statistic is compared to critical values. The z-test using a P-value compares the P-value to the level of significance α.

7.3 HYPOTHESIS TESTING FOR THE MEAN (SMALL SAMPLES)

7.3 Try It Yourself Solutions

1a. 2.650   **b.** $t_0 = -2.650$

2a. 1.860   **b.** $t_0 = +1.860$

3a. 2.947   **b.** $t_0 = \pm 2.947$

4a. $H_0: \mu \geq \$1240$ (claim); $H_a: \mu < \$1240$

 b. $\alpha = 0.01$ and d.f. $= n - 1 = 8$

 c. $t_0 = -2.896$; Reject H_0 if $t \leq -2.896$.

 d. $t = \dfrac{\bar{x} - \mu}{\dfrac{s}{\sqrt{n}}} = \dfrac{1190 - 1240}{\dfrac{62}{\sqrt{9}}} = \dfrac{-50}{20.667} \approx -2.419$

 e. Fail to reject H_0.

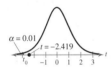

 f. There is not enough evidence to reject the claim.

5a. $H_0: \mu = 1890$ (claim); $H_a: \mu \neq 1890$

 b. $\alpha = 0.01$ and d.f. $= n - 1 = 18$

 c. $t_0 = \pm 2.878$; Reject H_0 if $t < -2.878$ or $t > 2.878$.

 d. $t = \dfrac{\bar{x} - \mu}{\dfrac{s}{\sqrt{n}}} = \dfrac{2500 - 1890}{\dfrac{700}{\sqrt{19}}} = \dfrac{610}{160.591} \approx 3.798$

 e. Reject H_0.

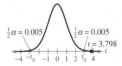

 f. There is enough evidence to reject the company's claim.

6a. $t = \dfrac{\bar{x} - \mu}{\dfrac{s}{\sqrt{n}}} = \dfrac{126 - 136}{\dfrac{12}{\sqrt{6}}} = \dfrac{-10}{4.899} \approx -2.041$

 P-value = {Area left of $t = -2.04$} ≈ 0.0484

© 2006 Pearson Education, Inc., Upper Saddle River, NJ. All rights reserved. This material is protected under all copyright laws as they currently exist. No portion of this material may be reproduced, in any form or by any means, without permission in writing from the publisher.

b. P-value $= 0.0484 < 0.05 = \alpha$

c. Reject H_0.

d. There is enough evidence to reject the claim.

7.3 EXERCISE SOLUTIONS

1. Identify the level of significance α and the degrees of freedom, d.f. $= n - 1$. Find the critical value(s) using the t-distribution table in the row with $n - 1$ d.f. If the hypothesis test is:

   (1) Left-tailed, use "One Tail, α" column with a negative sign.

   (2) Right-tailed, use "One Tail, α" column with a positive sign.

   (3) Two-tailed, use "Two Tail, α" column with a negative and a positive sign.

3. $t_0 = 1.717$ 5. $t_0 = -2.101$

7. $t_0 = \pm 2.779$ 9. 1.328

11. -2.473 13. ± 3.747

15. (a) Fail to reject H_0 since $t > -2.086$.

    (b) Fail to reject H_0 since $t > -2.086$.

    (c) Fail to reject H_0 since $t > -2.086$.

    (d) Reject H_0 since $t < -2.086$.

17. (a) Fail to reject H_0 since $-2.602 < t < 2.602$.

    (b) Fail to reject H_0 since $-2.602 < t < 2.602$.

    (c) Reject H_0 since $t > 2.602$.

    (d) Reject H_0 since $t < -2.602$.

19. $H_0: \mu = 15$ (claim); $H_a: \mu \neq 15$

    $\alpha = 0.01$ and d.f. $= n - 1 = 5$

    $t_0 = \pm 4.032$

    $t = \dfrac{\bar{x} - \mu}{\frac{s}{\sqrt{n}}} = \dfrac{13.9 - 15}{\frac{3.23}{\sqrt{6}}} = \dfrac{-1.1}{1.319} \approx -0.834$

    Fail to reject H_0. There is not enough evidence to reject the claim.

21. $H_0: \mu \geq 8000$ (claim); $H_a: \mu < 8000$

    $\alpha = 0.01$ and d.f. $= n - 1 = 24$

    $t_0 = -2.492$

    $t = \dfrac{\bar{x} - \mu}{\frac{s}{\sqrt{n}}} = \dfrac{7700 - 8000}{\frac{450}{\sqrt{25}}} = \dfrac{-300}{90} \approx -3.333$

    Reject H_0. There is enough evidence to reject the claim.

© 2006 Pearson Education, Inc., Upper Saddle River, NJ. All rights reserved. This material is protected under all copyright laws as they currently exist. No portion of this material may be reproduced, in any form or by any means, without permission in writing from the publisher.

23. (a) H_0: $\mu > 100$; H_a: $\mu < 100$ (claim)

   (b) $t_0 = -3.747$; Reject H_0 if $t < -3.747$.

   (c) $t = \dfrac{\bar{x} - \mu}{\frac{s}{\sqrt{n}}} = \dfrac{75 - 100}{\frac{12.50}{\sqrt{5}}} = \dfrac{-25}{5.590} \approx -4.472$

   (d) Reject H_0.

   (e) There is sufficient evidence at the 1% level to support the claim that the mean repair cost for damaged microwave ovens is less than \$100.

25. (a) H_0: $\mu \le 1$; H_a: $\mu > 1$ (claim)

   (b) $t_0 = 1.796$; Reject H_0 if $t > 1.796$.

   (c) $t = \dfrac{\bar{x} - \mu}{\frac{s}{\sqrt{n}}} = \dfrac{1.2 - 1}{\frac{0.3}{\sqrt{12}}} = \dfrac{0.2}{0.866} \approx 2.309$

   (d) Reject H_0.

   (e) There is sufficient evidence at the 5% level to support the claim that the mean waste recycled by adults in the United States is more than 1 pound per person per day.

27. (a) H_0: $\mu = \$22{,}300$ (claim); H_a: $\mu \ne \$22{,}300$

   (b) $t_0 = 2.262$; Reject H_0 if $t < -2.262$ or $t > 2.262$.

   (c) $\bar{x} \approx 21{,}824.3$ $s \approx \$2628.9$

   $t = \dfrac{\bar{x} - \mu}{\frac{s}{\sqrt{n}}} = \dfrac{21{,}824.3 - 22{,}300}{\frac{2628.9}{\sqrt{10}}} = \dfrac{-475.7}{831.3} \approx -0.572$

   (d) Fail to reject H_0.

   (e) There is insufficient evidence at the 5% level to reject the claim that the mean salary for full-time male workers over age 25 without a high school diploma is \$22,300.

29. (a) H_0: $\mu \ge 3.0$; H_a: $\mu < 3.0$ (claim)

   (b) $\bar{x} = 2.785$ $x = 0.828$

   $t = \dfrac{\bar{x} - \mu}{\frac{s}{\sqrt{n}}} = \dfrac{2.785 - 3.0}{\frac{0.828}{\sqrt{20}}} = \dfrac{-0.215}{0.185} \approx -1.161$

   P-value = {Area left of $t = -1.161$} = 0.130

   (c) Fail to reject H_0.

   (e) There is insufficient evidence at the 5% level to reject the claim that teenage males drink less than three 12-ounce servings of soda per day.

31. (a) H_0: $\mu \ge 32$; H_a: $\mu < 32$ (claim)

   (b) $\bar{x} = 30.167$ $s = 4.004$

   $t = \dfrac{\bar{x} - \mu}{\frac{s}{\sqrt{n}}} = \dfrac{30.167 - 32}{\frac{4.004}{\sqrt{18}}} = \dfrac{-1.833}{0.944} \approx -1.942$

   P-value = {Area left of $t = -1.942$} ≈ 0.034

© 2006 Pearson Education, Inc., Upper Saddle River, NJ. All rights reserved. This material is protected under all copyright laws as they currently exist. No portion of this material may be reproduced, in any form or by any means, without permission in writing from the publisher.

(c) Fail to reject H_0.

(e) There is insufficient evidence at the 1% level to support the claim that the mean class size for full-time faculty is less than 32.

33. (a) H_0: $\mu = \$2116$ (claim); H_a: $\mu = \$2116$

(b) $\bar{x} = \$2423.75$ $s = \$800.566$

$$t = \frac{\bar{x} - \mu}{\frac{s}{\sqrt{n}}} = \frac{2423.75 - 2116}{\frac{800.566}{\sqrt{12}}} = \frac{307.75}{231.103} = 1.332$$

P-value $= 2\{\text{Area right of } t = 1.332\} = 2\{0.105\} = 0.210$

(c) Fail to reject H_0.

(e) There is insufficient evidence at the 2% level to reject the claim that the typical household in the U.S. spends a mean amount of $2116 per year on food away from home.

35. H_0: $\mu \leq \$2294$; H_a: $\mu > 2294$ (claim)

$$t = \frac{\bar{x} - \mu}{\frac{s}{\sqrt{n}}} = \frac{2494 - 2294}{\frac{325}{\sqrt{6}}} = \frac{200}{132.681} \approx 1.507$$

P-value $= \{\text{Area right of } t = 1.507\} \approx 0.096$

Since $0.096 > 0.01 = \alpha$, fail to reject H_0.

37. Since σ is unknown, $n < 30$, and the gas mileage is normally distributed, use the t-distribution.

H_0: $\mu \geq 21$ (claim); H_a: $\mu < 21$

$$t = \frac{\bar{x} - \mu}{\frac{s}{\sqrt{n}}} = \frac{19 - 21}{\frac{4}{\sqrt{5}}} = \frac{-2}{1.789} \approx 1.118$$

P-value $= \{\text{Area left of } t = -1.118\} = 0.163$

Fail to reject H_0. There is insufficient evidence at the 5% level to reject the claim that the mean gas mileage for the luxury sedan is at least 21 mpg.

7.4 HYPOTHESIS TESTING FOR PROPORTIONS

7.4 Try It Yourself Solutions

1a. $np = (86)(0.30) = 25.8 > 5$, $nq = (86)(0.70) = 60.2 > 5$

b. H_0: $p \geq 0.30$; H_a: $p < 0.30$ (claim)

c. $\alpha = 0.05$

d. $z_0 = -1.645$; Reject H_0 if $z < -1.645$.

e. $z = \dfrac{\hat{p} - p}{\sqrt{\dfrac{pq}{n}}} = \dfrac{0.20 - 0.30}{\sqrt{\dfrac{(0.30)(0.70)}{86}}} = \dfrac{-0.1}{0.0494} \approx -2.024$

f. Reject H_0.

g. There is enough evidence to support the claim.

© 2006 Pearson Education, Inc., Upper Saddle River, NJ. All rights reserved. This material is protected under all copyright laws as they currently exist.
No portion of this material may be reproduced, in any form or by any means, without permission in writing from the publisher.

2a. $np = (250)(0.05) = 12.5 > 5, nq = (250)(0.95) = 237.5 > 5$

b. $H_0: p = 0.05$ (claim); $H_a: p \neq 0.05$

c. $\alpha = 0.01$

d. $z_0 = \pm 2.575$; Reject H_0 if $z < -2.575$ or $z > 2.575$.

e. $z = \dfrac{\hat{p} - p}{\sqrt{\dfrac{pq}{n}}} = \dfrac{0.08 - 0.05}{\sqrt{\dfrac{(0.05)(0.95)}{250}}} = \dfrac{0.03}{0.0138} \approx 2.176$

f. Fail to reject H_0.

g. There is not enough evidence to reject the claim.

3a. $np = (75)(0.38) = 28.5 > 5, nq = (75)(0.62) = 46.5 > 5$

b. $H_0: p \leq 0.38$; $H_a: p > 0.38$ (claim)

c. $\alpha = 0.01$

d. $z_0 = 2.33$; Reject H_0 if $z > 2.33$.

e. $\hat{p} = \dfrac{x}{n} = \dfrac{33}{75} = 0.440$

$z = \dfrac{\hat{p} - p}{\sqrt{\dfrac{pq}{n}}} = \dfrac{0.440 - 0.38}{\sqrt{\dfrac{(0.38)(0.62)}{75}}} = \dfrac{0.06}{0.056} \approx 1.071$

f. Fail to reject H_0.

g. There is not enough evidence to support the claim.

7.4 EXERCISE SOLUTIONS

1. Verify that $np \geq 5$ and $nq \geq 5$. State H_0 and H_a. Specify the level of significance α. Determine the critical value(s) and rejection region(s). Find the standardized test statistic. Make a decision and interpret in the context of the original claim.

3. $np = (105)(0.25) = 26.25 > 5$

$nq = (105)(0.75) = 78.75 > 5 \rightarrow$ use normal distribution

$H_0: p = 0.25$; $H_a: p \neq 0.25$ (claim)

$z_0 \pm 1.96$

$z = \dfrac{\hat{p} - p}{\sqrt{\dfrac{pq}{n}}} = \dfrac{0.239 - 0.25}{\sqrt{\dfrac{(0.25)(0.75)}{105}}} = \dfrac{-0.011}{0.0423} \approx -0.260$

Fail to reject H_0. There is not enough evidence to support the claim.

5. $np = (20)(0.12) = 2.4 < 5$

$nq = (20)(0.88) = 17.6 \geq 5 \rightarrow$ cannot use normal distribution

© 2006 Pearson Education, Inc., Upper Saddle River, NJ. All rights reserved. This material is protected under all copyright laws as they currently exist. No portion of this material may be reproduced, in any form or by any means, without permission in writing from the publisher.

7. $np = (70)(0.48) = 33.6 \geq 5$

$nq = (70)(0.52) = 36.4 \geq 5 \rightarrow$ use normal distribution

$H_0: p \geq 0.48$ (claim); $H_a: p < 0.48$

$z_0 = -1.29$

$$z = \frac{\hat{p} - p}{\sqrt{\dfrac{pz}{n}}} = \frac{0.40 - 0.48}{\sqrt{\dfrac{(0.48)(0.52)}{70}}} = \frac{-0.08}{0.060} \approx -1.34$$

Reject H_0. There is not enough evidence to support the claim.

9. (a) $H_0: p \geq 0.23$ (claim); $H_a: p < 0.23$

(b) $z_0 = -2.33$; Reject H_0 if $z < -2.33$.

(c) $z = \dfrac{\hat{p} - p}{\sqrt{\dfrac{pq}{n}}} = \dfrac{0.225 - 0.23}{\sqrt{\dfrac{(0.23)(0.77)}{200}}} = \dfrac{-0.005}{0.0298} \approx -0.168$

(d) Fail to reject H_0.

(e) There is insufficient evidence at the 1% level to reject the claim that at least 23% of U.S. adults are smokers.

11. (a) $H_0: p \leq 0.30$; $H_a: p > 0.30$ (claim)

(b) $z_0 = 1.88$; Reject H_0 if $z > 1.88$.

(c) $z = \dfrac{\hat{p} - p}{\sqrt{\dfrac{pq}{n}}} = \dfrac{0.32 - 0.3}{\sqrt{\dfrac{(0.30)(0.70)}{1050}}} = \dfrac{0.02}{0.0141} \approx 1.414$

(d) Fail to reject H_0.

(e) There is insufficient evidence at the 3% level to support the claim that more than 30% of U.S. consumers have stopped buying the product because the manufacturing of the product pollutes the environment.

13. (a) $H_0: p = 0.44$ (claim); $H_a: p \neq 0.44$

(b) $z_0 = \pm 2.33$; Reject H_0 if $z < -2.33$ or $z > 2.33$.

(c) $\hat{p} = \dfrac{722}{1762} \approx 0.410$

$$z = \frac{\hat{p} - p}{\sqrt{\dfrac{pq}{n}}} = \frac{0.410 - 0.44}{\sqrt{\dfrac{(0.44)(0.56)}{1762}}} = \frac{-0.03}{0.01} \approx -2.537$$

(d) Reject H_0.

(e) There is sufficient evidence at the 2% level to reject the claim that 44% of home buyers find their real estate agent through a friend.

15. $H_0: p \geq 0.52$ (claim); $H_a: p < 0.52$

$z_0 = -1.645$; Rejection region: $z < -1.645$

$$z = \frac{\hat{p} - p}{\sqrt{\dfrac{pq}{n}}} = \frac{0.48 - 0.52}{\sqrt{\dfrac{(0.52)(0.48)}{50}}} = \frac{-0.04}{0.0707} \approx -0.566$$

Fail to reject H_0. There is insufficient evidence to reject the claim.

© 2006 Pearson Education, Inc., Upper Saddle River, NJ. All rights reserved. This material is protected under all copyright laws as they currently exist.
No portion of this material may be reproduced, in any form or by any means, without permission in writing from the publisher.

17. $H_0: p = 0.44$ (claim); $H_a: p \neq 0.44$

$$z = \frac{x - np}{\sqrt{npq}} = \frac{722 - (1762)(0.44)}{\sqrt{(1762)(0.44)(0.56)}} = \frac{-53.28}{20.836} \approx -2.557$$

Reject H_0. The results are the same.

7.5 HYPOTHESIS TESTING FOR VARIANCE AND STANDARD DEVIATION

7.5 Try It Yourself Solutions

1a. $\chi_0^2 = 33.409$ **2a.** $\chi_0^2 = 17.708$ **3a.** $\chi_R^2 = 31.526$

b. $\chi_L^2 = 8.231$

4a. $H_0: \sigma^2 \leq 0.40$ (claim); $H_a: \sigma^2 > 0.40$

b. $\alpha = 0.01$ and d.f. $= n - 1 = 30$

c. $\chi_0^2 = 50.892$; Reject H_0 if $\chi^2 > 50.892$.

d. $\chi^2 = \frac{(n-1)s^2}{\sigma^2} = \frac{(30)(0.75)}{0.40} = 56.250$

e. Reject H_0.

f. There is enough evidence to reject the claim.

5a. $H_0: \sigma \geq 3.7$; $H_a: \sigma < 3.7$ (claim)

b. $\alpha = 0.05$ and d.f. $= n - 1 = 8$

c. $\chi_0^2 = 2.733$; Reject H_0 if $\chi^2 < 2.733$.

d. $\chi^2 = \frac{(n-1)s^2}{\sigma^2} = \frac{(8)(3.0)^2}{(3.7)^2} \approx 5.259$

e. Fail to reject H_0.

f. There is not enough evidence to support the claim.

6a. $H_0: \sigma^2 = 8.6$ (claim); $H_a: \sigma^2 \neq 8.6$

b. $\alpha = 0.01$ and d.f. $= n - 1 = 9$

c. $\chi_L^2 = 1.735$ and $\chi_R^2 = 23.589$

Reject H_0 if $\chi^2 > 23.589$ or $\chi^2 < 1.735$.

d. $\chi^2 = \frac{(n-1)s^2}{\sigma^2} = \frac{(9)(4.3)}{(8.6)} = 4.50$

e. Fail to reject H_0.

f. There is not enough evidence to reject the claim.

© 2006 Pearson Education, Inc., Upper Saddle River, NJ. All rights reserved. This material is protected under all copyright laws as they currently exist. No portion of this material may be reproduced, in any form or by any means, without permission in writing from the publisher.

7.5 EXERCISE SOLUTIONS

1. Specify the level of significance α. Determine the degrees of freedom. Determine the critical values using the χ^2 distribution. If (a) right-tailed test, use the value that corresponds to d.f. and α. (b) left-tailed test, use the value that corresponds to d.f. and $1 - \alpha$; and (c) two-tailed test, use the value that corresponds to d.f. and $\frac{1}{2}\alpha$ and $1 - \frac{1}{2}\alpha$.

3. $\chi_0^2 = 38.885$ **5.** $\chi_0^2 = 0.872$ **7.** $\chi_L^2 = 7.261, \chi_R^2 = 24.996$

9. (a) Fail to reject H_0.   (b) Fail to reject H_0.

    (c) Fail to reject H_0.   (d) Reject H_0.

11. (a) Fail to reject H_0.   (b) Reject H_0.

    (c) Reject H_0.   (d) Fail to reject H_0.

13. $H_0: \sigma^2 = 0.52$ (claim); $H_a: \sigma^2 \neq 0.52$

$\chi_L^2 = 7.564, \chi_R^2 = 30.191$

$\chi^2 = \dfrac{(n-1)s^2}{\sigma^2} = \dfrac{(17)(0.508)^2}{(0.52)} \approx 16.608$

Fail to reject H_0. There is insufficient evidence to reject the claim.

15. (a) $H_0: \sigma^2 = 3$ (claim); $H_a: \sigma^2 \neq 3$

    (b) $\chi_L^2 = 13.844, \chi_R^2 = 41.923$; Reject H_0 if $\chi^2 > 41.923$ or $\chi^2 < 13.844$.

    (c) $\chi^2 = \dfrac{(n-1)s^2}{\sigma^2} = \dfrac{(26)(2.8)}{3} \approx 24.267$

    (d) Fail to reject H_0.

    (e) There is insufficient evidence at the 5% level of significance to reject the claim that the variance of the life of the appliances is 3.

17. (a) $H_0: \sigma \geq 29$; $H_a: \sigma < 29$ (claim)

    (b) $\chi_0^2 = 13.240$; Reject H_0 if $\chi^2 < 13.240$.

    (c) $\chi^2 = \dfrac{(n-1)s^2}{\sigma^2} = \dfrac{(21)(27.7)^2}{(29)^2} \approx 19.159$

    (d) Fail to reject H_0.

    (e) There is insufficient evidence at the 10% level of significance to support the claim that the standard deviation for eighth graders on the examination is less than 29.

19. (a) $H_0: \sigma \leq 0.5$ (claim); $H_a: \sigma > 0.5$

    (b) $\chi_0^2 = 33.196$; Reject H_0 if $\chi^2 > 33.196$.

    (c) $\chi^2 = \dfrac{(n-1)s^2}{\sigma^2} = \dfrac{(24)(0.7)^2}{(0.5)^2} = 47.040$

    (d) Reject H_0.

    (e) There is sufficient evidence at the 10% level to reject the claim that the standard deviation of waiting times is no more than 0.5 minute.

21. (a) $H_0: \sigma > \$18,000$; $H_a: \sigma < \$18,000$ (claim)

    (b) $\chi_0^2 = 18.114$; Reject H_0 if $\chi^2 < 18.114$.

© 2006 Pearson Education, Inc., Upper Saddle River, NJ. All rights reserved. This material is protected under all copyright laws as they currently exist. No portion of this material may be reproduced, in any form or by any means, without permission in writing from the publisher.

(c) $\chi^2 = \dfrac{(n-1)s^2}{\sigma^2} = \dfrac{(27)(18,500)^2}{(18,000)^2} \approx 28.521$

(d) Fail to reject H_0.

(e) There is insufficient evidence at the 10% level to support the claim that the standard deviation of the total charge for patients involved in a crash where the vehicle struck a wall is less than $18,000.

23. (a) $H_0: \sigma \le 20,000$; $H_a: \sigma > 20,000$ (claim)

(b) $\chi_0^2 = 24.996$; Reject H_0 if $\chi^2 > 24.996$.

(c) $s = 20,662.992$

$\chi^2 = \dfrac{(n-1)s^2}{\sigma^2} = \dfrac{(15)(20,662.992)^2}{(20,000)^2} \approx 16.011$

(d) Fail to reject H_0.

(e) There is insufficient evidence at the 5% level to support the claim that the standard deviation of the annual salaries for actuaries is more than $20,000.

25. $\chi^2 = 28.521$

P-value $= \{$Area left of $\chi^2 = 28.521\} = 0.615$

Fail to reject H_0 because P-value $= 0.385 > 0.10 = \alpha$.

27. $\chi^2 = 16.011$

P-value $= \{$Area right of $\chi^2 = 16.011\} = 0.381$

Fail to reject H_0 because P-value $= 0.381 > 0.05 = \alpha$.

CHAPTER 7 REVIEW EXERCISE SOLUTIONS

1. $H_0: \mu \le 1593$ (claim); $H_a: \mu > 1593$

3. $H_0: p \ge 0.205$; $H_a: p < 0.205$ (claim)

5. $H_0: \sigma \le 4.5$; $H_a: \sigma > 4.5$ (claim)

7. (a) $H_0: p = 0.73$ (claim); $H_a: p \ne 0.73$

(b) Type I error will occur if H_0 is rejected when the actual proportion of American adults who use nonprescription pain relievers is 0.73.
Type II error if H_0 is not rejected when the actual proportion of American adults who use nonprescription pain relievers is not 0.73.

(c) Two-tailed, since hypothesis compares "$=$ vs $\ne$".

(d) There is enough evidence to reject the claim.

(e) There is not enough evidence to reject the claim.

9. (a) $H_0: \mu \le 50$ (claim); $H_a: \mu > 50$

(b) Type I error will occur if H_0 is rejected when the actual standard deviation sodium content is no more than 50 mg.
Type II error if H_0 is not rejected when the actual standard deviation sodium content is more than 50 mg.

© 2006 Pearson Education, Inc., Upper Saddle River, NJ. All rights reserved. This material is protected under all copyright laws as they currently exist. No portion of this material may be reproduced, in any form or by any means, without permission in writing from the publisher.

    (c) Right-tailed, since hypothesis compares "≤ vs >".

    (d) There is enough evidence to reject the claim.

    (e) There is not enough evidence to reject the claim.

11. $z_0 \approx -2.05$ **13.** $z_0 = 1.96$

15. $H_0: \mu \le 45$ (claim); $H_a: \mu > 45$

    $z_0 = 1.645$

$$z = \frac{\bar{x} - \mu}{\frac{s}{\sqrt{n}}} = \frac{47.2 - 45}{\frac{6.7}{\sqrt{42}}} = \frac{2.2}{1.0338} \approx 2.128$$

    Reject H_0. There is enough evidence to reject the claim.

17. $H_0: \mu \ge 5.500$; $H_a: \mu < 5.500$ (claim)

    $z_0 = -2.33$

$$z = \frac{\bar{x} - \mu}{\frac{s}{\sqrt{n}}} = \frac{5.497 - 5.500}{\frac{0.011}{\sqrt{36}}} = \frac{-0.003}{0.00183} \approx -1.636$$

    Fail to reject H_0. There is not enough evidence to support the claim.

19. $H_0: \mu \le 0.05$ (claim); $H_a: \mu > 0.05$

$$z = \frac{\bar{x} - \mu}{\frac{s}{\sqrt{n}}} = \frac{0.057 - 0.05}{\frac{0.018}{\sqrt{32}}} = \frac{0.007}{0.00318} \approx 2.200$$

    P-value = {Area right of $z = 2.20$} = 0.0139

    $\alpha = 0.10$; Reject H_0.

    $\alpha = 0.05$; Reject H_0.

    $\alpha = 0.01$; Fail to reject H_0.

21. $H_0: \mu = 284$ (claim); $H_a: \mu \ne 284$

$$z = \frac{x - \mu}{\frac{s}{\sqrt{n}}} = \frac{292 - 284}{\frac{25}{\sqrt{50}}} = \frac{8}{3.536} \approx 2.263$$

    P-value = 2{Area right of $z = 2.263$} = 2{0.012} = 0.024

    Reject H_0. There is sufficient evidence to reject the claim.

23. $t_0 = \pm 2.093$ **25.** $t_0 = -1.345$

27. $H_0: \mu = 95$; $H_a: \mu \ne 95$ (claim)

    $t_0 = \pm 2.201$

$$t = \frac{\bar{x} - \mu}{\frac{s}{\sqrt{n}}} = \frac{94.1 - 95}{\frac{1.53}{\sqrt{12}}} = \frac{-0.9}{0.442} \approx -2.038$$

    Fail to reject H_0. There is not enough evidence to support the claim.

© 2006 Pearson Education, Inc., Upper Saddle River, NJ. All rights reserved. This material is protected under all copyright laws as they currently exist. No portion of this material may be reproduced, in any form or by any means, without permission in writing from the publisher.

29. $H_0: \mu \geq 0$ (claim); $H_a: \mu < 0$

$t_0 = -1.341$

$$t = \frac{\bar{x} - \mu}{\frac{s}{\sqrt{n}}} = \frac{-0.45 - 0}{\frac{1.38}{\sqrt{16}}} = \frac{-0.45}{0.345} \approx -1.304$$

Fail to reject H_0. There is not enough evidence to reject the claim.

31. $H_0: \mu \leq 48$ (claim); $H_a: \mu > 48$

$t_0 = 3.148$

$$t = \frac{\bar{x} - \mu}{\frac{s}{\sqrt{n}}} = \frac{52 - 48}{\frac{2.5}{\sqrt{7}}} = \frac{4}{0.945} \approx 4.233$$

Reject H_0. There is enough evidence to reject the claim.

33. $H_0: \mu = \$25$ (claim); $H_a: \mu \neq \$25$

$t_0 = \pm 1.740$

$$t = \frac{\bar{x} - \mu}{\frac{s}{\sqrt{n}}} = \frac{26.25 - 25}{\frac{3.23}{\sqrt{18}}} = \frac{1.25}{0.761} \approx 1.642$$

Fail to reject H_0. There is not enough evidence to reject the claim.

35. $H_0: \mu \geq 6$ (claim); $H_a: \mu < 6$

$t_0 = -2.539$

$x = 5.765 \quad s = 1.709$

$$t = \frac{\bar{x} - \mu}{\frac{s}{\sqrt{n}}} = \frac{5.765 - 6}{\frac{1.709}{\sqrt{20}}} = \frac{-0.235}{0.382} \approx -0.615$$

P-value ≈ 0.273

Fail to reject H_0. There is not enough evidence to reject the claim.

37. $H_0: p = 0.15$ (claim); $H_a: p \neq 0.15$

$z_0 = \pm 1.96$

$$z = \frac{\hat{p} - p}{\sqrt{\frac{pq}{n}}} = \frac{0.09 - 0.15}{\sqrt{\frac{(0.15)(0.85)}{40}}} = \frac{-0.06}{0.0565} \approx -1.063$$

Fail to reject H_0. There is not enough evidence to reject the claim.

39. Because $np = 3.6$ is less than 5, the normal distribution cannot be used to approximate the binomial distribution.

41. Because $np = 1.2 < 5$, the normal distribution cannot be used to approximate the binomial distribution.

43. $H_0: p = 0.20$; $H_a: p \neq 0.20$ (claim)

$z_0 \pm 2.575$

$$z = \frac{\hat{p} - p}{\sqrt{\frac{pq}{n}}} = \frac{0.23 - 0.20}{\sqrt{\frac{(0.20)(0.80)}{56}}} = \frac{0.03}{0.0534} \approx 0.561$$

Fail to reject H_0. There is not enough evidence to support the claim.

© 2006 Pearson Education, Inc., Upper Saddle River, NJ. All rights reserved. This material is protected under all copyright laws as they currently exist. No portion of this material may be reproduced, in any form or by any means, without permission in writing from the publisher.

45. $H_0: p \leq 0.75$; $H_a: p > 0.75$ (claim)

$z_0 = 1.28$

$\hat{p} = \dfrac{x}{n} = \dfrac{818}{1036} \approx 0.790$

$z = \dfrac{\hat{p} - p}{\sqrt{\dfrac{pq}{n}}} = \dfrac{0.790 - 0.75}{\sqrt{\dfrac{(0.75)(0.25)}{1036}}} \approx \dfrac{0.04}{0.0134} \approx 2.973$

Reject H_0. There is enough evidence to support the claim.

47. $\chi_R^2 = 30.144$ **49.** $\chi_R^2 = 33.196$

51. $H_0: \sigma^2 \leq 2$; $H_a: \sigma^2 > 2$ (claim)

$\chi_0^2 = 24.769$

$\chi^2 = \dfrac{(n-1)s^2}{\sigma^2} = \dfrac{(17)(2.38)}{(2)} = 20.230$

Fail to reject H_0. There is not enough evidence to support the claim.

53. $H_0: \sigma^2 = 1.25$ (claim); $H_a: \sigma^2 \neq 1.25$

$\chi_L^2 = 0.831$, $\chi_R^2 = 12.833$

$\chi^2 = \dfrac{(n-1)s^2}{\sigma^2} = \dfrac{(5)(1.03)^2}{(1.25)^2} \approx 3.395$

Fail to reject H_0. There is not enough evidence to reject the claim.

55. $H_0: \sigma^2 \leq 0.01$ (claim); $H_a: \sigma^2 > 0.01$

$\chi_0^2 = 49.645$

$\chi^2 = \dfrac{(n-1)s^2}{\sigma^2} = \dfrac{(27)(0.064)}{(0.01)} = 172.800$

Reject H_0. There is not enough evidence to reject the claim.

CHAPTER 7 QUIZ SOLUTIONS

1. (a) $H_0: \mu \geq 94$ (claim); $H_a: \mu < 94$

(b) "$\geq$ vs $<$" $\rightarrow$ Left-tailed

σ is unknown and $n \geq 30 \rightarrow z$-test.

(c) $z_0 = -2.05$; Reject H_0 if $z < -2.05$.

(d) $z = \dfrac{\bar{x} - \mu}{\dfrac{s}{\sqrt{n}}} = \dfrac{93.5 - 94}{\dfrac{30}{\sqrt{103}}} = \dfrac{-0.5}{2.956} \approx -0.169$

(e) Fail to reject H_0. There is insufficient evidence at the 2% level to reject the claim that the mean consumption of fresh citrus fruits by people in the U.S. is at least 94 pounds per year.

2. (a) $H_0: \mu \geq 25$ (claim); $H_a: \mu < 25$

(b) "$\geq$ vs $<$" $\rightarrow$ Left-tailed

σ is unknown, the population is normal, and $n < 30 \rightarrow t$-test.

(c) $t_0 = -1.895$; Reject H_0 if $t < -1.895$.

(d) $z = \dfrac{\bar{x} - \mu}{\dfrac{s}{\sqrt{n}}} = \dfrac{23 - 25}{\dfrac{5}{\sqrt{8}}} = \dfrac{-2}{1.768} \approx -1.131$

© 2006 Pearson Education, Inc., Upper Saddle River, NJ. All rights reserved. This material is protected under all copyright laws as they currently exist.
No portion of this material may be reproduced, in any form or by any means, without permission in writing from the publisher.

(e) Fail to reject H_0. There is insufficient evidence at the 5% level to reject the claim that the mean gas mileage is at least 25 miles per gallon.

3. (a) H_0: $p \leq 0.10$ (claim); H_a: $p > 0.10$

(b) "$\leq$ vs $>$" $\rightarrow$ Right-tailed

$np \geq 5$ and $nq \geq 5 \rightarrow z$-test

(c) $z_0 = 1.75$; Reject H_0 if $z > 1.75$.

(d) $z = \dfrac{\hat{p} - p}{\sqrt{\dfrac{pq}{n}}} = \dfrac{0.13 - 0.10}{\sqrt{\dfrac{(0.10)(0.90)}{57}}} = \dfrac{0.03}{0.0397} \approx 0.755$

(e) Fail to reject H_0. There is insufficient evidence at the 4% level to reject the claim that no more than 10% of microwaves need repair during the first five years of use.

4. (a) H_0: $\sigma = 105$ (claim); H_a: $\sigma \neq 105$

(b) "$=$ vs $\neq$" $\rightarrow$ Two-tailed

Assuming the scores are normally distributed and you are testing the hypothesized standard deviation $\rightarrow \chi^2$ test.

(c) $\chi_L^2 = 3.565$, $\chi_R^2 = 29.819$; Reject H_0 if $\chi^2 < 3.565$ or if $\chi^2 > 29.819$.

(d) $\chi^2 = \dfrac{(n-1)s^2}{\sigma^2} = \dfrac{(13)(113)^2}{(105)^2} \approx 15.056$

(e) Fail to reject H_0. There is insufficient evidence at the 1% level to reject the claim that the standard deviation of the SAT verbal scores for the state is 105.

5. (a) H_0: $\mu = \$59,482$ (claim); H_a: $\mu \neq \$59,482$

(b) "$=$ vs $\neq$" $\rightarrow$ Two-tailed

σ is unknown, $n < 30$, and assuming the salaries are normally distributed $\rightarrow t$-test.

(c) not applicable

(d) $t = \dfrac{\bar{x} - \mu}{\dfrac{s}{\sqrt{n}}} = \dfrac{58,581 - 59,482}{\dfrac{6500}{\sqrt{12}}} = \dfrac{-901}{1876.388} \approx -0.480$

P-value $= 2\{$Area left of $t = -0.480\} = 2(0.320) = 0.640$

(e) Fail to reject H_0. There is insufficient evidence at the 5% level to reject the claim that the mean annual salary for full-time male workers age 25 to 34 with a bachelor's degree is $59,482.

6. (a) H_0: $\mu = \$276$ (claim); H_a: $\mu \neq \$276$

(b) "$=$ vs $\neq$" $\rightarrow$ Two-tailed

σ is unknown, $n \geq 30 \rightarrow z$-test.

(c) not applicable

(d) $z = \dfrac{\bar{x} - \mu}{\dfrac{s}{\sqrt{n}}} = \dfrac{285 - 276}{\dfrac{30}{\sqrt{35}}} = \dfrac{9}{5.071} \approx 1.775$

P-value $= 2\{$Area right of $z = 1.775\} = 2\{0.038\} = 0.0759$

(e) Fail to reject H_0. There is insufficient evidence at the 5% level to reject the claim that the mean daily cost of meals and lodging for a family of four traveling in Massachusetts is $276.

© 2006 Pearson Education, Inc., Upper Saddle River, NJ. All rights reserved. This material is protected under all copyright laws as they currently exist. No portion of this material may be reproduced, in any form or by any means, without permission in writing from the publisher.

8.1 Try It Yourself Solutions

1a. $H_0: \mu_1 = \mu_2; H_a: \mu_1 \neq \mu_2$ (claim)

b. $\alpha = 0.01$

c. $z_0 = \pm 2.575$; Reject H_0 if $z > 2.575$ or $z < -2.575$.

d. $z = \dfrac{(\bar{x}_1 - \bar{x}_2) - (\mu_1 - \mu_2)}{\sqrt{\dfrac{s_1^2}{n_1} + \dfrac{s_2^2}{n_2}}} = \dfrac{(3900 - 3500) - (0)}{\sqrt{\dfrac{(900)^2}{50} + \dfrac{(500)^2}{50}}} = \dfrac{400}{\sqrt{21200}} \approx 2.747$

e. Reject H_0.

f. There is enough evidence to support the claim.

2a. $z = \dfrac{(\bar{x}_1 - \bar{x}_2) - (\mu_1 - \mu_2)}{\sqrt{\dfrac{s_1^2}{n_1} + \dfrac{s_2^2}{n_2}}} = \dfrac{(252 - 242) - (0)}{\sqrt{\dfrac{(22)^2}{150} + \dfrac{(18)^2}{200}}} = \dfrac{10}{\sqrt{4.847}} \approx 4.542$

$\rightarrow P\text{-value} = \{\text{area right of } z = 4.542\} = 0.00000278$

b. Reject H_0.

8.1 EXERCISE SOLUTIONS

1. State the hypotheses and identify the claim. Specify the level of significance and find the critical value(s). Identify the rejection regions. Find the standardized test statistic. Make a decision and interpret in the context of the claim.

3. $H_0: \mu_1 = \mu_2$ (claim); $H_a: \mu_1 \neq \mu_2$

Rejection regions: $z_0 < -1.96$ and $z_0 > 1.96$ (Two-tailed test)

(a) $\bar{x}_1 - \bar{x}_2 = 16 - 14 = 2$

(b) $z = \dfrac{(\bar{x}_1 - \bar{x}_2) - (\mu_1 - \mu_2)}{\sqrt{\dfrac{s_1^2}{n_1} + \dfrac{s_2^2}{n_2}}} = \dfrac{(16 - 14) - (0)}{\sqrt{\dfrac{(1.1)^2}{50} + \dfrac{(1.5)^2}{50}}} = \dfrac{2}{\sqrt{0.0692}} \approx 7.603$

(c) z is in the rejection region because $7.603 > 1.96$.

(d) Reject H_0. There is enough evidence to reject the claim.

5. $H_0: \mu_1 \geq \mu_2; H_a: \mu_1 < \mu_2$ (claim)

Rejection region: $z_0 < -2.33$ (Left-tailed test)

(a) $\bar{x}_1 - \bar{x}_2 = 1225 - 1195 = 30$

© 2006 Pearson Education, Inc., Upper Saddle River, NJ. All rights reserved. This material is protected under all copyright laws as they currently exist. No portion of this material may be reproduced, in any form or by any means, without permission in writing from the publisher.

(b) $z = \dfrac{(\bar{x}_1 - \bar{x}_2) - (\mu_1 - \mu_2)}{\sqrt{\dfrac{s_1^2}{n_1} + \dfrac{s_2^2}{n_2}}} = \dfrac{(1225 - 1195) - (0)}{\sqrt{\dfrac{(75)^2}{35} + \dfrac{(105)^2}{105}}} = \dfrac{30}{\sqrt{265.714}} \approx 1.84$

(c) z is not in the rejection region because $1.84 > -2.330$.

(d) Fail to reject H_0. There is not enough evidence to support the claim.

7. $H_0: \mu_1 \leq \mu_2; H_a: \mu_1 > \mu_2$ (claim)

$z_0 = 2.33$; Reject H_0 if $z > 2.33$.

$z = \dfrac{(\bar{x}_1 - \bar{x}_2) - (\mu_1 - \mu_2)}{\sqrt{\dfrac{s_1^2}{n_1} + \dfrac{s_2^2}{n_2}}} = \dfrac{(5.2 - 5.5) - (0)}{\sqrt{\dfrac{(0.2)^2}{45} + \dfrac{(0.3)^2}{37}}} = \dfrac{-.30}{\sqrt{0.00332}} \approx -5.207$

Reject H_0. There is enough evidence to reject the claim.

9. (a) $H_0: \mu_1 = \mu_2; H_a: \mu_1 \neq \mu_2$ (claim)

(b) $z_0 = \pm 1.645$; Reject H_0 if $z < -1.645$ or $z > 1.645$.

(c) $z = \dfrac{(\bar{x}_1 - \bar{x}_2) - (\mu_1 - \mu_2)}{\sqrt{\dfrac{s_1^2}{n_1} + \dfrac{s_2^2}{n_2}}} = \dfrac{(42 - 45) - (0)}{\sqrt{\dfrac{(4.7)^2}{35} + \dfrac{(4.3)^2}{35}}} = \dfrac{-3}{\sqrt{1.159}} \approx -2.786$

(d) Reject H_0.

(e) There is sufficient evidence at the 10% level to support the claim that the mean braking distance is different for both types of tires.

11. (a) $H_0: \mu_1 \geq \mu_2; H_a: \mu_1 < \mu_2$ (claim)

(b) $z_0 = -2.33$; Reject H_0 if $z < -2.33$.

(c) $z = \dfrac{(\bar{x}_1 - \bar{x}_2) - (\mu_1 - \mu_2)}{\sqrt{\dfrac{s_1^2}{n_1} + \dfrac{s_2^2}{n_2}}} = \dfrac{(75 - 80) - (0)}{\sqrt{\dfrac{(12.50)^2}{47} + \dfrac{(20)^2}{55}}} = \dfrac{-5}{\sqrt{10.597}} \approx -1.536$

(d) Fail to reject H_0.

(e) There is insufficient evidence at the 1% level to conclude that the repair costs for Model A are lower than for Model B.

13. (a) $H_0: \mu_1 = \mu_2$ (claim); $H_a: \mu_1 \neq \mu_2$

(b) $z_0 = \pm 2.575$; Reject H_0 if $z < -2.575$ or $z > 2.575$.

(c) $z = \dfrac{(\bar{x}_1 - \bar{x}_2) - (\mu_1 - \mu_2)}{\sqrt{\dfrac{s_1^2}{n_1} + \dfrac{s_2^2}{n_2}}} = \dfrac{(21.0 - 20.8) - (0)}{\sqrt{\dfrac{(5.0)^2}{43} + \dfrac{(4.7)^2}{56}}} = \dfrac{0.2}{\sqrt{0.976}} \approx 0.202$

(d) Fail to reject H_0.

(e) There is insufficient evidence at the 1% level to reject the claim that the male and female high school students have equal ACT scores.

15. (a) $H_0: \mu_1 = \mu_2$ (claim); $H_a: \mu_1 \neq \mu_2$

(b) $z_0 = \pm 1.645$; Reject H_0 if $z < -1.645$ or $z > 1.645$.

© 2006 Pearson Education, Inc., Upper Saddle River, NJ. All rights reserved. This material is protected under all copyright laws as they currently exist. No portion of this material may be reproduced, in any form or by any means, without permission in writing from the publisher.

(c) $z = \dfrac{(\bar{x}_1 - \bar{x}_2) - (\mu_1 - \mu_2)}{\sqrt{\dfrac{s_1^2}{n_1} + \dfrac{s_2^2}{n_2}}} = \dfrac{(136 - 140) - (0)}{\sqrt{\dfrac{(25)^2}{35} + \dfrac{(30)^2}{35}}} = \dfrac{-4}{\sqrt{43.571}} \approx 0.606$

(d) Fail to reject H_0.

(e) There is insufficient evidence at the 10% level to reject the claim that the lodging cost for a family traveling in California is the same as Florida.

17. (a) $H_0: \mu_1 = \mu_2$ (claim); $H_a: \mu_1 \neq \mu_2$

(b) $z_0 = \pm 1.645$; Reject H_0 if $z < -1.645$ or $z > 1.645$.

(c) $z = \dfrac{(\bar{x}_1 - \bar{x}_2) - (\mu_1 - \mu_2)}{\sqrt{\dfrac{s_1^2}{n_1} + \dfrac{s_2^2}{n_2}}} = \dfrac{(146 - 142) - (0)}{\sqrt{\dfrac{(30)^2}{50} + \dfrac{(32)^2}{50}}} = \dfrac{4}{\sqrt{38.48}} \approx 0.645$

(d) Fail to reject H_0.

(e) There is insufficient evidence at the 10% level to reject the claim that the lodging cost for a family traveling in California is the same as Florida. The new samples do not lead to a different conclusion.

19. (a) $H_0: \mu_1 \leq \mu_2$; $H_a: \mu_1 > \mu_2$ (claim)

(b) $z_0 = 1.96$; Reject H_0 if $z > 1.96$.

(c) $\bar{x}_1 \approx 2.130, s_1 \approx 0.490, n_1 = 30$
$\bar{x}_2 \approx 1.593, s_2 \approx 0.328, n_2 = 30$

$z = \dfrac{(\bar{x}_1 - \bar{x}_2) - (\mu_1 - \mu_2)}{\sqrt{\dfrac{s_1^2}{n_1} + \dfrac{s_2^2}{n_2}}} = \dfrac{(2.130 - 1.593) - (0)}{\sqrt{\dfrac{(0.490)^2}{30} + \dfrac{(0.328)^2}{30}}} = \dfrac{0.537}{\sqrt{0.0116}} \approx 4.988$

(d) Reject H_0.

(e) At the 2.5% level of significance, there is sufficient evidence to support the claim.

21. (a) $H_0: \mu_1 = \mu_2$ (claim); $H_a: \mu_1 \neq \mu_2$

(b) $z_0 = \pm 2.575$; Reject H_0 if $z < -2.575$ or $z > 2.575$.

(c) $\bar{x}_1 \approx 0.875, s_1 \approx 0.011, n_1 = 35$
$\bar{x}_2 \approx 0.701, s_2 \approx 0.011, n_2 = 35$

$z = \dfrac{(\bar{x}_1 - \bar{x}_2) - (\mu_1 - \mu_2)}{\sqrt{\dfrac{s_1^2}{n_1} + \dfrac{s_2^2}{n_2}}} = \dfrac{(0.875 - 0.701) - (0)}{\sqrt{\dfrac{(0.011)^2}{35} + \dfrac{(0.011)^2}{35}}} = \dfrac{0.174}{\sqrt{0.0000006914}} \approx 66.172$

(d) Reject H_0.

(e) At the 1% level of significance, there is sufficient evidence to reject the claim.

23. They are equivalent through algebraic manipulation of the equation.
$\mu_1 = \mu_2 \rightarrow \mu_1 - \mu_2 = 0$

© 2006 Pearson Education, Inc., Upper Saddle River, NJ. All rights reserved. This material is protected under all copyright laws as they currently exist. No portion of this material may be reproduced, in any form or by any means, without permission in writing from the publisher.

25. $H_0: \mu_1 - \mu_2 = -9$ (claim); $H_a: \mu_1 - \mu_2 \neq -9$

$z_0 = \pm 2.575$; Reject H_0 if $z < -2.575$ or $z > 2.575$.

$$z = \frac{(\bar{x}_1 - \bar{x}_2) - (\mu_1 - \mu_2)}{\sqrt{\dfrac{s_1^2}{n_1} + \dfrac{s_2^2}{n_2}}} = \frac{(11.5 - 20) - (-9)}{\sqrt{\dfrac{(3.8)^2}{70} + \dfrac{(6.7)^2}{65}}} = \frac{0.5}{\sqrt{0.897}} \approx 0.528$$

Fail to reject H_0. There is not enough evidence to reject the claim.

27. $H_0: \mu_1 - \mu_2 \leq 6000$; $H_a: \mu_1 - \mu_2 > 6000$ (claim)

$z_0 = 1.28$; Reject H_0 if $z > 1.28$.

$$z = \frac{(\bar{x}_1 - \bar{x}_2) - (\mu_1 - \mu_2)}{\sqrt{\dfrac{s_1^2}{n_1} + \dfrac{s_2^2}{n_2}}} = \frac{(55{,}900 - 54{,}200) - (6000)}{\sqrt{\dfrac{(8875)^2}{45} + \dfrac{(9175)^2}{37}}} = \frac{-4300}{\sqrt{4{,}025{,}499.249}} \approx -2.143$$

Fail to reject H_0. There is not enough evidence to support the claim.

29. $(\bar{x}_1 - \bar{x}_2) - z_c \sqrt{\dfrac{s_1^2}{n_1} + \dfrac{s_2^2}{n_2}} < \mu_1 - \mu_2 < (\bar{x}_1 - \bar{x}_2) + z_c \sqrt{\dfrac{s_1^2}{n_1} + \dfrac{s_2^2}{n_2}}$

$(3.2 - 4.1) - 1.96 \sqrt{\dfrac{(3.3)^2}{42} + \dfrac{(3.9)^2}{42}} < \mu_1 - \mu_2 < (3.2 - 4.1) + 1.96 \sqrt{\dfrac{(3.3)^2}{42} + \dfrac{(3.9)^2}{42}}$

$-0.9 - 1.96\sqrt{0.621} < \mu_1 - \mu_2 < -0.9 + 1.96\sqrt{0.621}$

$-2.45 < \mu_1 - \mu_2 < 0.65$

31. $H_0: \mu_1 - \mu_2 \leq 0$; $H_a: \mu_1 - \mu_2 > 0$ (claim)

$z_0 = 1.645$; Reject H_0 if $z > 1.645$.

$$z = \frac{(\bar{x}_1 - \bar{x}_2) - (\mu_1 - \mu_2)}{\sqrt{\dfrac{s_1^2}{n_1} + \dfrac{s_2^2}{n_2}}} = \frac{(3.2 - 4.1) - (0)}{\sqrt{\dfrac{(3.3)^2}{42} + \dfrac{(3.9)^2}{42}}} = \frac{-0.9}{\sqrt{0.621}} \approx -1.14$$

Fail to reject H_0. There is not enough evidence to support the claim. I would not recommend using the herbal supplement with a high-fiber, low-calorie diet to lose weight because there was not a significant difference between the weight loss it produced and that of the placebo.

33. $H_0: \mu_1 - \mu_2 \leq 0$; $H_a: \mu_1 - \mu_2 > 0$ (claim)

The 95% CI for $\mu_1 - \mu_2$ in Exercise 29 contained values less than or equal to zero and, as found in Exercise 31, there was not enough evidence at the 5% level of significance to support the claim. If zero is contained in the CI for $\mu_1 - \mu_2$, you fail to reject H_0 because the null hypothesis states that $\mu_1 - \mu_2$ is less than or equal to zero.

8.2 TESTING THE DIFFERENCE BETWEEN MEANS (SMALL INDEPENDENT SAMPLES)

8.2 Try It Yourself Solutions

1a. $H_0: \mu_1 = \mu_2$; $H_a: \mu_1 \neq \mu_2$ (claim)   **b.** $\alpha = 0.05$

c. d.f. $= \min\{n_1 - 1, n_2 - 1\} = \min\{10 - 1, 12 - 1\} = 9$

d. $t_0 = \pm 2.262$; Reject H_0 if $t < -2.262$ or $t > 2.262$.

© 2006 Pearson Education, Inc., Upper Saddle River, NJ. All rights reserved. This material is protected under all copyright laws as they currently exist. No portion of this material may be reproduced, in any form or by any means, without permission in writing from the publisher.

e. $z = \dfrac{(\bar{x}_1 - \bar{x}_2) - (\mu_1 - \mu_2)}{\sqrt{\dfrac{s_1^2}{n_1} + \dfrac{s_2^2}{n_2}}} = \dfrac{(102 - 94) - (0)}{\sqrt{\dfrac{(10)^2}{10} + \dfrac{(4)^2}{12}}} = \dfrac{8}{\sqrt{11.333}} \approx 2.376$

f. Reject H_0.

g. There is enough evidence to support the claim.

2a. $H_0: \mu_1 \geq \mu_2; H_a: \mu_1 < \mu_2$ (claim)   **b.** $\alpha = 0.10$

c. d.f. $= n_1 = n_2 - 2 = 12 + 15 - 2 = 25$ **d.** $t_0 = -1.316$; Reject H_0 if $t < -1.316$.

e. $t = \dfrac{(\bar{x}_1 - \bar{x}_2) - (\mu_1 - \mu_2)}{\sqrt{\dfrac{(n_1 - 1)s_1^2 + (n_2 - 1)s_2^2}{n_1 + n_2 - 2}}\sqrt{\dfrac{1}{n_1} + \dfrac{1}{n_2}}} = \dfrac{(73 - 74) - (0)}{\sqrt{\dfrac{(12 - 1)(2.4)^2 + (15 - 1)(3.2)^2}{12 + 15 - 2}}\sqrt{\dfrac{1}{12} + \dfrac{1}{15}}}$

$= \dfrac{-1}{\sqrt{8.269}\sqrt{0.150}} \approx -0.898$

f. Fail to reject H_0.

g. There is not enough evidence to support the claim.

8.2 EXERCISE SOLUTIONS

1. State hypotheses and identify the claim. Specify the level of significance. Determine the degrees of freedom. Find the critical value(s) and identify the rejection region(s). Find the standardized test statistic. Make a decision and interpret in the context of the original claim.

3. (a) d.f. $= n_1 + n_2 - 2 = 20$ **5.** (a) d.f. $= n_1 + n_2 - 2 = 22$
    $t_0 = \pm1.725$ $t_0 = -2.074$

(b) d.f. $= \min\{n_1 - 1, n_2 - 1\} = 9$ (b) d.f. $= \min\{n_1 - 1, n_2 - 1\} = 8$
    $t_0 = \pm1.833$ $t_0 = -2.306$

7. (a) d.f. $= n_1 + n_2 - 2 = 19$ **9.** (a) d.f. $= n_1 + n_2 - 2 = 27$
    $t_0 = 1.729$ $t_0 = \pm2.771$

(b) d.f. $= \min\{n_1 - 1, n_2 - 1\} = 7$ (b) d.f. $= \min\{n_1 - 1, n_2 - 1\} = 11$
    $t_0 = 1.895$ $t_0 = \pm3.106$

11. $H_0: \mu_1 = \mu_2$ (claim); $H_a: \mu_1 \neq \mu_2$
    d.f. $= n_1 + n_2 - 2 = 15$
    $t_0 = \pm2.947$ (Two-tailed test)

(a) $\bar{x}_1 - \bar{x}_2 = 33.7 - 35.5 = -1.8$

(b) $t = \dfrac{(\bar{x}_1 - \bar{x}_2) - (\mu_1 - \mu_2)}{\sqrt{\dfrac{(n_1 - 1)s_1^2 + (n_2 - 1)s_2^2}{n_1 + n_2 - 2}}\sqrt{\dfrac{1}{n_1} + \dfrac{1}{n_2}}} = \dfrac{(33.7 - 35.5) - (0)}{\sqrt{\dfrac{(10 - 1)(3.5)^2 + (7 - 1)(2.2)^2}{10 + 7 - 2}}\sqrt{\dfrac{1}{10} + \dfrac{1}{7}}}$

$= \dfrac{-1.8}{\sqrt{9.286}\sqrt{0.243}} \approx -1.199$

(c) t is not in the rejection region.

(d) Fail to reject H_0. There is not enough evidence to reject the claim.

13. There is no need to run the test since this is a right-tailed test and the test statistic is negative. It is obvious that the standardized test statistic will also be negative and fall outside of the rejection region. So, the decision is to fail to reject H_0.

© 2006 Pearson Education, Inc., Upper Saddle River, NJ. All rights reserved. This material is protected under all copyright laws as they currently exist. No portion of this material may be reproduced, in any form or by any means, without permission in writing from the publisher.

15. (a) H_0: $\mu_1 = \mu_2$ (claim); H_a: $\mu_1 \neq \mu_2$

(b) d.f. $= n_1 + n_2 - 2 = 13 + 15 - 2 = 26$

$t_0 = \pm 1.706$; Reject H_0 if $t < -1.706$ or $t > 1.706$.

(c) $t = \dfrac{(\bar{x}_1 - \bar{x}_2) - (\mu_1 - \mu_2)}{\sqrt{\dfrac{(n_1 - 1)s_1^2 + (n_2 - 1)s_2^2}{n_1 + n_2 - 2}}\sqrt{\dfrac{1}{n_1} + \dfrac{1}{n_2}}}$

$= \dfrac{(15.1 - 12.8) - (0)}{\sqrt{\dfrac{(13 - 1)(7.55)^2 + (15 - 1)(6.35)^2}{13 + 15 - 2}}\sqrt{\dfrac{1}{13} + \dfrac{1}{15}}} = \dfrac{2.3}{\sqrt{48.021}\,\sqrt{0.144}} \approx 0.876$

(d) Fail to reject H_0.

(e) There is not enough evidence to reject the claim.

17. (a) H_0: $\mu_1 \geq \mu_2$; H_a: $\mu_1 < \mu_2$ (claim)

(b) d.f. $= \min\{n_1 - 1, n_2 - 1\} = 14$

$t_0 = -1.345$; Reject H_0 if $t < -1.345$.

(c) $t = \dfrac{(\bar{x}_1 - \bar{x}_2) - (\mu_1 - \mu_2)}{\sqrt{\dfrac{s_1^2}{n_1} + \dfrac{s_2^2}{n_2}}} = \dfrac{(473 - 741) - (0)}{\sqrt{\dfrac{(190)^2}{14} + \dfrac{(205)^2}{23}}} = \dfrac{-268}{\sqrt{4405.745}} = -4.038$

(d) Reject H_0.

(e) There is enough evidence to support the claim.

19. (a) H_0: $\mu_1 \leq \mu_2$; H_a: $\mu_1 > \mu_2$ (claim)

(b) d.f. $= \min\{n_1 - 1, n_2 - 1\} = 14$

$t_0 = 1.345$; Reject H_0 if $t > 1.345$.

(c) $z = \dfrac{(\bar{x}_1 - \bar{x}_2) - (\mu_1 - \mu_2)}{\sqrt{\dfrac{s_1^2}{n_1} + \dfrac{s_2^2}{n_2}}} = \dfrac{(41,300 - 37,800) - (0)}{\sqrt{\dfrac{(8600)^2}{19} + \dfrac{(5500)^2}{15}}} = \dfrac{3500}{\sqrt{5,909,298.246}} \approx 1.440$

(d) Reject H_0.

(e) There is enough evidence to support the claim.

21. (a) H_0: $\mu_1 = \mu_2$; H_a: $\mu_1 \neq \mu_2$ (claim)

(b) d.f. $= n_1 + n_2 - 2 = 21$

$t_0 \pm 2.831$; Reject H_0 if $t < -2.831$ or $t > 2.831$.

(c) $\bar{x}_1 = 340.300$, $s_1 = 22.301$, $n_1 = 10$

$\bar{x}_2 = 389.538$, $s_2 = 14.512$, $n_2 = 13$

$t = \dfrac{(\bar{x}_1 - \bar{x}_2) - (\mu_1 - \mu_2)}{\sqrt{\dfrac{(n_1 - 1)s_1^2 + (n_2 - 1)s_2^2}{n_1 + n_2 - 2}}\sqrt{\dfrac{1}{n_1} + \dfrac{1}{n_2}}}$

$= \dfrac{(340.300 - 389.538) - (0)}{\sqrt{\dfrac{(10 - 1)(22.301)^2 + (13 - 1)(14.512)^2}{10 + 13 - 2}}\sqrt{\dfrac{1}{10} + \dfrac{1}{13}}} = \dfrac{-49.238}{\sqrt{333.485}\,\sqrt{0.177}} \approx -6.410$

(d) Reject H_0.

(e) There is enough evidence to support the claim.

© 2006 Pearson Education, Inc., Upper Saddle River, NJ. All rights reserved. This material is protected under all copyright laws as they currently exist. No portion of this material may be reproduced, in any form or by any means, without permission in writing from the publisher.

23. (a) H_0: $\mu_1 \geq \mu_2$; H_a: $\mu_1 < \mu_2$ (claim)

(b) d.f. $= n_1 + n_2 - 2 = 42$

$t_0 = -1.282 \rightarrow t < -1.282$

(c) $\bar{x}_1 = 56.684$, $s_1 = 6.961$, $n_1 = 19$

$\bar{x}_2 = 67.400$, $s_2 = 9.014$, $n_2 = 25$

$$t = \frac{(\bar{x}_1 - \bar{x}_2) - (\mu_1 - \mu_2)}{\sqrt{\frac{(n_1 - 1)s_1^2 + (n_2 - 1)s_2^2}{n_1 + n_2 - 2}}\sqrt{\frac{1}{n_1} + \frac{1}{n_2}}}$$

$$= \frac{(56.684 - 67.400) - (0)}{\sqrt{\frac{(19 - 1)(6.961)^2 + (25 - 1)(9.014)^2}{19 + 25 - 2}}\sqrt{\frac{1}{19} + \frac{1}{25}}} = \frac{-10.716}{\sqrt{67.196}\sqrt{0.0926}} \approx -4.295$$

(d) Reject H_0.

(e) There is enough evidence to support the claim and to recommend changing to the new method.

25. $\hat{\sigma} = \sqrt{\frac{(n_1 - 1)s_1^2 + (n_2 - 1)s_2^2}{n_1 + n_2 - 2}} = \sqrt{\frac{(15 - 1)(6.2)^2 + (12 - 1)(8.1)^2}{15 + 12 - 2}} \approx 7.099$

$(\bar{x}_1 - \bar{x}_2) \pm t_c\hat{\sigma}\sqrt{\frac{1}{n_1} + \frac{1}{n_2}} \rightarrow (410 - 400) \pm 2.060 \cdot 7.099\sqrt{\frac{1}{15} + \frac{1}{12}}$

$\rightarrow 10 \pm 5.664 \rightarrow 4.336 < \mu_1 - \mu_2 < 15.644$

27. $(\bar{x}_1 - \bar{x}_2) \pm t_c\sqrt{\frac{s_1^2}{n_1} + \frac{s_2^2}{n_2}} \rightarrow (60 - 70) \pm 1.363\sqrt{\frac{(3.59)^2}{15} + \frac{(2.41)^2}{12}}$

$\rightarrow -10 \pm 1.580 \rightarrow -11.58 < \mu_1 - \mu_2 < -8.42$

8.3 TESTING THE DIFFERENCE BETWEEN MEANS (DEPENDENT SAMPLES)

8.3 Try It Yourself Solutions

1a. (1) Independent   (2) Dependent

2.

Before	After	d	d²
72	73	−1	1
81	80	1	1
76	79	−3	9
74	76	−2	4
75	76	−1	1
80	80	0	0
68	74	−6	36
75	77	−2	4
78	75	3	9
76	74	2	4
74	76	−2	4
77	78	−1	1
		$\Sigma d = -12$	$\Sigma d^2 = 74$

a. H_0: $\mu_d \geq 0$; H_a: $\mu_d < 0$ (claim)

b. $\alpha = 0.05$ and d.f. $= n - 1 = 11$

c. $t_0 \approx -1.796$; Reject H_0 if $t < -1.796$.

d. $\bar{d} = \frac{\Sigma d}{n} = \frac{-12}{12} = -1$

$s_d = \sqrt{\frac{n(\Sigma d^2) - (\Sigma d)^2}{n(n-1)}} = \sqrt{\frac{12(74) - (-12)^2}{12(11)}} \approx 2.374$

e. $t = \frac{\bar{d} - \mu_d}{\frac{s_d}{\sqrt{n}}} = \frac{-1 - 0}{\frac{2.374}{\sqrt{12}}} \approx -1.459$

f. Fail to reject H_0.

g. There is not enough evidence to support the claim.

© 2006 Pearson Education, Inc., Upper Saddle River, NJ. All rights reserved. This material is protected under all copyright laws as they currently exist. No portion of this material may be reproduced, in any form or by any means, without permission in writing from the publisher.

3.

Before	After	d	d^2
101.8	99.2	2.6	6.76
98.5	98.4	0.1	0.01
98.1	98.2	−0.1	0.01
99.4	99	0.4	0.16
98.9	98.6	0.3	0.09
100.2	99.7	0.5	0.25
97.9	97.8	0.1	0.01
		$\Sigma d = 3.9$	$\Sigma d^2 = 7.29$

a. $H_0: \mu_d = 0; H_a: \mu_d \neq 0$ (claim)

b. $\alpha = 0.05$ and d.f. $= n - 1 = 6$

c. $t_0 = \pm 2.447$; Reject H_0 if $t < -2.447$ or $t > 2.447$.

d. $\overline{d} = \dfrac{\Sigma d}{n} = \dfrac{3.9}{7} \approx 0.557$

$$s_d = \sqrt{\dfrac{n(\Sigma d^2) - (\Sigma d)^2}{n(n-1)}} = \sqrt{\dfrac{7(7.29) - (3.9)^2}{7(6)}} \approx 0.924$$

e. $t = \dfrac{\overline{d} - \mu_d}{\dfrac{s_d}{\sqrt{n}}} = \dfrac{0.557 - 0}{\dfrac{0.924}{\sqrt{7}}} \approx 1.595$

f. Fail to reject H_0.

g. There is not enough evidence to conclude that the drug changes the body's temperature at the specified level of significance.

8.3 EXERCISE SOLUTIONS

1. Two samples are dependent if each member of one sample corresponds to a member of the other sample. Example: The weights of 22 people before starting an exercise program and the weights of the same 22 people six weeks after starting the exercise program. Two samples are independent if the sample selected from one population is not related to the sample selected from the second population. Example: The weights of 25 cats and the weights of 20 dogs.

3. Independent because the scores are from different students.

5. Dependent because the same adults were sampled.

7. Independent because different boats were sampled.

9. Dependent because the same tire sets were sampled.

11. $H_0: \mu_d \geq 0; H_a: \mu_d < 0$ (claim)

$\alpha = 0.05$ and d.f. $= n - 1 = 9$

$t_0 = -1.833$ (Left-tailed)

$t = \dfrac{\overline{d} - \mu_d}{\dfrac{s_d}{\sqrt{n}}} = \dfrac{10 - 0}{\dfrac{1.5}{\sqrt{10}}} = \dfrac{10}{0.474} \approx 21.082$

Fail to reject H_0. There is not enough evidence to support the claim.

© 2006 Pearson Education, Inc., Upper Saddle River, NJ. All rights reserved. This material is protected under all copyright laws as they currently exist. No portion of this material may be reproduced, in any form or by any means, without permission in writing from the publisher.

13. H_0: $\mu_d \leq 0$ (claim); H_a: $\mu_d > 0$

$\alpha = 0.10$ and d.f. $= n - 1 = 15$

$t_0 = 1.341$ (Right-tailed)

$$t = \frac{\bar{d} - \mu_d}{\frac{s_d}{\sqrt{n}}} = \frac{6.1 - 0}{\frac{0.36}{\sqrt{16}}} = \frac{6.1}{0.09} \approx 67.778$$

Reject H_0. There is enough evidence to reject the claim.

15. H_0: $\mu_d \geq 0$ (claim); H_a: $\mu_d < 0$

$\alpha = 0.01$ and d.f. $= n - 1 = 14$

$t_0 = -2.624$ (Left-tailed)

$$t = \frac{\bar{d} - \mu_d}{\frac{s_d}{\sqrt{n}}} = \frac{-2.3 - 0}{\frac{1.2}{\sqrt{15}}} = \frac{-2.3}{0.3098} \approx -7.423$$

Reject H_0. There is enough evidence to reject the claim.

17. (a) H_0: $\mu_d \geq 0$; H_a: $\mu_d < 0$ (claim)

(b) $t_0 = -2.650$; Reject H_0 if $t < -2.650$.

(c) $\bar{d} \approx -33.714$ and $s_d \approx 42.034$

(d) $t = \dfrac{\bar{d} - \mu_d}{\frac{s_d}{\sqrt{n}}} = \dfrac{-33.714 - 0}{\frac{42.034}{\sqrt{14}}} = \dfrac{-33.714}{11.234} \approx -3.001$

(e) Reject H_0.

(f) There is enough evidence to support the claim that the second SAT scores are improved.

19. (a) H_0: $\mu_d \geq 0$; H_a: $\mu_d < 0$ (claim)

(b) $t_0 = -1.415$; Reject H_0 if $t > 1.415$.

(c) $\bar{d} \approx -1.125$ and $s_d \approx 0.871$

(d) $t = \dfrac{\bar{d} - \mu_d}{\frac{s_d}{\sqrt{n}}} = \dfrac{-1.125 - 0}{\frac{0.871}{\sqrt{8}}} = \dfrac{-1.125}{0.308} = -3.653$

(e) Reject H_0.

(f) There is enough evidence to support the fuel additive improved gas mileage.

21. (a) H_0: $\mu_d \leq 0$; H_a: $\mu > 0$ (claim)

(b) $t_0 = 1.363$; Reject H_0 if $t > 1.363$.

(c) $\bar{d} = 3.75$ and $s_d \approx 7.84$

(d) $t = \dfrac{\bar{d} - \mu_d}{\frac{s_d}{\sqrt{n}}} = \dfrac{3.75 - 0}{\frac{7.84}{\sqrt{12}}} = \dfrac{3.75}{2.26} = 1.657$

(e) Reject H_0.

(f) There is enough evidence to support the claim that the exercise program helps participants lose weight.

© 2006 Pearson Education, Inc., Upper Saddle River, NJ. All rights reserved. This material is protected under all copyright laws as they currently exist. No portion of this material may be reproduced, in any form or by any means, without permission in writing from the publisher.

23. (a) $H_0: \mu_d \le 0; H_a: \mu_d > 0$ (claim)

(b) $t_0 = 2.764$; Reject H_0 if $t > 2.764$.

(c) $\bar{d} \approx 1.255$ and $s_d \approx 0.441$

(d) $t = \dfrac{\bar{d} - \mu_d}{\frac{s_d}{\sqrt{n}}} = \dfrac{1.255 - 0}{\frac{0.441}{\sqrt{11}}} = \dfrac{1.255}{0.133} \approx 9.438$

(e) Reject H_0.

(f) There is enough evidence to support the claim that soft tissue therapy and spinal manipulation help reduce the length of time patients suffer from headaches.

25. (a) $H_0: \mu_d \le 0; H_a: \mu_d > 0$ (claim)

(b) $t_0 = 1.895$; Reject H_0 if $t > 1.895$.

(c) $\bar{d} = 14.75$ and $s_d \approx 6.86$

(d) $t = \dfrac{\bar{d} - \mu_d}{\frac{s_d}{\sqrt{n}}} = \dfrac{14.75 - 0}{\frac{6.86}{\sqrt{8}}} = \dfrac{14.75}{2.425} \approx 6.082$

(e) Reject H_0.

(f) There is enough evidence to support the claim that the new drug reduces systolic blood pressure.

27. (a) $H_0: \mu_d = 0; H_a: \mu_d \ne 0$ (claim)

(b) $t_0 = \pm 2.365$; Reject H_0 if $t < -2.365$ or $t > 2.365$.

(c) $\bar{d} = -1$ and $s_d = 1.31$

(d) $t = \dfrac{\bar{d} - \mu_d}{\frac{s_d}{\sqrt{n}}} = \dfrac{-1 - 0}{\frac{1.31}{\sqrt{8}}} = \dfrac{-1}{0.463} = -2.159$

(e) Fail to reject H_0.

(f) There is not enough evidence to support the claim that the product ratings have changed.

29. $\bar{d} \approx -1.525$ and $s_d \approx 0.542$

$$\bar{d} - t_{\alpha/2}\frac{s_d}{\sqrt{n}} < \mu_d < \bar{d} - t_{\alpha/2}\frac{s_d}{\sqrt{n}}$$

$$-1.525 - 1.753\left(\frac{0.542}{\sqrt{16}}\right) < \mu_d < -1.525 + 1.753\left(\frac{0.542}{\sqrt{16}}\right)$$

$$-1.525 - 0.238 < \mu_d < -1.525 + 0.238$$

$$-1.763 < \mu_d < -1.287$$

© 2006 Pearson Education, Inc., Upper Saddle River, NJ. All rights reserved. This material is protected under all copyright laws as they currently exist. No portion of this material may be reproduced, in any form or by any means, without permission in writing from the publisher.

8.4 TESTING THE DIFFERENCE BETWEEN PROPORTIONS

8.4 Try It Yourself Solutions

1a. $H_0: p_1 = p_2; H_a: p_1 \neq p_2$ (claim)   **b.** $\alpha = 0.05$

c. $z_0 = \pm 1.96$; Reject H_0 if $z < -1.96$ or $z > 1.96$.

d. $\bar{p} = \dfrac{x_1 + x_2}{n_1 + n_2} = \dfrac{1666 + 1435}{6771 + 6767} = 0.229$

$\bar{q} = 0.771$

e. $n_1 \bar{p} \approx 1550.559 > 5, n_1 \bar{q} \approx 5220.411 > 5, n_2 \bar{p} \approx 1549.643 > 5$, and $n_2 \bar{q} \approx 5217.357 > 5$.

f. $z = \dfrac{(\hat{p}_1 - \hat{p}_2) - (p_1 - p_2)}{\sqrt{\bar{p}\bar{q}\left(\dfrac{1}{n_1} + \dfrac{1}{n_2}\right)}} = \dfrac{(0.246 - 0.212) - (0)}{\sqrt{0.229 \cdot 0.771\left(\dfrac{1}{6771} + \dfrac{1}{6767}\right)}} = \dfrac{0.034}{\sqrt{0.000052167}} \approx 4.707$

g. Reject H_0.

h. There is enough evidence to support the claim.

2a. $H_0: p_1 \leq p_2; H_a: p_1 > p_2$ (claim)   **b.** $\alpha = 0.05$

c. $z_0 = 1.645$; Reject H_0 if $z > 1.645$.

d. $\bar{p} = \dfrac{x_1 + x_2}{n_1 + n_2} = \dfrac{1144 + 420}{6771 + 6767} = 0.116$

$\bar{q} = 0.884$

e. $n_1 \bar{p} \approx 785.436 > 5, n_1 \bar{q} \approx 5985.564 > 5, n_2 \bar{p} \approx 778.205 > 5$, and $n_2 \bar{q} \approx 5982.028 > 5$.

f. $z = \dfrac{(\hat{p}_1 - \hat{p}_2) - (p_1 - p_2)}{\sqrt{\bar{p}\bar{q}\left(\dfrac{1}{n_1} + \dfrac{1}{n_2}\right)}} = \dfrac{(0.169 - 0.062) - (0)}{\sqrt{0.116 \cdot 0.884\left(\dfrac{1}{6771} + \dfrac{1}{6767}\right)}} = \dfrac{0.107}{\sqrt{0.000030298}} \approx 19.44$

g. Reject H_0.

h. There is enough evidence to support the claim.

8.4 EXERCISE SOLUTIONS

1. State the hypotheses and identify the claim. Specify the level of significance. Find the critical value(s) and rejection region(s). Find $\bar{p}$ and $\bar{q}$. Find the standardized test statistic. Make a decision and interpret in the context of the claim.

3. $H_0: p_1 = p_2; H_a: p_1 \neq p_2$ (claim)

$z_0 = \pm 2.575$ (Two-tailed test)

$\bar{p} = \dfrac{x_1 + x_2}{n_1 + n_2} = \dfrac{35 + 36}{70 + 60} = 0.546$

$\bar{q} = 0.454$

$z = \dfrac{(\hat{p}_1 - \hat{p}_2) - (p_1 - p_2)}{\sqrt{\bar{p}\bar{q}\left(\dfrac{1}{n_1} + \dfrac{1}{n_2}\right)}} = \dfrac{(0.500 - 0.600) - (0)}{\sqrt{0.546 \cdot 0.454\left(\dfrac{1}{70} + \dfrac{1}{60}\right)}} = \dfrac{-0.100}{\sqrt{0.00767}} \approx -1.142$

Fail to reject H_0. There is not enough evidence to support the claim.

© 2006 Pearson Education, Inc., Upper Saddle River, NJ. All rights reserved. This material is protected under all copyright laws as they currently exist. No portion of this material may be reproduced, in any form or by any means, without permission in writing from the publisher.

5. $H_0: p_1 \leq p_2$ (claim); $H_a: p_1 > p_2$

$z_0 = 1.282$ (Right-tailed test)

$\bar{p} = \dfrac{x_1 + x_2}{n_1 + n_2} = \dfrac{344 + 304}{860 + 800} = 0.390$

$\bar{q} = 0.610$

$z = \dfrac{(\hat{p}_1 - \hat{p}_2) - (p_1 - p_2)}{\sqrt{\bar{p}\,\bar{q}\left(\dfrac{1}{n_1} + \dfrac{1}{n_2}\right)}} = \dfrac{(0.400 - 0.380) - (0)}{\sqrt{0.390 \cdot 0.610\left(\dfrac{1}{860} + \dfrac{1}{800}\right)}} = \dfrac{0.020}{\sqrt{0.0000574003}} \approx 0.835$

Fail to reject H_0. There is not enough evidence to reject the claim.

7. (a) $H_0: p_1 = p_2$ (claim); $H_a: p_1 \neq p_2$

(b) $z_0 = \pm 1.96$; Reject H_0 if $z < -1.96$ or $z > 1.96$.

$\bar{p} = \dfrac{x_1 + x_2}{n_1 + n_2} = \dfrac{520 + 865}{1539 + 2055} = 0.385$

$\bar{q} = 0.615$

(c) $z = \dfrac{(\hat{p}_1 - \hat{p}_2) - (p_1 - p_2)}{\sqrt{\bar{p}\,\bar{q}\left(\dfrac{1}{n_1} + \dfrac{1}{n_2}\right)}} = \dfrac{(0.338 - 0.421) - (0)}{\sqrt{0.385 \cdot 0.615\left(\dfrac{1}{1539} + \dfrac{1}{2055}\right)}}$

$= \dfrac{-0.083}{\sqrt{0.0000269069}} \approx -5.060$

(d) Reject H_0. There is sufficient evidence at the 5% level to reject the claim that the proportion of adults using alternative medicines has not changed since 1990.

9. (a) $H_0: p_1 = p_2$ (claim); $H_a: p_1 \neq p_2$

(b) $z_0 = \pm 1.645$; Reject H_0 if $z < -1.645$ or $z > 1.645$.

$\bar{p} = \dfrac{x_1 + x_2}{n_1 + n_2} = \dfrac{2201 + 2348}{5240 + 6180} = 0.398$

$\bar{q} = 0.602$

(c) $z = \dfrac{(\hat{p}_1 - \hat{p}_2) - (p_1 - p_2)}{\sqrt{\bar{p}\,\bar{q}\left(\dfrac{1}{n_1} + \dfrac{1}{n_2}\right)}} = \dfrac{(0.420 - 0.380) - 0}{\sqrt{(0.398)(0.602)\left(\dfrac{1}{5240} + \dfrac{1}{6180}\right)}}$

$= \dfrac{0.04}{\sqrt{0.00008449}} = 4.351$

(d) Reject H_0.

(e) There is sufficient evidence at the 10% level to reject the claim that the proportions of male and female senior citizens that eat the daily recommended number of servings of vegetables is not different.

11. (a) $H_0: p_1 \geq p_2$; $H_a: p_1 < p_2$ (claim)

(b) $z_0 = -2.33$; Reject H_0 if $z < -2.33$.

$\bar{p} = \dfrac{x_1 + x_2}{n_1 + n_2} = \dfrac{488 + 532}{2000 + 2000} = 0.255$

$\bar{q} = 0.745$

© 2006 Pearson Education, Inc., Upper Saddle River, NJ. All rights reserved. This material is protected under all copyright laws as they currently exist. No portion of this material may be reproduced, in any form or by any means, without permission in writing from the publisher.

(c) $z = \dfrac{(\hat{p}_1 - \hat{p}_2) - (p_1 - p_2)}{\sqrt{\bar{p}\,\bar{q}\left(\dfrac{1}{n_1} + \dfrac{1}{n_2}\right)}} = \dfrac{(0.244 - 0.266) - (0)}{\sqrt{0.255 \cdot 0.745\left(\dfrac{1}{2000} + \dfrac{1}{2000}\right)}} = \dfrac{-0.022}{\sqrt{0.00018997}} \approx -1.596$

(d) Fail to reject H_0.

(e) There is not sufficient evidence at the 1% level to support the claim that the proportion of adults who are smokers is lower in Alabama than in Missouri.

13. (a) $H_0 \colon p_1 \geq p_2$; $H_a \colon p_1 < p_2$ (claim)

(b) $z_0 = -2.33$; Reject H_0 if $z < -2.33$.

$\bar{p} = \dfrac{x_1 + x_2}{n_1 + n_2} = \dfrac{1589 + 1683}{5800 + 6600} = 0.264$

$\bar{q} = 0.736$

(c) $z = \dfrac{(\hat{p}_1 - \hat{p}_2) - (p_1 - p_2)}{\sqrt{\bar{p}\,\bar{q}\left(\dfrac{1}{n_1} + \dfrac{1}{n_2}\right)}} = \dfrac{(0.274 - 0.255) - (0)}{\sqrt{0.264 \cdot 0.736\left(\dfrac{1}{5800} + \dfrac{1}{6600}\right)}} = \dfrac{0.019}{\sqrt{0.00006294}} \approx 2.395$

(d) Fail to reject H_0.

(e) There is sufficient evidence at the 1% level to support the claim that the proportion of males who said they had smoked in the last 30 days is less than the proportion of females.

15. (a) $H_0 \colon p_1 = p_2$ (claim); $H_a \colon p_1 \neq p_2$

(b) $z_0 = \pm 1.96$; Reject H_0 if $z < -1.96$ or $z > 1.96$.

$\bar{p} = \dfrac{x_1 + x_2}{n_1 + n_2} = \dfrac{2496 + 1380}{9600 + 11{,}500} = 0.184$

$\bar{q} = 0.816$

(c) $z = \dfrac{(\hat{p}_1 - \hat{p}_2) - (p_1 - p_2)}{\sqrt{\bar{p}\,\bar{q}\left(\dfrac{1}{n_1} + \dfrac{1}{n_2}\right)}} = \dfrac{(0.260 - 0.120) - 0}{\sqrt{(0.184)(0.816)\left(\dfrac{1}{9600} + \dfrac{1}{11{,}500}\right)}} = \dfrac{0.14}{\sqrt{0.00002869}} = 26.135$

(d) Reject H_0.

(e) There is insufficient evidence at the 5% level to reject the claim that the proportions of adults that have chronic backs are the same for both groups.

17. $H_0 \colon p_1 \geq p_2$; $H_a \colon p_1 < p_2$ (claim)

$z_0 = -2.33$

$\bar{p} = \dfrac{x_1 + x_2}{n_1 + n_2} = \dfrac{28 + 35}{700 + 500} = 0.053$

$\bar{q} = 0.947$

$z = \dfrac{(\hat{p}_1 - \hat{p}_2) - (p_1 - p_2)}{\sqrt{\bar{p}\,\bar{q}\left(\dfrac{1}{n_1} + \dfrac{1}{n_2}\right)}} = \dfrac{(0.04 - 0.07) - (0)}{\sqrt{0.053 \cdot 0.947\left(\dfrac{1}{700} + \dfrac{1}{500}\right)}} = \dfrac{-0.03}{\sqrt{0.0001721}} \approx -2.287$

Fail to reject H_0. There is insufficient evidence at the 1% level to support the claim.

© 2006 Pearson Education, Inc., Upper Saddle River, NJ. All rights reserved. This material is protected under all copyright laws as they currently exist.
No portion of this material may be reproduced, in any form or by any means, without permission in writing from the publisher.

19. $H_0: p_1 = p_2$ (claim); $H_a: p_1 \neq p_2$

$z_0 = \pm 1.96$

$\bar{p} = \dfrac{x_1 + x_2}{n_1 + n_2} = \dfrac{189 + 185}{700 + 500} = 0.312$

$\bar{q} = 0.688$

$z = \dfrac{(\hat{p}_1 - \hat{p}_2) - (p_1 - p_2)}{\sqrt{\bar{p}\bar{q}\left(\dfrac{1}{n_1} + \dfrac{1}{n_2}\right)}} = \dfrac{(0.27 - 0.37) - (0)}{\sqrt{0.312 \cdot 0.688\left(\dfrac{1}{700} + \dfrac{1}{500}\right)}} = \dfrac{-0.10}{\sqrt{0.0007359}} \approx -3.686$

Reject H_0. There is sufficient evidence at the 5% level to reject the advocate's claim.

21. $H_0: p_1 \leq p_2$; $H_a: p_1 > p_2$ (claim)

$z_0 = 1.645$

$\bar{p} = \dfrac{x_1 + x_2}{n_1 + n_2} = \dfrac{348 + 275}{580 + 500} = 0.577$

$\bar{q} = 0.423$

$z = \dfrac{(\hat{p}_1 - \hat{p}_2) - (p_1 - p_2)}{\sqrt{\bar{p}\bar{q}\left(\dfrac{1}{n_1} + \dfrac{1}{n_2}\right)}} = \dfrac{(0.60 - 0.55) - (0)}{\sqrt{(0.577)(0.423)\left(\dfrac{1}{580} + \dfrac{1}{500}\right)}} = \dfrac{0.05}{\sqrt{0.0009089}} \approx 1.658$

Reject H_0. There is sufficient evidence at the 5% level to support the claim.

23. $H_0: p_1 = p_2$ (claim); $H_a: p_1 \neq p_2$

$z_0 = \pm 2.576$

$\bar{p} = \dfrac{x_1 + x_2}{n_1 + n_2} = \dfrac{348 + 240}{580 + 500} = 0.544$

$\bar{q} = 0.456$

$z = \dfrac{(\hat{p}_1 - \hat{p}_2) - (p_1 - p_2)}{\sqrt{\bar{p}\bar{q}\left(\dfrac{1}{n_1} + \dfrac{1}{n_2}\right)}} = \dfrac{(0.60 - 0.48) - (0)}{\sqrt{(0.544)(0.456)\left(\dfrac{1}{580} + \dfrac{1}{500}\right)}} = \dfrac{0.12}{\sqrt{0.0009238}} \approx 3.948$

Reject H_0. There is sufficient evidence at the 1% level to reject the claim.

25. $(\hat{p}_1 - \hat{p}_2) \pm z_c \sqrt{\dfrac{\hat{p}_1 \hat{q}_1}{n_1} + \dfrac{\hat{p}_2 \hat{q}_2}{n_2}} \rightarrow (0.117 - 0.085) \pm 1.96 \sqrt{\dfrac{0.117 \cdot 0.883}{977,000} + \dfrac{0.085 \cdot 0.915}{1,085,000}}$

$$\rightarrow 0.032 \pm 1.96 \sqrt{0.000000177425}$$

$$\rightarrow 0.0312 < p_1 - p_2 < 0.0328$$

CHAPTER 8 REVIEW EXERCISE SOLUTIONS

1. $H_0: \mu_1 \geq \mu_2$ (claim); $H_1: \mu_1 < \mu_2$

$z_0 = -1.645$

$z = \dfrac{(\bar{x}_1 - \bar{x}_2) - (\mu_1 - \mu_2)}{\sqrt{\dfrac{s_1^2}{n_1} + \dfrac{s_2^2}{n_2}}} = \dfrac{(1.28 - 1.36) - (0)}{\sqrt{\dfrac{(0.28)^2}{76} + \dfrac{(0.23)^2}{65}}} = \dfrac{-0.08}{\sqrt{0.00185}} \approx -.1862$

Reject H_0. There is enough evidence to reject the claim.

© 2006 Pearson Education, Inc., Upper Saddle River, NJ. All rights reserved. This material is protected under all copyright laws as they currently exist. No portion of this material may be reproduced, in any form or by any means, without permission in writing from the publisher.

3. $H_0: \mu_1 \geq \mu_2; H_1: \mu_1 < \mu_2$ (claim)

$z_0 = -1.282$

$$z = \frac{(\bar{x}_1 - \bar{x}_2) - (\mu_1 - \mu_2)}{\sqrt{\dfrac{s_1^2}{n_1} + \dfrac{s_2^2}{n_2}}} = \frac{(0.28 - 0.33) - (0)}{\sqrt{\dfrac{(0.11)^2}{41} + \dfrac{(0.10)^2}{34}}} = \frac{-0.50}{\sqrt{0.00058924}} \approx -2.060$$

Reject H_0. There is enough evidence to support the claim.

5. (a) $H_0: \mu_1 1 \leq \mu_2; H_1: \mu_1 > \mu_2$ (claim)

(b) $z_0 = 1.645$; Reject H_0 if $z > 1.645$.

(c) $z = \dfrac{(\bar{x}_1 - \bar{x}_2) - (\mu_1 - \mu_2)}{\sqrt{\dfrac{s_1^2}{n_1} + \dfrac{s_2^2}{n_2}}} = \dfrac{(430 - 410) - (0)}{\sqrt{\dfrac{(43)^2}{36} + \dfrac{(57)^2}{41}}} = \dfrac{20}{\sqrt{130.605}} \approx 1.750$

(d) Reject H_0.

(e) There is enough evidence to support the claim.

7. $H_0: \mu_1 = \mu_2$ (claim); $H_a: \mu_1 \neq \mu_2$

d.f. $= n_1 + n_2 - 2 = 31$

$t_0 = \pm 1.96$

$$t = \frac{(\bar{x}_1 - \bar{x}_2) - (\mu_1 - \mu_2)}{\sqrt{\dfrac{(n_1 - 1)s_1^2 + (n_2 - 1)s_2^2}{n_1 + n_2 - 2}} \sqrt{\dfrac{1}{n_1} + \dfrac{1}{n_2}}} = \frac{(250 - 240) - (0)}{\sqrt{\dfrac{(21 - 1)(26)^2 + (12 - 1)(22)^2}{21 + 12 - 2}} \sqrt{\dfrac{1}{21} + \dfrac{1}{12}}}$$

$$= \frac{10}{\sqrt{607.871}\sqrt{0.13095}} \approx 1.121$$

Fail to reject H_0. There is not enough evidence to reject the claim.

9. $H_0: \mu_1 \leq \mu_2$ (claim); $H_a: \mu_1 > \mu_2$

d.f. $= \min\{n_1 - 1, n_2 - 1\} = 24$

$t_0 = 1.711$

$$t = \frac{(\bar{x}_1 - \bar{x}_2) - (\mu_1 - \mu_2)}{\sqrt{\dfrac{s_1^2}{n_1} + \dfrac{s_2^2}{n_2}}} = \frac{(183.5 - 184.7) - (0)}{\sqrt{\dfrac{(1.3)^2}{25} + \dfrac{(3.9)^2}{25}}} = \frac{-1.2}{\sqrt{0.676}} \approx -1.460$$

Fail to reject H_0. There is not enough evidence to reject the claim.

11. $H_0: \mu_1 = \mu_2; H_a: \mu_1 \neq \mu_2$ (claim)

d.f. $= n_1 + n_2 - 2 = 10$

$t_0 = \pm 3.169$

$$t = \frac{(\bar{x}_1 - \bar{x}_2) - (\mu_1 - \mu_2)}{\sqrt{\dfrac{(n_1 - 1)s_1^2 + (n_2 - 1)s_2^2}{n_1 + n_2 - 2}} \cdot \sqrt{\dfrac{1}{n_1} + \dfrac{1}{n_2}}} = \frac{(61 - 55) - (0)}{\sqrt{\dfrac{(5 - 1)3.3^2 + (7 - 1)1.2^2}{5 + 7 - 2}} \cdot \sqrt{\dfrac{1}{5} + \dfrac{1}{7}}}$$

$$= \frac{6}{\sqrt{5.22}\sqrt{0.343}} \approx 4.484$$

Reject H_0. There is enough evidence to support the claim.

© 2006 Pearson Education, Inc., Upper Saddle River, NJ. All rights reserved. This material is protected under all copyright laws as they currently exist.
No portion of this material may be reproduced, in any form or by any means, without permission in writing from the publisher.

13. (a) $H_0: \mu_1 \leq \mu_2; H_a: \mu_1 > \mu_2$ (claim)

(b) d.f. $= n_1 + n_2 - 2 = 42$

$t_0 = 1.645$; Reject H_0 if $t > 1.645$.

(c) $\bar{x}_1 = 51.476, s_1 = 11.007, n_1 = 21$

$\bar{x}_2 = 41.522, s_2 = 17.149, n_2 = 23$

$$t = \frac{(\bar{x}_1 - \bar{x}_2) - (\mu_1 - \mu_2)}{\sqrt{\dfrac{(n_1 - 1)s_1^2 + (n_2 - 1)s_2^2}{n_1 + n_2 - 2}} \sqrt{\dfrac{1}{n_1} + \dfrac{1}{n_2}}} = \frac{(51.476 - 41.522) - (0)}{\sqrt{\dfrac{(21 - 1)(11.007)^2 + (23 - 1)(17.149)^2}{21 + 23 - 2}} \sqrt{\dfrac{1}{21} + \dfrac{1}{23}}}$$

$$= \frac{9.954}{\sqrt{211.7386} \sqrt{0.0911}} \approx 2.266$$

(d) Reject H_0.

(e) There is sufficient evidence at the 5% level to support the claim that the third graders taught with the direct reading activities scored higher than those taught without the activities.

15. Independent since the two samples of laboratory mice are different groups.

17. $H_0: \mu_d = 0$ (claim); $H_a: \mu_d \neq 0$

$\alpha = 0.05$ and d.f. $= n - 1 = 99$

$t_0 = \pm 1.96$ (Two-tailed test)

$$t = \frac{\bar{d} - \mu_d}{\dfrac{s_d}{\sqrt{n}}} = \frac{10 - 0}{\dfrac{12.4}{\sqrt{100}}} = \frac{10}{1.24} \approx 8.065$$

Reject H_0. There is enough evidence to reject the claim.

19. $H_0: \mu_d \leq 6$ (claim); $H_a: \mu_d > 6$

$\alpha = 0.10$ and d.f. $= n - 1 = 32$

$t_0 = 1.282$ (Right-tailed test)

$$t = \frac{\bar{d} - \mu_d}{\dfrac{s_d}{\sqrt{n}}} = \frac{10.3 - 6}{\dfrac{1.24}{\sqrt{33}}} = \frac{4.3}{0.21586} \approx 19.921$$

Reject H_0. There is enough evidence to reject the claim.

21. (a) $H_0: \mu_d \leq 0; H_a: \mu_d > 0$ (claim)

(b) $t_0 = 1.383$; Reject H_0 if $t > 1.383$.

(c) $\bar{d} = 5$ and $s_d \approx 8.743$

(d) $t = \dfrac{\bar{d} - \mu_d}{\dfrac{s_d}{\sqrt{n}}} = \dfrac{5 - 0}{\dfrac{8.743}{\sqrt{10}}} = \dfrac{5}{2.765} \approx 1.808$

(e) Reject H_0.

(f) There is enough evidence to support the claim.

© 2006 Pearson Education, Inc., Upper Saddle River, NJ. All rights reserved. This material is protected under all copyright laws as they currently exist. No portion of this material may be reproduced, in any form or by any means, without permission in writing from the publisher.

23. $H_0: p_1 = p_2$; $H_a: p_1 \neq p_2$ (claim)

$z_0 = \pm 1.96$ (Two-tailed test)

$\bar{p} = \dfrac{x_1 + x_2}{n_1 + n_2} = \dfrac{375 + 365}{720 + 660} = 0.536$

$\bar{q} = 0.464$

$z = \dfrac{(\hat{p}_1 - \hat{p}_2) - (p_1 - p_2)}{\sqrt{\bar{p}\,\bar{q}\left(\dfrac{1}{n_1} + \dfrac{1}{n_2}\right)}} = \dfrac{(0.521 - 0.553) - (0)}{\sqrt{0.536 \cdot 0.464\left(\dfrac{1}{720} + \dfrac{1}{660}\right)}} = \dfrac{-0.032}{\sqrt{0.000722246}} \approx -1.198$

Fail to reject H_0. There is not enough evidence to reject the claim.

25. $H_0: p_1 \leq p_2$; $H_a: p_1 > p_2$ (claim)

$z_0 = 1.282$ (Right-tailed test)

$\bar{p} = \dfrac{x_1 + x_2}{n_1 + n_2} = \dfrac{227 + 198}{556 + 420} = 0.435$

$\bar{q} = 0.565$

$z = \dfrac{(\hat{p}_1 - \hat{p}_2) - (p_1 - p_2)}{\sqrt{\bar{p}\,\bar{q}\left(\dfrac{1}{n_1} + \dfrac{1}{n_2}\right)}} = \dfrac{(0.408 - 0.471) - (0)}{\sqrt{0.435 \cdot 0.565\left(\dfrac{1}{556} + \dfrac{1}{420}\right)}} = \dfrac{-0.063}{\sqrt{0.001027}} \approx -1.970$

Fail to reject H_0. There is not enough evidence to support the claim.

27. (a) $H_0: p_1 = p_2$ (claim); $H_a: p_1 \neq p_2$

(b) $z_0 = \pm 1.645$; Reject H_0 if $z < -1.645$ or $z > 1.645$.

$\bar{p} = \dfrac{x_1 + x_2}{n_1 + n_2} = \dfrac{26 + 46}{200 + 300} = 0.144$

$\bar{q} = 0.856$

(c) $z = \dfrac{(\hat{p}_1 - \hat{p}_2) - (p_1 - p_2)}{\sqrt{\bar{p}\,\bar{q}\left(\dfrac{1}{n_1} + \dfrac{1}{n_2}\right)}} = \dfrac{(0.130 - 0.153) - (0)}{\sqrt{0.144 \cdot 0.856\left(\dfrac{1}{200} + \dfrac{1}{300}\right)}} = \dfrac{-0.023}{\sqrt{0.001027}} \approx -0.718$

(d) Fail to reject H_0.

(e) There is not enough evidence to reject the claim.

CHAPTER 8 QUIZ SOLUTIONS

1. (a) $H_0: \mu_1 \leq \mu_2$; $H_a: \mu_1 > \mu_2$ (claim)

(b) n_1 and $n_2 > 30$ and the samples are independent $\rightarrow$ Right tailed z-test

(c) $z_0 = 1.645$; Reject H_0 if $z > 1.645$.

(d) $z = \dfrac{(\bar{x}_1 - \bar{x}_2) - (\mu_1 - \mu_2)}{\sqrt{\dfrac{s_1^2}{n_1} + \dfrac{s_2^2}{n_2}}} = \dfrac{(300.4 - 290.6) - (0)}{\sqrt{\dfrac{(1.6)^2}{49} + \dfrac{(1.5)^2}{50}}} = \dfrac{9.8}{\sqrt{0.0972}} \approx 31.426$

(e) Reject H_0.

(f) There is sufficient evidence at the 5% level to support the claim that the mean score on the science assessment for male high school students was higher than for the female high school students.

© 2006 Pearson Education, Inc., Upper Saddle River, NJ. All rights reserved. This material is protected under all copyright laws as they currently exist. No portion of this material may be reproduced, in any form or by any means, without permission in writing from the publisher.

2. (a) $H_0: \mu_1 = \mu_2$ (claim); $H_a: \mu_1 \neq \mu_2$

(b) n_1 and $n_2 < 30$, the samples are independent, and the populations are normally distributed. → Two-tailed t-test (assume vars are equal)

(c) d.f. $= n_1 + n_2 - 2 = 26$
$t_0 = \pm 2.779$; Reject H_0 if $t < -2.779$ or $t > 2.779$.

(d) $t = \dfrac{(\bar{x}_1 - \bar{x}_2) - (\mu_1 - \mu_2)}{\sqrt{\dfrac{(n_1 - 1)s_1^2 + (n_2 - 1)s_2^2}{n_1 + n_2 - 2}}\sqrt{\dfrac{1}{n_1} + \dfrac{1}{n_2}}} = \dfrac{(230.9 - 227.9) - (0)}{\sqrt{\dfrac{(13 - 1)(1.3)^2 + (15 - 1)(1.1)^2}{13 + 15 - 2}}\sqrt{\dfrac{1}{13} + \dfrac{1}{15}}}$

$= \dfrac{3.0}{\sqrt{1.43154}\sqrt{0.14359}} \approx 6.617$

(e) Reject H_0.

(f) There is sufficient evidence at the 1% level to reject the teacher's suggestion that the mean scores on the science assessment test are the same for nine-year old boys and girls.

3. (a) $H_0: p_1 \leq p_2$; $H_a: p_1 > p_2$ (claim)

(b) Testing 2 proportions, $n_1\bar{p}$, $n_1\bar{q}$, $n_2\bar{p}$, and $n_2\bar{q} \geq 5$, and the samples are independent → Right-tailed z-test

(c) $z_0 = 1.282$; Reject H_0 if $z > 1.282$.

(d) $\bar{p} = \dfrac{x_1 + x_2}{n_1 + n_2} = \dfrac{64{,}800 + 8560}{1{,}296{,}000 + 856{,}000} = 0.034$

$\bar{q} = 0.966$

$z = \dfrac{(\hat{p}_1 - \hat{p}_2) - (p_1 - p_2)}{\sqrt{\bar{p}\,\bar{q}\left(\dfrac{1}{n_1} + \dfrac{1}{n_2}\right)}} = \dfrac{(0.05 - 0.01) - (0)}{\sqrt{0.034 \cdot 0.966\left(\dfrac{1}{1{,}296{,}000} + \dfrac{1}{856{,}000}\right)}}$

$= \dfrac{0.04}{\sqrt{0.0000000637118}} \approx 158.471$

(e) Reject H_0.

(f) There is sufficient evidence at the 10% level to support the claim that the proportion of accidents involving alcohol is higher for drivers in the 21 to 24 age group than for drivers aged 65 and older.

4. (a) $H_0: \mu_d \geq 0$; $H_a: \mu_d < 0$ (claim)

(b) Dependent samples and both populations are normally distributed. → Dependent t-test

(c) $t_0 = -1.796$; Reject H_0 if $t < -1.796$.

(d) $t = \dfrac{\bar{d} - \mu_d}{\dfrac{s_d}{\sqrt{n}}} = \dfrac{0 - 68.5}{\dfrac{26.318}{\sqrt{12}}} = \dfrac{-68.5}{7.597} \approx 9.016$

(e) Reject H_0.

(f) There is sufficient evidence at the 5% level to conclude that the students' SAT scores improved on the second test.

© 2006 Pearson Education, Inc., Upper Saddle River, NJ. All rights reserved. This material is protected under all copyright laws as they currently exist. No portion of this material may be reproduced, in any form or by any means, without permission in writing from the publisher.

Correlation and Regression

9.1 Try It Yourself Solutions

1ab.

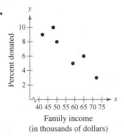

c. Yes, it appears that there is a negative linear correlation. As family income increases, the percent of income donated to charity decreases.

2ab.

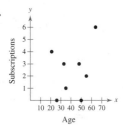

c. No, it appears that there is no correlation between age and subscriptions.

3ab.

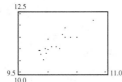

c. Yes, there appears to be a positive linear relationship between men's winning time and women's winning time.

4a. $n = 6$

b.

x	y	xy	x^2	y^2
42	9	378	1764	81
48	10	480	2304	100
50	8	400	2500	64
59	5	295	3481	25
65	6	390	4225	36
72	3	216	5184	9
$\Sigma x = 336$	$\Sigma y = 41$	$\Sigma xy = 2159$	$\Sigma x^2 = 19458$	$\Sigma y^2 = 315$

c. $r = \dfrac{n\Sigma xy - (\Sigma x)(\Sigma y)}{\sqrt{n\Sigma x^2 - (\Sigma x)^2}\sqrt{n\Sigma y^2 - (\Sigma y)^2}} = \dfrac{6(2159) - (336)(41)}{\sqrt{6(19{,}458) - (336)^2}\sqrt{6(315) - (41)^2}}$

$= \dfrac{-822}{\sqrt{3852}\,\sqrt{209}} \approx -0.916$

© 2006 Pearson Education, Inc., Upper Saddle River, NJ. All rights reserved. This material is protected under all copyright laws as they currently exist. No portion of this material may be reproduced, in any form or by any means, without permission in writing from the publisher.

d. Since r is close to -1, there appears to be a strong negative linear correlation between income level and donating percent.

5a. Enter the data.

b. $r \approx 0.849$

c. Since r is close to 1, there appears to be a strong positive linear correlation between men's winning time and women's winning time.

6a. $n = 6$

b. $\alpha = 0.01$

c. $cu = 0.917$

d. Since $|r| \approx 0.916 < 0.917$, the correlation is not significant.

e. There is not enough evidence to conclude that there is a significant correlation between income level and the donating percent.

7a. $H_0: \rho = 0; H_a: \rho \neq 0$

b. $\alpha = 0.01$

c. d.f. $= n - 2 = 16$

d. ± 2.921; Reject H_0 if $t < -2.947$ or $t > 2.947$.

e. $t = \dfrac{r}{\sqrt{\dfrac{1 - r^2}{n - 2}}} = \dfrac{0.849}{\sqrt{\dfrac{1 - (0.849)^2}{18 - 2}}} = \dfrac{0.849}{\sqrt{0.01777}} \approx 6.427$

f. Reject H_0.

g. There is enough evidence in the sample to conclude that a significant correlation exists.

9.1 EXERCISE SOLUTIONS

1. $r = -0.845$ represents a stronger correlation since it is closer to -1 than $r = 0.731$ is to $+1$.

3. State the null and alternative hypotheses. Specify the level of significance and determine the degrees of freedom. Identify the rejection regions and calculate the standardized test statistic. Make a decision and interpret in the context of the original claim.

5. Positive linear correlation

7. No linear correlation (but there is a nonlinear correlation between the variables)

9. (c), You would expect a positive linear correlation between age and income.

11. (b), You would expect a negative linear correlation between age and balance on student loans.

13. Explanatory variable: Amount of water consumed.
Response variable: Weight loss.

15. (a)

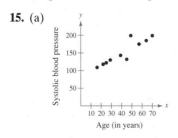

© 2006 Pearson Education, Inc., Upper Saddle River, NJ. All rights reserved. This material is protected under all copyright laws as they currently exist. No portion of this material may be reproduced, in any form or by any means, without permission in writing from the publisher.

(b)

x	y	xy	x^2	y^2
16	109	1744	256	11,881
25	122	3050	625	14,884
39	143	5577	1521	20,449
45	132	5940	2025	17,424
49	199	9751	2401	39,601
64	185	11,840	4096	34,225
70	199	13,930	4900	39,601
29	130	3770	841	16,900
57	175	9975	3249	30,625
20	118	2360	400	13,924
$\Sigma x = 414$	$\Sigma y = 1512$	$\Sigma xy = 67{,}937$	$\Sigma x^2 = 20{,}314$	$\Sigma y^2 = 239{,}514$

$$r = \frac{n\Sigma xy - (\Sigma x)(\Sigma y)}{\sqrt{n\Sigma x^2 - (\Sigma x)^2}\sqrt{n\Sigma y^2 - (\Sigma y)^2}} = \frac{10(67{,}937) - (414)(1512)}{\sqrt{10(20{,}314) - (414)^2}\sqrt{10(239{,}514) - (1512)^2}}$$

$$= \frac{53{,}402}{\sqrt{31{,}744}\ \sqrt{108{,}996}} \approx 0.908$$

(c) Strong positive linear correlation

17. (a)

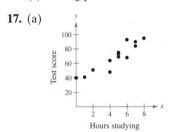

(b)

x	y	xy	x^2	y^2
0	40	0	0	1600
1	41	41	1	1681
2	51	102	4	2601
4	48	192	16	2304
4	64	256	16	4096
5	69	345	25	4761
5	73	365	25	5329
5	75	375	25	5625
6	68	408	36	4624
6	93	558	36	8649
7	84	588	49	7056
7	90	630	49	8100
8	95	760	64	9025
$\Sigma x = 60$	$\Sigma y = 891$	$\Sigma xy = 4620$	$\Sigma x^2 = 346$	$\Sigma y^2 = 65{,}451$

$$r = \frac{n\Sigma xy - (\Sigma x)(\Sigma y)}{\sqrt{n\Sigma x^2 - (\Sigma x)^2}\sqrt{n\Sigma y^2 - (\Sigma y)^2}} = \frac{13(4620) - (60)(891)}{\sqrt{13(346) - (60)^2}\sqrt{13(65{,}451) - (891)^2}}$$

$$= \frac{6600}{\sqrt{898}\ \sqrt{56{,}982}} \approx 0.923$$

(c) Strong positive linear correlation

© 2006 Pearson Education, Inc., Upper Saddle River, NJ. All rights reserved. This material is protected under all copyright laws as they currently exist. No portion of this material may be reproduced, in any form or by any means, without permission in writing from the publisher.

19. (a)

Coffee sales (in hundreds of dollars) vs Temperature (in °F)

(b)

x	y	xy	x^2	y^2
32	26.2	838.4	1024	686.44
39	24.8	967.2	1521	615.04
51	19.7	1004.7	2601	388.09
60	20.0	1200.0	3600	400.00
65	13.3	864.5	4225	176.89
72	13.9	1000.8	5184	193.21
78	11.4	889.2	6084	129.96
81	11.2	907.2	6561	125.44
$\Sigma x = 478$	$\Sigma y = 140.5$	$\Sigma xy = 7672$	$\Sigma x^2 = 30{,}800$	$\Sigma y^2 = 2715.07$

$$r = \frac{n\Sigma xy - (\Sigma x)(\Sigma y)}{\sqrt{n\Sigma x^2 - (\Sigma x)^2}\sqrt{n\Sigma y^2 - (\Sigma y)^2}} = \frac{8(7672) - (478)(140.5)}{\sqrt{8(30800) - (478)^2}\sqrt{8(2715.07) - (140.5)^2}}$$

$$= \frac{-5783}{\sqrt{17{,}916}\sqrt{1980.31}} \approx -0.971$$

(c) Strong negative linear correlation

21. (a)

Dividends per share vs Earnings per share

(b)

x	y	xy	x^2	y^2
2.78	2.16	6.005	7.728	4.666
1.41	0.88	1.241	1.988	0.774
2.74	1.04	2.850	7.508	1.082
0.92	1.1	1.012	0.846	1.210
2.44	0.96	2.342	5.954	0.922
3.5	2.18	7.630	12.250	4.752
3.68	1.54	5.667	13.542	2.372
1.97	1.39	2.738	3.881	1.932
1.95	1.41	2.750	3.803	1.988
2.07	2.88	5.962	4.285	8.294
$\Sigma x = 23.460$	$\Sigma y = 15.540$	$\Sigma xy = 38.196$	$\Sigma x^2 = 61.785$	$\Sigma y^2 = 27.992$

$$r = \frac{n\Sigma xy - (\Sigma x)(\Sigma y)}{\sqrt{n\Sigma x^2 - (\Sigma x)^2}\sqrt{n\Sigma y^2 - (\Sigma y)^2}} = \frac{10(38.196) - (23.460)(15.540)}{\sqrt{10(61.785) - (23.460)^2}\sqrt{10(27.992) - (15.540)^2}}$$

$$= \frac{17.392}{\sqrt{67.478}\sqrt{38.428}} = 0.342$$

(c) No linear correlation

© 2006 Pearson Education, Inc., Upper Saddle River, NJ. All rights reserved. This material is protected under all copyright laws as they currently exist. No portion of this material may be reproduced, in any form or by any means, without permission in writing from the publisher.

23. $r \approx 0.623$

    $n = 8$ and $\alpha = 0.01$

    $cv = 0.834$

    $|r| \approx 0.623 < 0.834 \Rightarrow$ The correlation is not significant.

    or

    $H_0: \rho = 0$; and $H_a: \rho \neq 0$

    $\alpha = 0.01$

    d.f. $= n - 2 = 6$

    $cu = \pm 3.703$; Reject H_0 if $t < -3.707$ or $t > 3.707$.

$$t = \frac{r}{\sqrt{\dfrac{1 - r^2}{n - 2}}} = \frac{0.623}{\sqrt{\dfrac{1 - (0.623)^2}{8 - 2}}} = \frac{0.623}{\sqrt{0.10198}} = 1.951$$

    Fail to reject H_0. There is not a significant linear correlation between vehicle weight and the variability in braking distance.

25. $r \approx 0.923$

    $n = 8$ and $\alpha = 0.01$

    $cv = 0.834$

    $|r| \approx 0.923 > 0.834 \Rightarrow$ The correlation is significant.

    or

    $H_0: \rho = 0$; $H_a: \rho \neq 0$

    $\alpha = 0.01$

    d.f. $= n - 2 = 11$

    $cu = \pm 3.106$; Reject H_0 if $t < -3.106$ or $t > 3.106$.

    $r \approx 0.923$

$$t = \frac{r}{\sqrt{\dfrac{1 - r^2}{n - 2}}} = \frac{0.923}{\sqrt{\dfrac{1 - (0.923)^2}{13 - 2}}} = \frac{0.923}{\sqrt{0.01346}} \approx 7.955$$

    Reject H_0. There is enough evidence to conclude that a significant linear correlation exists.

27. $r \approx 0.341$

    $n = 10$ and $\alpha = 0.01$

    $cv = 0.765$

    $|r| \approx 0.341 < 0.765 \Rightarrow$ The correlation is not significant.

    or

    $H_0: \rho = 0$; $H_a: \rho \neq 0$

    $\alpha = 0.01$

    d.f. $= n - 2 = 8$

    $cu = \pm 3.355$; Reject H_0 if $t < -3.355$ or $t > 3.355$.

    $r \approx 0.341$

$$t = \frac{r}{\sqrt{\dfrac{1 - r^2}{n - 2}}} = \frac{0.341}{\sqrt{\dfrac{1 - (0.341)^2}{10 - 2}}} = \frac{0.341}{\sqrt{0.110}} = 1.026$$

    Fail to reject H_0. There is enough not evidence at the 1% level to conclude there is a significant linear correlation between earnings per share and dividends per share.

29. The correlation coefficient remains unchanged when the x-values and y-values are switched.

31. Answers will vary.

© 2006 Pearson Education, Inc., Upper Saddle River, NJ. All rights reserved. This material is protected under all copyright laws as they currently exist. No portion of this material may be reproduced, in any form or by any means, without permission in writing from the publisher.

9.2 LINEAR REGRESSION

9.2 Try It Yourself Solutions

1a. $n = 6$

x	y	xy	x^2
42	9	378	1764
48	10	480	2304
50	8	400	2500
59	5	295	3481
65	6	390	4225
72	3	216	5184
$\Sigma x = 336$	$\Sigma y = 41$	$\Sigma xy = 2159$	$\Sigma x^2 = 19{,}458$

b. $m = \dfrac{n\Sigma xy - (\Sigma x)(\Sigma y)}{n\Sigma x^2 - (\Sigma x)^2} = \dfrac{6(2159) - (336)(41)}{6(19{,}458) - (336)^2} = \dfrac{-840}{3852} \approx -0.2134$

c. $b = \bar{y} - m\bar{x} = \left(\dfrac{41}{6}\right) - (-0.2134)\left(\dfrac{336}{6}\right) \approx 18.7837$

d. $\hat{y} = -0.213x + 18.784$

2a. Enter the data.

b. $m \approx 1.486; b \approx -3.819$

c. $\hat{y} = 1.486x - 3.819$

3a. (1) $\hat{y} = 11.824(2) + 35.301$ (2) $\hat{y} = 11.824(3.32) + 35.301$

b. (1) 58.949   (2) 74.557

c. (1) 58.949 minutes   (2) 74.557 minutes

9.2 EXERCISE SOLUTIONS

1. c   **3.** d   **5.** g

7. h   **9.** c   **11.** a

13.

x	y	xy	x^2
17	110	1870	289
26	124	3224	676
37	146	5402	1369
48	140	6720	2304
50	200	10,000	2500
68	192	13,056	4624
72	200	14,400	5184
$\Sigma x = 318$	$\Sigma y = 1112$	$\Sigma xy = 54{,}672$	$\Sigma x^2 = 16{,}946$

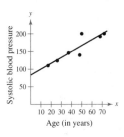

$m = \dfrac{n\Sigma xy - (\Sigma x)(\Sigma y)}{n\Sigma x^2 - (\Sigma x)^2} = \dfrac{7(54{,}672) - (318)(1112)}{7(16{,}946) - (318)^2} = \dfrac{29{,}088}{17{,}498} \approx 1.662$

$b = \bar{y} - m\bar{x} = \left(\dfrac{1112}{7}\right) - (1.662)\left(\dfrac{318}{7}\right) \approx 83.338$

$\hat{y} = 1.662x + 83.338$

© 2006 Pearson Education, Inc., Upper Saddle River, NJ. All rights reserved. This material is protected under all copyright laws as they currently exist. No portion of this material may be reproduced, in any form or by any means, without permission in writing from the publisher.

(a) $\hat{y} = 1.662(18) + 83.338 \approx 113.254$

(b) $\hat{y} = 1.662(71) + 83.338 \approx 201.340$

(c) $\hat{y} = 1.662(29) + 83.338 \approx 131.536$

(d) $\hat{y} = 1.662(55) + 83.338 \approx 174.748$

15.

x	y	xy	x^2
0	40	0	0
1	41	41	1
2	51	102	4
4	48	192	16
4	64	256	16
5	69	345	25
5	73	365	25
5	75	375	25
6	68	408	36
6	93	558	36
7	84	588	49
7	90	630	49
8	95	760	64
$\Sigma x = 60$	$\Sigma y = 891$	$\Sigma xy = 4620$	$\Sigma x^2 = 346$

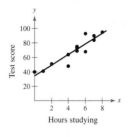

$$m = \frac{n\Sigma xy - (\Sigma x)(\Sigma y)}{n\Sigma x^2 - (\Sigma x)^2} = \frac{13(4620) - (60)(891)}{13(346) - (60)^2} = \frac{6600}{898} \approx 7.350$$

$$b = \bar{y} - m\bar{x} = \left(\frac{60}{13}\right) - (7.350)\left(\frac{891}{13}\right) \approx 34.617$$

$$\hat{y} = 7.350x + 34.617$$

(a) $\hat{y} = 7.350(3) + 34.617 \approx 56.7$

(b) $\hat{y} = 7.350(6.5) + 34.617 \approx 82.4$

(c) It is not meaningful to predict the value of y for $x = 13$ because $x = 13$ is outside the range of the original data.

(d) $\hat{y} = 7.350(4.5) + 34.617 \approx 67.7$

17.

x	y	xy	x^2
186	495	92,070	34,596
181	477	86,337	32,761
176	425	74,800	30,976
149	322	47,978	22,201
184	482	88,688	33,856
190	587	111,530	36,100
158	370	58,460	24,964
139	322	44,758	19,321
175	479	83,825	30,625
148	375	55,500	21,904
$\Sigma x = 1686$	$\Sigma y = 4334$	$\Sigma xy = 743,946$	$\Sigma x^2 = 287,304$

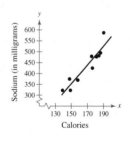

$$m = \frac{n\Sigma xy - (\Sigma x)(\Sigma y)}{n\Sigma x^2 - (\Sigma x)^2} = \frac{10(743,946) - (1686)(4334)}{10(287,304) - (1686)^2} = \frac{132,336}{30,444} \approx 4.347$$

$$b = \bar{y} - m\bar{x} = \left(\frac{4334}{10}\right) - 4.347\left(\frac{1686}{10}\right) = -299.482$$

$$\hat{y} = 4.347x - 299.482$$

© 2006 Pearson Education, Inc., Upper Saddle River, NJ. All rights reserved. This material is protected under all copyright laws as they currently exist. No portion of this material may be reproduced, in any form or by any means, without permission in writing from the publisher.

(a) $\hat{y} = 4.347(170) - 299.482 = 439.508$

(b) It is not meaningful to predict the value of y for $x = 136$ because $x = 136$ is outside the range of the original data.

(c) $\hat{y} = 4.347(145) - 299.482 = 330.833$

(d) $\hat{y} = 4.347(183) - 299.482 = 496.019$

19.

x	y	xy	x^2
8.5	66.0	561.00	72.25
9.0	68.5	616.50	81.00
9.0	67.5	607.50	81.00
9.5	70.0	665.00	90.25
10.0	70.0	700.00	100.00
10.0	72.0	720.00	100.00
10.5	71.5	750.75	110.25
10.5	69.5	729.75	110.25
11.0	71.5	786.50	121.00
11.0	72.0	792.00	121.00
11.0	73.0	803.00	121.00
12.0	73.5	882.00	144.00
12.0	74.0	888.00	144.00
12.5	74.0	925.00	156.25
$\Sigma x = 146.5$	$\Sigma y = 993.0$	$\Sigma xy = 10,427.0$	$\Sigma x^2 = 1552.3$

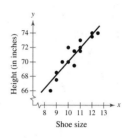

$$m = \frac{n\Sigma xy - (\Sigma x)(\Sigma y)}{n\Sigma x^2 - (\Sigma x)^2} = \frac{14(10,427.0) - (146.5)(993.0)}{14(1552.3) - (146.5)^2} = \frac{503.5}{269.95} \approx 1.870$$

$$b = \bar{y} - m\bar{x} = \left(\frac{993.0}{14}\right) - (1.870)\left(\frac{146.5}{14}\right) \approx 51.360$$

$$\hat{y} = 1.870x + 51.360$$

(a) $\hat{y} = 1.870(11.5) + 51.360 \approx 72.865$

(b) $\hat{y} = 1.870(8.0) + 51.360 \approx 66.320$

(c) It is not meaningful to predict the value of y for $x = 15.5$ because $x = 15.5$ is outside the range of the original data.

(d) $\hat{y} = 1.870(10.0) + 51.360 \approx 70.060$

21.

x	y	xy	x^2
5720	2.19	12,527	32,718,400
4050	1.36	5508	16,402,500
6130	2.58	15,815	37,576,900
5000	1.74	8700	25,000,000
5010	1.78	8917.8	25,100,100
4270	1.69	7216.3	18,232,900
5500	1.80	9900	30,250,000
5550	1.87	10,379	30,802,500
$\Sigma x = 41,230$	$\Sigma y = 15.01$	$\Sigma xy = 78,962.8$	$\Sigma x^2 = 216,083,300$

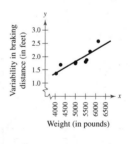

$$m = \frac{n\Sigma xy - (\Sigma x)(\Sigma y)}{n\Sigma x^2 - (\Sigma x)^2} = \frac{8(78,962.8) - (41,230)(15.01)}{8(216,083,300) - (41,230)^2} = \frac{12,833.7}{28,753,500} = 0.000447$$

$$b = \bar{y} - m\bar{x} = \left(\frac{15.01}{8}\right) - (0.000447)\left(\frac{41,230}{8}\right) = -0.425$$

$$\hat{y} = 0.000447x - 0.425$$

© 2006 Pearson Education, Inc., Upper Saddle River, NJ. All rights reserved. This material is protected under all copyright laws as they currently exist. No portion of this material may be reproduced, in any form or by any means, without permission in writing from the publisher.

(a) $\hat{y} = 0.000447(4500) - 0.425 = 1.587$

(b) $\hat{y} = 0.000447(6000) - 0.425 = 2.257$

(c) It is not meaningful to predict the value of y for $x = 7500$ because $x = 7500$ is outside the range of the original data.

(d) $\hat{y} = 0.000447(5750) - 0.425 = 2.145$

23. Substitute a value x into the equation of a regression line and solve for y.

25. (a) $\hat{y} = 1.724x + 79.733$ (b) $\hat{y} = 0.453x - 26.448$ (c) The slope of the line keeps the same sign, but the values of m and b change.

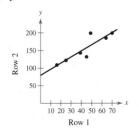

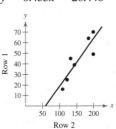

27. Strong negative non-linear correlation; as the number of subscribers increases, the average monthly bill decreases.

29. $\hat{y} = -0.294(180) + 70.652 \approx 17.73$

This is not a valid prediction because $x = 180$ is outside the range of the original data.

31. As the number of cellular phone subscribers increases, the average monthly cellular phone bill decreases. (Answers will vary).

33. The exponential equation is a better fit to the data.

35. $\hat{y} = a + b \ln x = 13.667 - 0.471 \ln x$

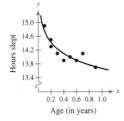

37. The logarithmic equation is a better fitting model to the data.

9.3 MEASURES OF REGRESSION AND PREDICTION INTERVALS

9.3 Try It Yourself Solutions

1a. $r = 0.970$

 b. $r^2 = (0.970)^2 = 0.941$

 c. 94.1% of the variation in the times is explained.
5.9% of the variation is unexplained.

© 2006 Pearson Education, Inc., Upper Saddle River, NJ. All rights reserved. This material is protected under all copyright laws as they currently exist.
No portion of this material may be reproduced, in any form or by any means, without permission in writing from the publisher.

2a.

x_i	y_i	$\hat{y}_i$	$(y_i - \hat{y}_i)^2$
15	26	28.386	5.693
20	32	35.411	11.635
20	38	35.411	6.703
30	56	49.461	42.759
40	54	63.511	90.459
45	78	70.536	55.711
50	80	77.561	5.949
60	88	91.611	13.039
			$\Sigma = 231.948$

b. $n = 8$

c. $s_e = \sqrt{\dfrac{\Sigma(y_i - \hat{y}_i)^2}{n - 2}} = \sqrt{\dfrac{231.948}{6}} \approx 6.218$

d. The standard deviation of the weekly sales for a specific radio ad time is about $621.80.

3a. $n = 8$, d.f. $= 6$, $t_c = 2.447$, $s_e \approx 10.290$

b. $\hat{y} = 50.729x + 104.061 = 50.729(2.5) + 104.061 \approx 230.884$

c. $E = t_c s_e \sqrt{1 + \dfrac{1}{n} + \dfrac{n(x - \bar{x})^2}{n(\Sigma x^2) - (\Sigma x)^2}} = (2.447)(10.290)\sqrt{1 + \dfrac{1}{8} + \dfrac{8(2.5 - 1.975)^2}{8(32.44) - (15.8)^2}}$

$= (2.447)(10.290)\sqrt{1.34818} \approx 29.236$

d. $\hat{y} \pm E \rightarrow (201.648, 260.120)$

e. You can be 95% confident that the company sales will be between $201,648 and $260,120 when advertising expenditures are $2500.

9.3 EXERCISE SOLUTIONS

1. Total variation $= \Sigma(y_i - \bar{y})^2$; the sum of the squares of the differences between the y-values of each ordered pair and the mean of the y-values of the ordered pairs.

3. Unexplained variation $= \Sigma(y_i - \hat{y}_i)^2$; the sum of the squares of the differences between the observed y-values and the predicted y-values.

5. $r^2 = (0.250)^2 \approx 0.063$

6.3% of the variation is explained. 93.7% of the variation is unexplained.

7. $r = (-0.891)^2 \approx 0.794$

79.4% of the variation is explained. 20.6% of the variation is unexplained.

9. (a) $r^2 = \dfrac{\Sigma(\hat{y}_i - \bar{y})^2}{\Sigma(y_i - \bar{y})^2} \approx 0.623$

62.3% of the variation in proceeds can be explained by the variation in the number of issues and 37.7% of the variation is unexplained.

(b) $s_e = \sqrt{\dfrac{\Sigma(y_i - \hat{y}_i)^2}{n - 2}} = \sqrt{\dfrac{770,153,382.32}{10}} \approx 8775.838$

The standard deviation of the proceeds for a specific number of issues is about $8,775,838,000.

© 2006 Pearson Education, Inc., Upper Saddle River, NJ. All rights reserved. This material is protected under all copyright laws as they currently exist. No portion of this material may be reproduced, in any form or by any means, without permission in writing from the publisher.

11. (a) $r^2 = \dfrac{\Sigma(\hat{y}_i - \bar{y})^2}{\Sigma(y_i - \bar{y})^2} \approx 0.985$

98.5% of the variation in sales can be explained by the variation in the total square footage and 1.5% of the variation is unexplained.

(b) $s_e = \sqrt{\dfrac{\Sigma(y_i - \hat{y}_i)^2}{n-2}} = \sqrt{\dfrac{11,439.531}{9}} \approx 35.652$

The standard deviation of the sales for a specific total square footage is about 35,652,000,000.

13. (a) $r^2 = \dfrac{\Sigma(\hat{y}_i - \bar{y})^2}{\Sigma(y_i - \bar{y})^2} \approx 0.982$

98.2% of the variation in the median weekly earnings of female workers can be explained by the variation in the median weekly earnings of male workers and 1.8% of the variation is unexplained.

(b) $s_e = \sqrt{\dfrac{\Sigma(y_i - \hat{y}_i)^2}{n-2}} = \sqrt{\dfrac{203.004}{3}} \approx 8.226$

The standard deviation of the median weekly earnings of female workers for a specific median weekly earnings of male workers is about $8.226.

15. (a) $r^2 = \dfrac{\Sigma(\hat{y}_i - \bar{y})^2}{\Sigma(y_i - \bar{y})^2} \approx 0.992$

99.2% of the variation in the money spent can be explained by the variation in the money raised and 0.8% of the variation is unexplained.

(b) $s_e = \sqrt{\dfrac{\Sigma(y_i - \hat{y}_i)^2}{n-2}} = \sqrt{\dfrac{1,551.176}{6}} \approx 16.079$

The standard deviation of the money spent for a specified amount of money raised is about $16,079,000.

17. $n = 12$, d.f. $= 10$, $t_c = 2.228$, $s_e = 8775.838$

$\hat{y} = 51.185x - 35.462 = 51.185(712) - 35.462 \approx 36,408.258$

$E = t_c s_e \sqrt{1 + \dfrac{1}{n} + \dfrac{n(x - \bar{x})^2}{n(\Sigma x^2) - (\Sigma x)^2}} = (2.228)(8775.838)\sqrt{1 + \dfrac{1}{12} + \dfrac{12(712 - 5376/12)^2}{12(2,894,666) - (5376)^2}}$

$= (2.228)(8775.838)\sqrt{1.22667} \approx 21,655.529$

$\hat{y} \pm E \rightarrow (14,752.729, 58,063.787) \rightarrow (\$14,752,729,000, \$58,063,787,000)$

You can be 95% confident that the proceeds will be between 14,752,729,000 and $58,063,787,000 when the number of initial offerings is 712.

19. $n = 11$, d.f. $= 9$, $t_c = 1.833$, $s_e \approx 35.652$

$\hat{y} = 230.831x - 289.809 = 230.831(4.5) - 289.809 \approx 748.931$

$E = t_c s_e \sqrt{1 + \dfrac{1}{n} + \dfrac{n(x - \bar{x})^2}{n(\Sigma x^2) - (\Sigma x)^2}} = (1.833)(35.652)\sqrt{1 + \dfrac{1}{11} + \dfrac{11[4.5 - (43.3/11)]^2}{11(184.93) - (43.3)^2}}$

$= (1.833)(35.652)\sqrt{1.11284} \approx 68.939$

$\hat{y} \pm E \rightarrow (679.992, 817.870) \rightarrow (\$679,992,000, \$817,870,000)$

You can be 90% confident that the sales will be between $679,992,000,000 and $817,870,000,000 when the total square footage is 4.5 billion.

© 2006 Pearson Education, Inc., Upper Saddle River, NJ. All rights reserved. This material is protected under all copyright laws as they currently exist.
No portion of this material may be reproduced, in any form or by any means, without permission in writing from the publisher.

21. $n = 5$, d.f. $= 3$, $t_c = 5.841$, $s_e \approx 8.226$

$\hat{y} = 0.919x - 95.462 = 0.919(500) - 95.462 \approx 364.038$

$$E = t_c s_e \sqrt{1 + \frac{1}{n} + \frac{n(x - \bar{x})^2}{n(\Sigma x^2) - (\Sigma x)^2}} = (5.841)(8.226)\sqrt{1 + \frac{1}{5} + \frac{5[500 - (3221/5)]^2}{5(2,087,823) - (3221)^2}}$$

$$= (5.841)(8.226)\sqrt{2.81758} \approx 80.652$$

$\hat{y} \pm E \to (283.386, 444.690)$

You can be 99% confident that the median earnings of female workers will be between $283.386 and $444.690 when the median weekly earnings of male workers is $500.

23. $n = 8$, d.f. $= 6$, $t_c = 2.447$, $s_e \approx 16.079$

$\hat{y} = 1.020x - 25.854 = 1.020(775.8) - 25.854 \approx 765.462$

$$E = t_c s_e \sqrt{1 + \frac{1}{n} + \frac{n(x - \bar{x})^2}{n(\Sigma x^2) - (\Sigma x)^2}} = (2.447)(16.079)\sqrt{1 + \frac{1}{8} + \frac{8[775.8 - (4363.5/8)]^2}{8(2,564,874) - (4363.5)^2}}$$

$$= (2.447)(16.079)\sqrt{1.41207} \approx 46.754$$

$\hat{y} \pm E \to (\$718.708 \text{ million}, \$812.216 \text{ million})$

You can be 95% confident that the money spent in congressional campaigns will be between $729.046 million and $822.554 million when the money raised is $775.8 million.

25.

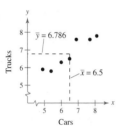

27.

x_i	y_i	$\hat{y}_i$	$\hat{y}_i - \bar{y}$	$y_i - \hat{y}_i$	$y_i - \bar{y}$
8.1	7.8	7.893	1.107	−0.093	1.014
7.7	7.6	7.616	0.830	−0.016	0.814
6.5	6.5	6.785	−0.001	−0.285	−0.286
6.9	7.6	7.062	0.276	0.538	0.814
6.0	6.3	6.438	−0.348	−0.138	−0.486
5.4	5.8	6.022	−0.764	−0.222	−0.986
4.9	5.9	5.676	−1.11	0.224	−0.886

29. $r^2 \approx 0.887$; About 88.7% of the variation in the median age of tracks can be explained by the variation in the median age of cars, and 11.3% of the variation is unexplained.

31. $\hat{y} = 0.693x + 2.280 = 0.693(7.3) + 2.280 \approx 7.339$

$$E = t_c s_e \sqrt{1 + \frac{1}{n} + \frac{n(x - \bar{x})^2}{n(\Sigma x^2) - (\Sigma x)^2}} = (2.571)(0.316)\sqrt{1 + \frac{1}{7} + \frac{7[7.3 - (45.5/7)]^2}{7(303.930) - (45.5)^2}}$$

$$= (2.571)(0.316)\sqrt{1.22110} \approx 0.898$$

$\hat{y} \pm E \to (6.441, 8.237)$

9.4 MULTIPLE REGRESSION

9.4 Try It Yourself Solutions

1a. Enter the data. **b.** $\hat{y} = 46.385 + 0.540x_1 - 4.897x_2$

2ab. (1) $\hat{y} = 46.385 + 0.540(89) - 4.897(1)$ (2) $\hat{y} = 46.385 + 0.540(78) - 4.897(3)$

 (3) $\hat{y} = 46.385 + 0.540(83) - 4.897(2)$

c. (1) $\hat{y} = 89.548$ (2) $\hat{y} = 73.814$ (3) $\hat{y} = 81.411$

d. (1) 90 (2) 74 (3) 81

© 2006 Pearson Education, Inc., Upper Saddle River, NJ. All rights reserved. This material is protected under all copyright laws as they currently exist. No portion of this material may be reproduced, in any form or by any means, without permission in writing from the publisher.

9.4 EXERCISE SOLUTIONS

1. $\hat{y} = 6503 - 14.8x_1 + 12.2x_2$

   (a) $\hat{y} = 6503 - 14.8(1458) + 12.2(1450) = 2614.6$

   (b) $\hat{y} = 6503 - 14.8(1500) + 12.2(1475) = 2298$

   (c) $\hat{y} = 6503 - 14.8(1400) + 12.2(1385) = 2680$

   (d) $\hat{y} = 6503 - 14.8(1525) + 12.2(1500) = 2233$

3. $\hat{y} = -52.2 + 0.3x_1 + 4.5x_2$

   (a) $\hat{y} = -52.2 + 0.3(70) + 4.5(8.6) = 7.5$

   (b) $\hat{y} = -52.2 + 0.3(65) + 4.5(11.0) = 16.8$

   (c) $\hat{y} = -52.2 + 0.3(83) + 4.5(17.6) = 51.9$

   (d) $\hat{y} = -52.2 + 0.3(87) + 4.5(19.6) = 62.1$

5. $\hat{y} = -256.293 + 103.502x_1 + 14.649x_2$

   (a) $s = 34.16$

   (b) $r^2 = 0.988$

   (c) The standard deviation of the predicted sales given a specific total square footage and number of shopping centers is $34.16 billion. The multiple regression model explains 98.8% of the variation in y.

7. $n = 11, k = 2, r = 0.988$

$$r^2_{adj} = 1 - \left[\frac{(1 - r^2)(n - 1)}{n - k - 1}\right] = 0.985$$

CHAPTER 9 REVIEW EXERCISE SOLUTIONS

1.

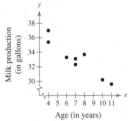

$r \approx -0.939$; negative linear correlation; milk production decreases with age.

3.

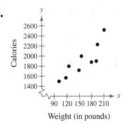

$r \approx 0.868$; positive linear correlation; calorie intake increases with weight.

5. $H_0: \rho = 0; H_a: \rho \neq 0$

$\alpha = 0.01$, d.f. $= n - 2 = 24$

$t_0 = 2.797$

$$t = \frac{r}{\sqrt{\dfrac{1 - r^2}{n - 2}}} = \frac{0.24}{\sqrt{\dfrac{1 - (0.24)^2}{26 - 2}}} = \frac{0.24}{\sqrt{0.03927}} = 1.211$$

Fail to reject H_0. There is not enough evidence to conclude that a significant linear correlation exists.

© 2006 Pearson Education, Inc., Upper Saddle River, NJ. All rights reserved. This material is protected under all copyright laws as they currently exist. No portion of this material may be reproduced, in any form or by any means, without permission in writing from the publisher.

7. $H_0: \rho = 0; H_a: \rho \neq 0$

$\alpha = 0.05$, d.f. $= n - 2 = 6$

$t_0 = \pm 2.447$

$$t = \frac{r}{\sqrt{\dfrac{1 - r^2}{n - 2}}} = \frac{-0.939}{\sqrt{\dfrac{1 - (-0.939)^2}{8 - 2}}} = \frac{-0.939}{\sqrt{0.01971}} = -6.688$$

Reject H_0. There is enough evidence to conclude that there is a significant linear correlation between the age of a cow and its milk production.

9. $H_0: \rho = 0; H_a: \rho \neq 0$

$\alpha = 0.01$, d.f. $= n - 2 = 7$

$t_0 = \pm 3.499$

$$t = \frac{r}{\sqrt{\dfrac{1 - r^2}{n - 2}}} = \frac{0.868}{\sqrt{\dfrac{1 - (0.868)^2}{7}}} = 4.625$$

Reject H_0. There is enough evidence to conclude a significant linear correlation exists between weight and calories.

11. $\hat{y} = 0.757x + 21.5$

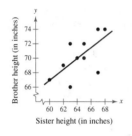

$r \approx 0.688$ (Moderate positive linear correlation)

13. $\hat{y} = 10.450 - 0.086x$

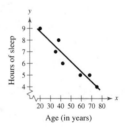

$r \approx -0.949$ (Strong negative linear correlation)

15. (a) $\hat{y} = 0.757(61) + 21.5 = 67.677 \approx 68$ inches

(b) $\hat{y} = 0.757(66) + 21.5 = 71.462 \approx 71$ inches

(c) Not meaningful since $x = 71$ inches is outside range of data.

(d) Not meaningful since $x = 50$ inches is outside range of data.

17. (a) Not meaningful since $x = 18$ years is outside range of data.

(b) $\hat{y} = 10.450 = 0.086x = 10.450 - 0.086(25) = 8.3$

(c) Not meaningful since $x = 80$ years is outside range of data.

(d) $\hat{y} = 10.450 - 0.086x = 10.450 - 0.086(50) = 6.15$

19. $r^2 = (-0.553)^2 = 0.306$

30.6% of the variation in y is explained by the model.
69.4% of the variation in y is unexplained by the model.

21. $r^2 = (0.181)^2 = 0.033$

3.3% of the variation in y is explained by the model.
96.7% of the variation in y is unexplained by the model.

© 2006 Pearson Education, Inc., Upper Saddle River, NJ. All rights reserved. This material is protected under all copyright laws as they currently exist. No portion of this material may be reproduced, in any form or by any means, without permission in writing from the publisher.

23. (a) $r^2 = 0.897$

89.7% of the variation in y is explained by the model.
10.3% of the variation in y is unexplained by the model.

(b) $s_e = 568.011$

The standard error of the cooling capacity for a specific living area is 568.0 Btu/hr.

25. $\hat{y} = 0.757(64) + 21.5 = 69.948$

$$E = t_c s_e \sqrt{1 + \frac{1}{n} + \frac{n(x - \bar{x})^2}{n\Sigma x^2 - (\Sigma x)^2}} \approx (1.833)(2.206)\sqrt{1 + \frac{1}{11} + \frac{11(64 - 64.727)^2}{11(46,154) - 712^2}}$$

$$= (1.833)(2.206)\sqrt{1.09866} \approx 4.238$$

$$\hat{y} - E < y < \hat{y} + E$$
$$69.948 - 4.238 < y < 69.948 + 4.238$$
$$65.71 < y < 74.19$$

27. $\hat{y} = -0.086(45) + 10.450 = 6.580$

$$E = t_c s_e \sqrt{1 + \frac{1}{n} + \frac{n(x - \bar{x})^2}{n\Sigma x^2 - (\Sigma x)^2}} \approx (2.571)(0.623)\sqrt{1 + \frac{1}{7} + \frac{7[45 - (337/7)]^2}{7(18,563) - (337)^2}}$$

$$= (2.571)(0.623)\sqrt{1.14708} = 1.715$$

$$\hat{y} - E < y < \hat{y} + E$$
$$6.580 - 1.715 < y < 6.58 + 1.715$$
$$4.865 < y < 8.295$$

29. $\hat{y} = 3002.991 + 9.468(720)$

$$= 9819.95$$

$$E = t_c s_e \sqrt{1 + \frac{1}{n} + \frac{n(x - \bar{x})^2}{n\Sigma x^2 - (\Sigma x)^2}} = (3.707)(568)\sqrt{1 + \frac{1}{8} + \frac{8(720 - 499.4)^2}{8(2,182,275) - 3995^2}}$$

$$= (3.707)(568)\sqrt{1.38486} \approx 2477.94$$

$$\hat{y} - E < y < \hat{y} + E$$
$$9819.96 - 2477.94 < y < 9819.96 + 2477.94$$
$$7342.01 < y < 12,297.89$$

31. $\hat{y} = 6.317 + 0.8227x_1 + 0.031x_2 - 0.004x_3$

33. (a) 21.705   (b) 25.210   (c) 30.100   (d) 25.860

CHAPTER 9 QUIZ SOLUTIONS

1.

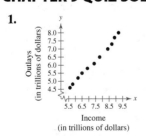

The data appear to have a positive correlation. The outlays increase as the incomes increase.

© 2006 Pearson Education, Inc., Upper Saddle River, NJ. All rights reserved. This material is protected under all copyright laws as they currently exist.
No portion of this material may be reproduced, in any form or by any means, without permission in writing from the publisher.

2. $r \approx 0.996 \rightarrow$ Strong positive linear correlation

3. $H_0: \rho = 0; H_a: \rho \neq 0$

$\alpha = 0.05$, d.f. $= n - 2 = 9$

$t_0 = \pm 2.262$

$$t = \frac{r}{\sqrt{\dfrac{1 - r^2}{n - 2}}} = \frac{0.996}{\sqrt{\dfrac{1 - (0.996)^2}{11 - 2}}} = \frac{0.996}{\sqrt{0.00088711}} \approx 33.44$$

Reject H_0. There is enough evidence to conclude that a significant correlation exists.

4. $\Sigma y^2 = 441.140$

$\Sigma y = 68.600$

$\Sigma xy = 522.470$

$b = -0.359$

$m = 0.891$

$\hat{y} = 0.891x - 0.359$

5. $\hat{y} = 0.891(5.3) - 0.359 = 4.363$

6. $r^2 = 0.992$

99.2% of the variation in y is explained by the regression model.
0.8% of the variation in y is unexplained by the regression model.

7. $s_e = 0.110$

The standard deviation of personal outlays for a specified personal income is $0.110 trillion.

8. $\hat{y} = 0.891(6.4) - 0.359$

$\quad\ = 5.343$

$$E = t_c s_e \sqrt{1 + \frac{1}{n} + \frac{n(x - \bar{x})^2}{n\Sigma x^2 - (\Sigma x)^2}}$$

$$= 2.262(0.110)\sqrt{1 + \frac{1}{11} + \frac{11[6.4 - (81.4/11)]^2}{11(619) - 81.4^2}} \approx (2.262)(0.110)\sqrt{1.15101}$$

$$\approx 0.267$$

$$\hat{y} - E < y < \hat{y} + E$$

$$5.343 - 0.267 < y < 5.343 + 0.267$$

$$5.076 < y < 5.610 \rightarrow (\$5.076 \text{ trillion}, \$5.610 \text{ trillion})$$

You can be 95% confident that the personal outlays will be between $5.076 trillion and $5.610 trillion when personal income is $6.4 trillion.

9. (a) 1311.150

(b) 961.110

(c) 1120.900

(d) 1386.740; x_2 has the greatest influence on y.

© 2006 Pearson Education, Inc., Upper Saddle River, NJ. All rights reserved. This material is protected under all copyright laws as they currently exist. No portion of this material may be reproduced, in any form or by any means, without permission in writing from the publisher.

10.1 Try It Yourself Solutions

1a.

Music	% of Listeners	Expected Frequency
Classical	4%	12
Country	36%	108
Gospel	11%	33
Oldies	2%	6
Pop	18%	54
Rock	29%	87

2a. The expected frequencies are 64, 80, 32, 56, 60, 48, 40, and 20, all of which are at least 5.

b. Claimed Distribution:

Ages	Distribution
0–9	16%
10–19	20%
20–29	8%
30–39	14%
40–49	15%
50–59	12%
60–69	10%
70+	5%

H_0: Distribution of ages is as shown in table above.
H_a: Distribution of ages differs from the claimed distribution.

c. $\alpha = 0.05$ **d.** d.f. $= n - 1 = 7$

e. $\chi_0^2 = 14.067$; Reject H_0 if $\chi^2 > 14.067$.

f.

Ages	Distribution	Observed	Expected	$\frac{(O - E)^2}{E}$
0–9	16%	76	64	2.250
10–19	20%	84	80	0.200
20–29	8%	30	32	0.125
30–39	14%	60	56	0.286
40–49	15%	54	60	0.600
50–59	12%	40	48	1.333
60–69	10%	42	40	0.100
70+	5%	14	20	1.800
				6.694

$\chi^2 \approx 6.694$

g. Fail to reject H_0.

h. There is not enough evidence to conclude that the distribution of ages differs from the claimed distribution.

© 2006 Pearson Education, Inc., Upper Saddle River, NJ. All rights reserved. This material is protected under all copyright laws as they currently exist.
No portion of this material may be reproduced, in any form or by any means, without permission in writing from the publisher.

3a. The expected frequencies are 88, 54, and 58, all of which are at least 5.

b. Claimed Distribution:

Response	Distribution
In favor of	44%
Against	27%
No Opinion	29%

H_0: Distribution of responses is as shown in table above.

H_a: Distribution of responses differs from the claimed distribution.

c. $\alpha = 0.01$ **d.** d.f. $= n - 1 = 2$ **e.** $\chi_0^2 = 9.210$; Reject H_0 if $\chi^2 > 9.210$.

f.

Response	Distribution	Observed	Expected	$\frac{(O - E)^2}{E}$
In favor of	44%	100	88	1.636
Against	27%	48	54	0.667
No opinion	29%	52	58	0.621
				2.924

$\chi^2 \approx 2.924$

g. Fail to reject H_0.

h. There is not enough evidence to conclude that the distribution of responses differs from the claimed distribution.

10.1 EXERCISE SOLUTIONS

1. A multinomial experiment is a probability experiment consisting of a fixed number of trials in which there are more than two possible outcomes for each independent trial.

3. $E_i = np_i = (150)(0.3) = 45$

5. $E_i = np_i = (230)(0.25) = 57.5$

7. (a) Claimed distribution:

Response	Distribution
Agree	78%
Disagree	17%
Neither	5%

H_0: Distribution of responses is as shown in the table above.

H_a: Distribution of responses differs from the claimed distribution.

(b) $\chi_0^2 = 5.991$; Reject H_0 if $\chi^2 > 5.991$.

(c)

Response	Distribution	Observed	Expected	$\frac{(O - E)^2}{E}$
Agree	78%	311	331.50	1.268
Disagree	17%	84	72.25	1.911
Neither	5%	30	21.25	3.603
				6.782

$\chi^2 = 6.782$

(d) Reject H_0. There is enough evidence at the 5% level to conclude that the distribution of responses differs from the claimed distribution.

© 2006 Pearson Education, Inc., Upper Saddle River, NJ. All rights reserved. This material is protected under all copyright laws as they currently exist. No portion of this material may be reproduced, in any form or by any means, without permission in writing from the publisher.

9. (a) Claimed distribution:

Response	Distribution
Keeping Medicare, Social Security, and Medicaid	77%
Tax cuts	15%
Not sure	8%

H_0: Distribution of responses is as shown in the table above.

H_a: Distribution of responses differs from the claimed distribution.

(b) $\chi_0^2 = 9.210$; Reject H_0 if $\chi^2 > 9.210$.

(c)

Response	Distribution	Observed	Expected	$\frac{(O - E)^2}{E}$
Keeping Medicare, Social Security, and Medicaid	77%	431	462	2.080
Tax cuts	15%	107	90	3.211
Not sure	8%	62	48	4.083
				9.374

$\chi^2 = 9.374$

(d) Reject H_0. There is enough evidence at the 1% level to conclude that the distribution of responses differs from the claimed distribution.

11. (a) Claimed distribution:

Day	Distribution
Sunday	14.286%
Monday	14.286%
Tuesday	14.286%
Wednesday	14.286%
Thursday	14.286%
Friday	14.286%
Saturday	14.286%

H_0: The distribution of fatal bicycle accidents throughout the week is uniform as shown in the table above.

H_a: The distribution of fatal bicycle accidents throughout the week is not uniform.

(b) $\chi_0^2 = 10.645$; Reject H_0 if $\chi^2 > 10.645$.

(c)

Day	Distribution	Observed	Expected	$\frac{(O - E)^2}{E}$
Sunday	14.286%	118	130.15	1.133
Monday	14.286%	119	130.15	0.954
Tuesday	14.286%	127	130.15	0.076
Wednesday	14.286%	137	130.15	0.361
Thursday	14.286%	129	130.15	0.010
Friday	14.286%	146	130.15	1.931
Saturday	14.286%	135	130.15	0.181
				4.648

$\chi^2 \approx 4.648$

(d) Fail to reject H_0. There is not enough evidence at the 10% level to conclude that the distribution of fatal bicycle accidents throughout the week is not uniform.

© 2006 Pearson Education, Inc., Upper Saddle River, NJ. All rights reserved. This material is protected under all copyright laws as they currently exist. No portion of this material may be reproduced, in any form or by any means, without permission in writing from the publisher.

13. (a) Claimed distribution:

Object struck	Distribution
Tree	28%
Embankment	10%
Utility pole	10%
Guardrail	9%
Ditch	7%
Curb	6%
Culvert	5%
Sign/Post/Fence	10%
Other	15%

H_0: Distribution of objects struck is as shown in table above.

H_a: Distribution of objects struck differs from the claimed distribution.

(b) $\chi_0^2 = 20.090$; Reject H_0 if $\chi^2 > 20.090$.

(c)

Object Struck	Distribution	Observed	Expected	$\frac{(O-E)^2}{E}$
Tree	28%	179	193.48	1.084
Embankment	10%	100	69.10	13.818
Utility pole	10%	107	69.10	20.787
Guardrail	9%	57	62.19	0.433
Ditch	7%	36	48.37	3.163
Curb	6%	43	41.46	0.057
Culvert	5%	28	34.55	1.242
Sign/Post/Fence	10%	68	69.10	0.018
Other	15%	73	103.65	9.063
			691	49.665

$\chi^2 \approx 49.665$

(d) Reject H_0. There is enough evidence at the 1% level to conclude that the distribution of the objects struck changed after warning signs were erected.

15. (a) Claimed distribution:

Response	Distribution
Not a HS grad	33.333%
HS graduate	33.333%
College (1yr+)	33.333%

H_0: Distribution of the responses is uniform as shown in table above.

H_a: Distribution of the responses is not uniform.

(b) $\chi_0^2 = 7.378$; Reject H_0 if $\chi^2 > 7.378$.

(c)

Response	Distribution	Observed	Expected	$\frac{(O-E)^2}{E}$
Not a HS grad	33.333%	37	33	0.485
HS graduate	33.333%	40	33	1.485
College (1yr+)	33.333%	22	33	3.667
			99	5.637

$\chi^2 \approx 5.637$

(d) Fail to reject H_0. There is not enough evidence at the 2.5% level to conclude that the distribution of the responses is not uniform.

© 2006 Pearson Education, Inc., Upper Saddle River, NJ. All rights reserved. This material is protected under all copyright laws as they currently exist. No portion of this material may be reproduced, in any form or by any means, without permission in writing from the publisher.

17. (a) Claimed distribution:

Cause	Distribution
Trans. Accidents	41%
Assaults	20%
Objects/equipment	15%
Falls	10%
Exposure	10%
Other	4%

H_0: Distribution of the causes is as shown in table above.

H_a: Distribution of the causes differs from the claimed distribution.

(b) $\chi_0^2 = 11.071$; Reject H_0 if $\chi^2 > 11.071$.

(c)

Cause	Distribution	Observed	Expected	$\dfrac{(O - E)^2}{E}$
Trans. Accidents	41%	2500	2554.71	1.172
Assaults	20%	1300	1246.20	2.323
Objects/equipment	15%	985	934.65	2.712
Falls	10%	620	623.10	0.015
Exposure	10%	602	623.10	0.715
Other	4%	224	249.24	2.556
		6231		9.493

$\chi^2 \approx 9.493$

(d) Fail to reject H_0. There is not enough evidence at the 5% level to conclude that the distributions of the causes in the Western U.S. differs from the national distribution.

19. (a) Frequency distribution: $\mu = 69.435$; $\sigma \approx 8.337$

Lower Boundary	Upper Boundary	Lower z-score	Upper z-score	Area
49.5	58.5	−2.39	−1.31	0.0867
58.5	67.5	−1.31	−0.23	0.3139
67.5	76.5	−0.23	0.85	0.3933
76.5	85.5	0.85	1.93	0.1709
85.5	94.5	1.93	3.01	0.0255

Class Boundaries	Distribution	Frequency	Expected	$\dfrac{(O - E)^2}{E}$
49.5–58.5	8.67%	19	17	0.235
58.5–67.5	31.39%	61	63	0.063
67.5–76.5	39.33%	82	79	0.114
76.5–85.5	17.09%	34	34	0
85.5–94.5	2.55%	4	5	0.2
		200		0.612

H_0: Variable has a normal distribution

H_a: Variable does not have a normal distribution

(b) $\chi_0^2 = 13.277$; Reject H_0 if $\chi^2 > 13.277$.

(c) $\chi^2 = 0.612$

(d) Fail to reject H_0. There is not enough evidence at the 1% level to conclude that the distribution of test scores is not normal.

© 2006 Pearson Education, Inc., Upper Saddle River, NJ. All rights reserved. This material is protected under all copyright laws as they currently exist. No portion of this material may be reproduced, in any form or by any means, without permission in writing from the publisher.

10.2 INDEPENDENCE

10.2 Try It Yourself Solutions

1ab.

	Hotel	Leg Room	Rental Size	Other	Total
Business	36	108	14	22	180
Leisure	38	54	14	14	120
Total	74	162	28	36	300

c. $n = 300$

d.

	Hotel	Leg Room	Rental Size	Other
Business	44.4	97.2	16.8	21.6
Leisure	29.6	64.8	11.2	14.4

2a. H_0: Travel concern is independent of travel purpose.

H_a: Travel concern is dependent on travel purpose. (claim)

b. $\alpha = 0.01$ **c.** $(r - 1)(c - 1) = 3$ **d.** $\chi_0^2 = 11.345$; Reject H_0 if $\chi^2 > 11.345$.

e. $\chi^2 = \sum \dfrac{(O - E)^2}{E} = \dfrac{(36 - 44.4)^2}{44.4} + \dfrac{(108 - 97.2)^2}{97.2} + \cdots + \dfrac{(14 - 14.4)^2}{14.4} \approx 8.158$

f. Fail to reject H_0.

g. There is not enough evidence to conclude that travel concern is dependent on travel purpose.

3a. $\chi_0^2 = 9.488$; Reject H_0 if $\chi^2 > 9.488$.   **b.** Enter the data.

c. $\chi^2 \approx 65.619$ **d.** Reject H_0.

e. There is enough evidence to conclude that minutes spent online per day is dependent on gender.

10.2 EXERCISE SOLUTIONS

1. $E_{r,c} = \dfrac{(\text{Sum of row } r)(\text{Sum of column } c)}{\text{Sample size}}$

3. False. A contingency table with two rows and five columns will have $(2 - 1)(5 - 1) = 4$ degrees of freedom.

5.

	Athlete has	
Result	Stretched	Not stretched
Injury	20.818	19.182
No injury	208.182	191.818

7.

	Treatment		
Result	Brand-name	Generic	Placebo
Improvement	24	21	10
No change	12	13	45

9. (a) H_0: Skill level in a subject is independent of location. (claim)

H_a: Skill level in a subject is dependent on location.

© 2006 Pearson Education, Inc., Upper Saddle River, NJ. All rights reserved. This material is protected under all copyright laws as they currently exist. No portion of this material may be reproduced, in any form or by any means, without permission in writing from the publisher.

(b) d.f. $= (r - 1)(c - 1) = 2$

$\chi_0^2 = 9.210$; Reject H_0 if $\chi^2 > 9.210$.

(c) $\chi^2 \approx 0.297$

(d) Fail to reject H_0. There is not enough evidence at the 1% level to conclude that skill level in a subject is dependent on location.

11. (a) H_0: Grades are independent of the institution.

H_a: Grades are dependent on the institution. (claim)

(b) d.f. $= (r - 1)(c - 1) = 8$

$\chi_0^2 = 15.507$; Reject H_0 if $\chi^2 > 15.507$.

(c) $\chi^2 \approx 48.488$

(d) Reject H_0. There is enough evidence at the 5% level to conclude that grades are dependent on the institution.

13. (a) H_0: Results are independent of the type of treatment.

H_a: Results are dependent on the type of treatment. (claim)

(b) d.f. $= (r - 1)(c - 1) = 1$

$\chi_0^2 = 2.706$; Reject H_0 if $\chi^2 > 2.706$.

(c) $\chi^2 \approx 5.106$

(d) Reject H_0. There is not enough evidence at the 10% level to conclude that results are dependent on the type of treatment. I would recommend using the drug.

15. (a) H_0: Reasons are independent of the type of worker.

H_a: Reasons are dependent on the type of worker. (claim)

(b) d.f. $= (r - 1)(c - 1) = 2$

$\chi_0^2 = 9.210$; Reject H_0 if $\chi^2 > 9.210$.

(c) $\chi^2 \approx 7.326$

(d) Fail to reject H_0. There is not enough evidence at the 1% level to conclude that the reason(s) for continuing education are dependent on the type of worker. Based on these results, marketing strategies should not differ between technical and non-technical audiences in regard to reason(s) for continuing education.

17. (a) H_0: Type of crash is independent of the type of vehicle.

H_a: Type of crash is dependent on the type of vehicle. (claim)

(b) d.f. $= (r - 1)(c - 1) = 2$

$\chi_0^2 = 5.991$; Reject H_0 if $\chi^2 > 5.991$.

(c) $\chi^2 \approx 106.390$

(d) Reject H_0. There is enough evidence at the 5% level to conclude that type of crash is dependent on the type of vehicle.

19. (a) H_0: Subject is independent of coauthorship.

H_a: Subject and coauthorship are dependent. (claim)

© 2006 Pearson Education, Inc., Upper Saddle River, NJ. All rights reserved. This material is protected under all copyright laws as they currently exist. No portion of this material may be reproduced, in any form or by any means, without permission in writing from the publisher.

(b) d.f. $= (r - 1)(c - 1) = 4$

$\chi_0^2 = 7.779$; Reject H_0 if $\chi^2 > 7.779$.

(c) $\chi^2 \approx 5.610$

(d) Fail to reject H_0. There is not enough evidence at the 10% level to conclude that the subject matter and coauthorship are related.

21. H_0: The proportions are equal. (claim)

H_a: At least one of the proportions is different from the others.

d.f. $= (r - 1)(c - 1) = 1$

Critical value is 2.706; Reject H_0 if $\chi^2 > 2.706$.

$\chi^2 \approx 5.106$

Reject H_0. There is enough evidence at the 10% level to conclude that at least one of the proportions is different from the others.

10.3 COMPARING TWO VARIANCES

10.3 Try It Yourself Solutions

1a. $\alpha = 0.01$ **b.** $F = 5.42$

2a. $\alpha = 0.01$ **b.** $F = 18.31$

3a. H_0: $\sigma_1^2 \le \sigma_2^2$; H_a: $\sigma_1^2 > \sigma_2^2$ (claim)

b. $\alpha = 0.01$

c. d.f.$_N = n_1 - 1 = 24$
   d.f.$_D = n_2 - 1 = 19$

d. $F_0 = 2.92$; Reject H_0 if $F > 2.92$.

e. $F = \dfrac{s_1^2}{s_2^2} = \dfrac{180}{56} \approx 3.214$

f. Reject H_0.

g. There is enough evidence to support the claim.

4a. H_0: $\sigma_1 = \sigma_2$ (claim); H_a: $\sigma_1 \ne \sigma_2$

b. $\alpha = 0.01$

c. d.f.$_N = n_1 - 1 = 15$
   d.f.$_D = n_2 - 1 = 21$

d. $F_0 = 3.43$; Reject H_0 if $F > 3.43$.

e. $F = \dfrac{s_1^2}{s_2^2} = \dfrac{(0.95)^2}{(0.78)^2} \approx 1.483$

f. Fail to reject H_0.

g. There is not enough evidence to reject the claim.

© 2006 Pearson Education, Inc., Upper Saddle River, NJ. All rights reserved. This material is protected under all copyright laws as they currently exist. No portion of this material may be reproduced, in any form or by any means, without permission in writing from the publisher.

10.3 EXERCISE SOLUTIONS

1. Specify the level of significance α. Determine the degrees of freedom for the numerator and denominator. Use Table 7 to find the critical value F.

3. $F = 2.93$

5. $F = 5.32$

7. $F = 2.06$

9. $H_0: \sigma_1^2 \leq \sigma_2^2; H_a: \sigma_1^2 > \sigma_2^2$ (claim)

d.f.$_N = 4$
d.f.$_D = 5$

$F_0 = 3.52$; Reject H_0 if $F > 3.52$.

$$F = \frac{s_1^2}{s_2^2} = \frac{773}{765} \approx 1.010$$

Fail to reject H_0. There is not enough evidence to support the claim.

11. $H_0: \sigma_1^2 \leq \sigma_2^2$ (claim); $H_a: \sigma_1^2 > \sigma_2^2$

d.f.$_N = 10$
d.f.$_D = 9$

$F_0 = 5.26$; Reject H_0 if $F > 5.26$.

$$F = \frac{s_1^2}{s_2^2} = \frac{842}{836} \approx 1.007$$

Fail to reject H_0. There is not enough evidence to reject the claim.

13. $H_0: \sigma_1^2 = \sigma_2^2$ (claim); $H_a: \sigma_1^2 \neq \sigma_2^2$

d.f.$_N = 6$
d.f.$_D = 8$

$F_0 = 4.65$; Reject H_0 if $F > 4.65$.

$$F = \frac{s_1^2}{s_2^2} = \frac{5.2}{4.8} \approx 1.083$$

Fail to reject H_0. There is not enough evidence to reject the claim.

15. Population 1: Company B
Population 2: Company A

(a) $H_0: \sigma_1^2 \leq \sigma_2^2; H_a: \sigma_1^2 > \sigma_2^2$ (claim)

(b) d.f.$_N = 22$
d.f.$_D = 19$

$F_0 = 2.13$; Reject H_0 if $F > 2.13$.

(c) $F = \frac{s_1^2}{s_2^2} = \frac{2.8}{2.6} \approx 1.077$

(d) Fail to reject H_0. There is not enough evidence at the 5% level to support the Company A's claim that the variance of life of its appliances is less than the variance of life of Company B appliances.

© 2006 Pearson Education, Inc., Upper Saddle River, NJ. All rights reserved. This material is protected under all copyright laws as they currently exist. No portion of this material may be reproduced, in any form or by any means, without permission in writing from the publisher.

17. Population 1: District 1

Population 2: District 2

(a) $H_0: \sigma_1^2 = \sigma_2^2$ (claim); $H_a: \sigma_1^2 \neq \sigma_2^2$

(b) $\text{d.f.}_N = 11$

$\text{d.f.}_D = 13$

$F_0 = 2.63$; Reject H_0 if $F > 2.63$.

(c) $F = \dfrac{s_1^2}{s_2^2} = \dfrac{(27.7)^2}{(26.1)^2} \approx 1.126$

(d) Fail to reject H_0. There is not enough evidence at the 10% level to reject the claim that the standard deviation of physical science assessment test scores for eighth-grade students is the same in Districts 1 and 2.

19. Population 1: Before new admissions procedure

Population 2: After new admissions procedure

(a) $H_0: \sigma_1^2 \leq \sigma_2^2$; $H_a: \sigma_1^2 > \sigma_2^2$ (claim)

(b) $\text{d.f.}_N = 24$

$\text{d.f.}_D = 20$

$F_0 = 1.77$; Reject H_0 if $F > 1.77$.

(c) $F = \dfrac{s_1^2}{s_2^2} = \dfrac{(0.7)^2}{(0.5)^2} \approx 1.96$

(d) Reject H_0. There is enough evidence at the 10% level to support the claim that the standard deviation of waiting times has decreased.

21. (a) Population 1: California

Population 2: New York

$H_0: \sigma_1^2 \leq \sigma_2^2$; $H_a: \sigma_1^2 > \sigma_2^2$ (claim)

(b) $\text{d.f.}_N = 15$

$\text{d.f.}_D = 16$

$F_0 = 2.35$; Reject H_0 if $F > 2.35$.

(c) $F = \dfrac{s_1^2}{s_2^2} = \dfrac{(13,900)^2}{(8,800)^2} \approx 2.495$

(d) Reject H_0. There is enough evidence at the 5% level to conclude the standard deviation of annual salaries for actuaries is greater in California than in New York.

23. Right-tailed: $F_R = 14.73$

Left-tailed:

(1) $\text{d.f.}_N = 3$ and $\text{d.f.}_D = 6$

(2) $F = 6.60$

(3) Critical value is $\dfrac{1}{F} = \dfrac{1}{6.60} \approx 0.152$.

25. $\dfrac{s_1^2}{s_2^2} F_L < \dfrac{\sigma_1^2}{\sigma_2^2} < \dfrac{s_1^2}{s_2^2} F_R \rightarrow \dfrac{9.61}{8.41} \, 0.32 < \dfrac{\sigma_1^2}{\sigma_2^2} < \dfrac{9.61}{8.41} \, 3.36 \rightarrow 0.366 < \dfrac{\sigma_1^2}{\sigma_2^2} < 3.839$

© 2006 Pearson Education, Inc., Upper Saddle River, NJ. All rights reserved. This material is protected under all copyright laws as they currently exist. No portion of this material may be reproduced, in any form or by any means, without permission in writing from the publisher.

10.4 ANALYSIS OF VARIANCE

10.4 Try It Yourself Solutions

1a. H_0: $\mu_1 = \mu_2 = \mu_3 = \mu_4$
H_a: At least one mean is different from the others.

b. $\alpha = 0.05$

c. $\text{d.f.}_N = 3$
$\text{d.f.}_D = 14$

d. $F_0 = 3.34$; Reject H_0 if $F > 3.34$.

e.

Variation	Sum of Squares	Degrees of Freedom	Mean Squares	F
Between	549.8	3	183.3	4.22
Within	608.0	14	43.4	

$F \approx 4.22$

f. Reject H_0.

g. There is enough evidence to conclude that at least one mean is different from the others.

2a. Enter the data.

b. H_0: $\mu_1 = \mu_2 = \mu_3 = \mu_4$
H_a: At least one mean is different from the others.

Variation	Sum of Squares	Degrees of Freedom	Mean Squares	F
Between	0.584	3	0.195	1.34
Within	4.360	30	0.145	

$F = 1.34 \rightarrow P\text{-value} = 0.280$

c. Fail to reject H_0.

d. There is not enough evidence to conclude that at least one mean is different from the others.

10.4 EXERCISE SOLUTIONS

1. H_0: $\mu_1 = \mu_2 = \ldots = \mu_k$
H_a: At least one of the means is different from the others.

3. MS_B measures the differences related to the treatment given to each sample.
MS_W measures the differences related to entries within the same sample.

5. (a) H_0: $\mu_1 = \mu_2 = \mu_3$
H_a: At least one mean is different from the others. (claim)

(b) $\text{d.f.}_N = k - 1 = 2$
$\text{d.f.}_D = N - k = 21$

$F_0 = 3.47$; Reject H_0 if $F > 3.47$.

© 2006 Pearson Education, Inc., Upper Saddle River, NJ. All rights reserved. This material is protected under all copyright laws as they currently exist. No portion of this material may be reproduced, in any form or by any means, without permission in writing from the publisher.

(c)

Variation	Sum of Squares	Degrees of Freedom	Mean Squares	F
Between	1.253	2	0.627	0.771
Within	17.067	21	0.813	

$F \approx 0.771$

(d) Fail to reject H_0. There is not enough evidence at the 5% level to conclude that the mean costs per month are different.

7. (a) $H_0: \mu_1 = \mu_2 = \mu_3$ (claim)

H_a: At least one mean is different from the others.

(b) $\text{d.f.}_N = k - 1 = 2$

$\text{d.f.}_D = N - k = 12$

$F_0 = 2.8l$; Reject H_0 if $F > 2.81$.

(c)

Variation	Sum of Squares	Degrees of Freedom	Mean Squares	F
Between	302.6	2	151.3	1.77
Within	1024.2	12	85.4	

$F \approx 1.77$

(d) Fail to reject H_0. There is not enough evidence at the 10% level to reject the claim that the mean prices are all the same for the three types of treatment.

9. (a) $H_0: \mu_1 = \mu_2 = \mu_3 = \mu_4$ (claim)

H_a: At least one mean is different from the others.

(b) $\text{d.f.}_N = k - 1 = 3$

$\text{d.f.}_D = N - k = 29$

$F_0 = 4.54$; Reject H_0 if $F > 4.54$.

(c)

Variation	Sum of Squares	Degrees of Freedom	Mean Squares	F
Between	37.703	3	12.568	4.979
Within	73.206	29	2.524	

$F \approx 4.979$

(d) Reject H_0. There is enough evidence at the 1% level to reject the claim that the mean number of days patients spend in the hospital is the same for all four regions.

11. (a) $H_0: \mu_1 = \mu_2 = \mu_3 = \mu_4$ (claim)

H_a: At least one mean is different from the others.

(b) $\text{d.f.}_N = k - 1 = 3$

$\text{d.f.}_D = N - k = 43$

$F_0 = 2.22$; Reject H_0 if $F > 2.22$.

(c)

Variation	Sum of Squares	Degrees of Freedom	Mean Squares	F
Between	15,532	3	5177	3.04
Within	73,350	43	1706	

$F \approx 3.04$

© 2006 Pearson Education, Inc., Upper Saddle River, NJ. All rights reserved. This material is protected under all copyright laws as they currently exist. No portion of this material may be reproduced, in any form or by any means, without permission in writing from the publisher.

(d) Reject H_0. There is not enough evidence at the 10% level to reject the claim that the mean price is the same for all four cities.

13. (a) H_0: $\mu_1 = \mu_2 = \mu_3 = \mu_4$

H_a: At least one mean is different from the others. (claim)

(b) d.f.$_N = k - 1 = 3$

d.f.$_D = N - k = 26$

$F_0 = 2.31$; Reject H_0 if $F > 2.31$

(c)

Variation	Sum of Squares	Degrees of Freedom	Mean Squares	F
Between	877,803,059	3	292,601,020	6.36
Within	1,195,691,981	26	45,988,153	

$F \approx 6.36$

(d) Reject H_0. There is enough evidence at the 10% level to conclude that at least one of the mean prices is different.

15. (a) H_0: $\mu_1 = \mu_2 = \mu_3$ (claim)

H_a: At least one mean is different from the others.

(b) d.f.$_N = k - 1 = 3$

d.f.$_D = N - k = 19$

$F_0 = 5.01$; Reject H_0 if $F > 5.01$.

(c)

Variation	Sum of Squares	Degrees of Freedom	Mean Squares	F
Between	1,711.791	3	570.597	0.19
Within	57,303.65	19	3015.982	

$F \approx 0.19$

(d) Fail to reject H_0. There is not enough evidence at the 1% level to reject the claim that the mean numbers of female students are equal for all grades.

17. H_0: Advertising medium has no effect on mean rating.

H_a: Advertising medium has an effect on mean ratings.

H_0: Length of ad has no effect on mean ratings.

H_a: Length of ad has an effect on mean ratings.

H_0: There is no interaction effect between advertising medium and length of ad on mean ratings.

H_a: There is an interaction effect between advertising medium and length of ad on mean ratings.

Source	d.f.	SS	MS	F	P
Ad medium	1	1.25	1.25	0.57	0.459
Length of ad	1	0.45	0.45	0.21	0.655
Interaction	1	0.45	0.45	0.21	0.655
Error	16	34.80	2.17		
Total	19	36.95			

None of the null hypotheses can be rejected at the 10% level.

© 2006 Pearson Education, Inc., Upper Saddle River, NJ. All rights reserved. This material is protected under all copyright laws as they currently exist. No portion of this material may be reproduced, in any form or by any means, without permission in writing from the publisher.

19. H_0: Age has no effect on mean GPA.

H_a: Age has an effect on mean GPA.

H_0: Gender has no effect on mean GPA.

H_a: Gender has an effect on mean GPA.

H_0: There is no interaction effect between age and gender on mean GPA.

H_a: There is an interaction effect between age and gender on mean GPA.

Source	d.f.	SS	MS	F	P
Age	3	0.41	0.14	0.12	0.948
Gender	1	0.18	0.18	0.16	0.697
Interaction	3	0.29	0.10	0.08	0.968
Error	16	18.66	1.17		
Total	23	19.55			

None of the null hypotheses can be rejected at the 10% level.

21.

	Mean	Size
Pop 1	15.62	13
Pop 2	11.60	13
Pop 3	14.16	13
Pop 4	11.81	13

$SS_w = 1024.5$

$\Sigma(n_i - 1) = N - k = 48$

$F_0 = 2.20 \rightarrow CV_{\text{Scheffé}} = 2.20(4 - 1) = 6.60$

$$\frac{(\bar{x}_1 - \bar{x}_2)^2}{\dfrac{SS_w}{\Sigma(n_i - 1)}\left[\dfrac{1}{n_1} + \dfrac{1}{n_2}\right]} \approx 4.927 \rightarrow \text{No difference}$$

$$\frac{(\bar{x}_1 - \bar{x}_3)^2}{\dfrac{SS_w}{\Sigma(n_i - 1)}\left[\dfrac{1}{n_1} + \dfrac{1}{n_3}\right]} \approx 0.650 \rightarrow \text{No difference}$$

$$\frac{(\bar{x}_1 - \bar{x}_4)^2}{\dfrac{SS_w}{\Sigma(n_i - 1)}\left[\dfrac{1}{n_1} + \dfrac{1}{n_4}\right]} \approx 4.426 \rightarrow \text{No difference}$$

$$\frac{(\bar{x}_2 - \bar{x}_3)^2}{\dfrac{SS_w}{\Sigma(n_i - 1)}\left[\dfrac{1}{n_2} + \dfrac{1}{n_3}\right]} \approx 1.998 \rightarrow \text{No difference}$$

$$\frac{(\bar{x}_2 - \bar{x}_4)^2}{\dfrac{SS_w}{\Sigma(n_i - 1)}\left[\dfrac{1}{n_2} + \dfrac{1}{n_4}\right]} \approx 0.013 \rightarrow \text{No difference}$$

$$\frac{(\bar{x}_3 - \bar{x}_4)^2}{\dfrac{SS_w}{\Sigma(n_i - 1)}\left[\dfrac{1}{n_3} + \dfrac{1}{n_4}\right]} \approx 1.684 \rightarrow \text{No difference}$$

© 2006 Pearson Education, Inc., Upper Saddle River, NJ. All rights reserved. This material is protected under all copyright laws as they currently exist. No portion of this material may be reproduced, in any form or by any means, without permission in writing from the publisher.

23.

	Mean	Size
Pop 1	135.3	10
Pop 2	156.373	11
Pop 3	65.478	9
Pop 4	73.62	10

$SSw \approx 86{,}713.313$

$\Sigma(n_i - 1) = N - k = 36$

$F_0 = 4.38 \rightarrow CV_{\text{Scheffé}} = 4.38(4 - 1) = 13.14$

$$\frac{(\bar{x}_1 - \bar{x}_2)^2}{\dfrac{SS_w}{\Sigma(n_i - 1)}\left[\dfrac{1}{n_1} + \dfrac{1}{n_2}\right]} \approx 0.966 \rightarrow \text{No difference}$$

$$\frac{(\bar{x}_1 - \bar{x}_3)^2}{\dfrac{SS_w}{\Sigma(n_i - 1)}\left[\dfrac{1}{n_1} + \dfrac{1}{n_3}\right]} \approx 9.587 \rightarrow \text{No difference}$$

$$\frac{(\bar{x}_1 - \bar{x}_4)^2}{\dfrac{SS_w}{\Sigma(n_i - 1)}\left[\dfrac{1}{n_1} + \dfrac{1}{n_4}\right]} \approx 7.897 \rightarrow \text{No difference}$$

$$\frac{(\bar{x}_2 - \bar{x}_3)^2}{\dfrac{SS_w}{\Sigma(n_i - 1)}\left[\dfrac{1}{n_2} + \dfrac{1}{n_3}\right]} \approx 16.979 \rightarrow \text{Significant difference}$$

$$\frac{(\bar{x}_2 - \bar{x}_4)^2}{\dfrac{SS_w}{\Sigma(n_i - 1)}\left[\dfrac{1}{n_2} + \dfrac{1}{n_4}\right]} \approx 14.892 \rightarrow \text{Significant difference}$$

$$\frac{(\bar{x}_3 - \bar{x}_4)^2}{\dfrac{SS_w}{\Sigma(n_i - 1)}\left[\dfrac{1}{n_3} + \dfrac{1}{n_4}\right]} \approx 0.130 \rightarrow \text{No difference}$$

CHAPTER 10 REVIEW EXERCISE SOLUTIONS

1. Claimed distribution:

Category	Distribution
New parents	25%
Old/New	25%
Old/Recurring	50%

H_0: Distribution of office visits is as shown in table above.

H_a: Distribution of office visits differs from the claimed distribution.

$\chi_0^2 = 5.991$

Category	Distribution	Observed	Expected	$\dfrac{(O - E)^2}{E}$
New parents	25%	97	174	34.075
Old/New	25%	142	174	5.885
Old/Recurring	50%	457	348	34.141
		696		74.101

© 2006 Pearson Education, Inc., Upper Saddle River, NJ. All rights reserved. This material is protected under all copyright laws as they currently exist. No portion of this material may be reproduced, in any form or by any means, without permission in writing from the publisher.

3. Claimed distribution:

Price	Distribution
Less than $1.50	6%
$1.50–$1.99	22%
$2.00	29%
$2.01–$2.49	5%
$2.50 or more	38%

H_0: Distribution of prices is as shown in the table above.

H_a: Distribution of prices differs from the claimed distribution.

$\chi_0^2 = 7.779$

Price	Distribution	Observed	Expected	$\frac{(O - E)^2}{E}$
Less than $1.50	6%	54	48	0.750
$1.50–$1.99	22%	172	176	0.091
$2.00	29%	244	232	0.621
$2.01–$2.49	5%	28	40	3.600
$2.50 or more	38%	302	304	0.013
		800		5.075

$\chi^2 \approx 5.075$

Fail to reject H_0. There is not enough evidence at the 10% level to reject the claimed distribution.

5. (a) Expected frequencies:

	HS–did not complete	HS complete	College 1–3 years	College 4+ years	Total
25–44	13,836.62	27,733.60	20,686.43	20,962.35	83,219
45+	15,047.38	30,160.40	22,496.57	22,796.65	90,501
Total	28,884	57,894	43,183	43,759	173,720

(b) H_0: Education is independent of age.

H_a: Education is dependent on age.

d.f. = 3

$\chi_0^2 = 6.251$

$\chi^2 = \sum \frac{(O - E)^2}{E} \approx 2,904,408$

Reject H_0.

(c) There is enough evidence at the 10% level of significance to conclude that education level of people in the U.S. and their age are dependent.

7. (a) Expected frequencies:

Gender	\multicolumn{6}{c}{Age Group}	Total
	16–20	21–30	31–40	41–50	51–60	61+	Total
Male	143.76	284.17	274.14	237.37	147.10	43.46	1130
Female	71.24	140.83	135.86	117.63	72.90	21.54	560
Total	215	425	410	355	220	65	1690

© 2006 Pearson Education, Inc., Upper Saddle River, NJ. All rights reserved. This material is protected under all copyright laws as they currently exist. No portion of this material may be reproduced, in any form or by any means, without permission in writing from the publisher.

(b) H_0: Gender is independent of age.

H_a: Gender and age are dependent.

d.f. = 5

$\chi_0^2 = 11.071$

$\chi^2 = \sum \dfrac{(O - E)^2}{E} = 9.951$

Fail to reject H_0.

(c) There is not enough evidence at the 10% level to conclude that gender and age are dependent.

9. $F_0 \approx 2.295$

11. $F_0 = 2.39$

13. H_0: $\sigma_1^2 \le \sigma_2^2$ (claim); H_a: $\sigma_1^2 > \sigma_2^2$

d.f.$_N$ = 15

d.f.$_D$ = 20

$F_0 = 3.09$; Reject H_0 if $F > 3.09$.

$F = \dfrac{s_1^2}{s_2^2} = \dfrac{653}{270} \approx 2.419$

Fail to reject H_0. There is not enough evidence to reject the claim.

15. Population 1: Garfield County

Population 2: Kay County

H_0: $\sigma_1^2 \le \sigma_2^2$; H_a: $\sigma_1^2 > \sigma_2^2$ (claim)

d.f.$_N$ = 20

d.f.$_D$ = 15

$F_0 = 1.92$; Reject H_0 if $F > 1.92$.

$F = \dfrac{s_1^2}{s_2^2} = \dfrac{(0.76)^2}{(0.58)^2} \approx 1.717$

Fail to reject H_0. There is not enough evidence at the 10% level to support the claim that the variation in wheat production is greater in Garfield County than in Kay County.

17. Population 1: Male $\rightarrow s_1^2 = 18{,}486.26$

Population 2: Female $\rightarrow s_2^2 = 12{,}102.78$

H_0: $\sigma_1^2 = \sigma_2^2$; H_a: $\sigma_1^2 \ne \sigma_2^2$ (claim)

d.f.$_N$ = 13

d.f.$_D$ = 8

$F_0 = 6.94$; Reject H_0 if $F > 6.94$.

$F = \dfrac{s_1^2}{s_2^2} = \dfrac{18{,}486.26}{12{,}102.78} \approx 1.527$

Fail to reject H_0. There is not enough evidence at the 1% level to support the claim that the test score variance for females is different than that for males.

© 2006 Pearson Education, Inc., Upper Saddle River, NJ. All rights reserved. This material is protected under all copyright laws as they currently exist. No portion of this material may be reproduced, in any form or by any means, without permission in writing from the publisher.

19. $H_0: \mu_1 = \mu_2 = \mu_3 = \mu_4$

H_a: At least one mean is different from the others. (claim)

d.f.$_N = k - 1 = 3$
d.f.$_D = N - k = 28$

$F_0 = 2.29$; Reject H_0 if $F > 2.29$.

Variation	Sum of Squares	Degrees of Freedom	Mean Squares	F
Between	2,318,032	3	772,677	6.60
Within	3,277,311	28	117,047	

$F \approx 6.60$

Reject H_0. There is enough evidence at the 10% level to conclude that the mean residential energy expenditures are not the same for all four regions.

CHAPTER 10 QUIZ SOLUTIONS

1. (a) Population 1: San Jose $\rightarrow s_1^2 \approx 429.984$
Population 2: Dallas $\rightarrow s_2^2 \approx 112.779$

$H_0: \sigma_1^2 = \sigma_2^2$; $H_a: \sigma_1^2 \neq \sigma_2^2$ (claim)

(b) $\alpha = 0.01$

(cd) d.f.$_N = 12$
d.f.$_D = 17$

$F_0 = 3.97$; Reject H_0 if $F > 3.97$.

(e) $F = \dfrac{s_1^2}{s_2^2} = \dfrac{429.984}{112.779} \approx 3.813$

(f) Fail to reject H_0.

(g) There is not enough evidence at the 1% level to conclude that the variances in annual wages for San Jose, CA and Dallas, TX are different.

2. (a) $H_0: \mu_1 = \mu_2 = \mu_3$ (claim)
H_a: At least one mean is different from the others.

(b) $\alpha = 0.10$

(cd) d.f.$_N = k - 1 = 2$
d.f.$_D = N - k = 44$

$F_0 = 2.43$; Reject H_0 if $F > 2.43$.

Variation	Sum of Squares	Degrees of Freedom	Mean Squares	F
Between	2676	2	1338	7.39
Within	7962	44	181	

(e) $F \approx 7.39$

(f) Reject H_0.

(g) There is enough evidence at the 10% level to conclude that the mean annual wages for the three cities are not all equal.

© 2006 Pearson Education, Inc., Upper Saddle River, NJ. All rights reserved. This material is protected under all copyright laws as they currently exist. No portion of this material may be reproduced, in any form or by any means, without permission in writing from the publisher.

3. (a) Claimed distribution:

Education	25 & Over
Not a HS graduate	16.6%
HS graduate	33.3%
Some college, no degree	17.3%
Associate degree	7.5%
Bachelor's degree	17.0%
Advanced degree	8.2%

H_0: Distribution of educational achievement for people in the United States aged 35–44 is as shown in table above.

H_a: Distribution of educational achievement for people in the United States aged 35–44 differs from the claimed distribution.

(b) $\alpha = 0.01$

(cd) $\chi_0^2 = 15.086$; Reject H_0 if $\chi^2 > 15.086$.

(e)

Education	25 & Over	Observed	Expected	$\frac{(O - E)^2}{E}$
Not a HS graduate	16.6%	37	49.966	3.365
HS graduate	33.3%	102	100.233	0.0312
Some college, no degree	17.3%	59	52.073	0.921
Associate degree	7.5%	27	22.575	0.867
Bachelor's degree	17.0%	51	51.17	0.001
Advanced degree	8.2%	25	24.682	0.004
		301		5.189

$\chi^2 = 5.189$

(f) Fail to reject H_0.

(g) There is not enough evidence at the 1% level to conclude that the distribution of educational achievement for people in the United States aged 35–44 differs from the claimed distribution.

4. (a) Claimed distribution:

Education	25 & Over
Not a HS graduate	16.6%
HS graduate	33.3%
Some college, no degree	17.3%
Associate degree	7.5%
Bachelor's degree	17.0%
Advanced degree	8.2%

H_0: Distribution of educational achievement for people in the United States aged 65–74 is as shown in table above.

H_a: Distribution of educational achievement for people in the United States aged 65–74 differs from the claimed distribution.

(b) $\alpha = 0.05$

(c) $\chi_0^2 = 11.071$

(d) Reject H_0 if $\chi^2 > 11.071$.

© 2006 Pearson Education, Inc., Upper Saddle River, NJ. All rights reserved. This material is protected under all copyright laws as they currently exist. No portion of this material may be reproduced, in any form or by any means, without permission in writing from the publisher.

(e)

Education	25 & Over	Observed	Expected	$\frac{(O-E)^2}{E}$
Not a HS graduate	16.6%	124	67.562	47.146
HS graduate	33.3%	148	135.531	1.147
Some college, no degree	17.3%	61	70.411	1.258
Associate degree	7.5%	15	30.525	7.896
Bachelor's degree	17.0%	37	69.19	14.976
Advanced degree	8.3%	22	33.781	4.109
		407		76.532

$\chi^2 = 76.532$

(f) Reject H_0.

(g) There is enough evidence at the 5% level to conclude that the distribution of educational achievement for people in the United States aged 65–74 differs from the claimed distribution.

© 2006 Pearson Education, Inc., Upper Saddle River, NJ. All rights reserved. This material is protected under all copyright laws as they currently exist. No portion of this material may be reproduced, in any form or by any means, without permission in writing from the publisher.

Nonparametric Tests

11.1 Try It Yourself Solutions

1a. H_0: median ≤ 2500; H_a: median > 2500 (claim)

b. $\alpha = 0.025$

c. $n = 22$

d. The critical value is 5.

e. $x = 10$

f. Fail to reject H_0.

g. There is not enough evidence to support the claim.

2a. H_0: median $= 134{,}500$ (claim); H_a: median $\neq 134{,}500$

b. $\alpha = 0.10$

c. $n = 81$

d. The critical value is $z_0 = -1.645$.

e. $x = 30$

$$z = \frac{(x + 0.5) - 0.5(n)}{\dfrac{\sqrt{n}}{2}} = \frac{(30 + 0.5) - 0.5(81)}{\dfrac{\sqrt{81}}{2}} = \frac{-10}{4.5} = -2.22$$

f. Reject H_0.

g. There is enough evidence to reject the claim.

3a. H_0: The number of colds will not decrease.
H_a: The number of colds will decrease. (claim)

b. $\alpha = 0.05$

c. $n = 11$

d. The critical value is 2.

e. $x = 2$

f. Reject H_0.

g. There is enough evidence to support the claim.

11.1 EXERCISE SOLUTIONS

1. A nonparametric test is a hypothesis test that does not require any specific conditions concerning the shape of populations or the value of any population parameters.

A nonparametric test is usually easier to perform than its corresponding parametric test, but the nonparametric test is usually less efficient.

© 2006 Pearson Education, Inc., Upper Saddle River, NJ. All rights reserved. This material is protected under all copyright laws as they currently exist.
No portion of this material may be reproduced, in any form or by any means, without permission in writing from the publisher.

3. (a) H_0: median $\leq$ 200; H_a: median > 200 (claim)

    (b) Critical value is 1.

    (c) $x = 5$

    (d) Fail to reject H_0.

    (e) There is not enough evidence at the 1% level to support the claim that the median amount of new credit card charges for the previous month was more than $200.

5. (a) H_0: median $\leq$ 148,000 (claim); H_a: median > 148,000

    (b) Critical value is 1.

    (c) $x = 3$

    (d) Fail to reject H_0.

    (e) There is not enough evidence at the 5% level to reject the claim that the median sales price of new privately owned one-family homes sold in the past year is $148,000 or less.

7. (a) H_0: median $\geq$ 1900 (claim); H_a: median < 1900

    (b) Critical value is $z_0 = -2.055$.

    (c) $x = 36$

$$z = \frac{(x + 0.5) - 0.5(n)}{\frac{\sqrt{n}}{2}} = \frac{(36 + 0.5) - 0.5(104)}{\frac{\sqrt{104}}{2}} = \frac{-15.5}{5.099} \approx -3.040$$

    (d) Reject H_0.

    (e) There is enough evidence at the 2% level to reject the claim that the median amount of credit card debt for families holding such debts is at least $1900.

9. (a) H_0: median $\leq$ 34; H_a: median > 34 (claim)

    (b) Critical value is 3.

    (c) $x = 8$

    (d) Fail to reject H_0.

    (e) There is not enough evidence at the 1% level to support the claim that the median age of recipients of social science doctorates is greater than 34.

11. (a) H_0: median $=$ 4 (claim); H_a: median $\neq$ 4

    (b) Critical value is $z_0 = -1.96$.

    (c) $x = 15$

$$z = \frac{(x + 0.5) - 0.5(n)}{\frac{\sqrt{n}}{2}} = \frac{(15 + 0.5) - 0.5(47)}{\frac{\sqrt{47}}{2}} = \frac{-8}{3.429} \approx -2.334$$

    (d) Reject H_0.

    (e) There is enough evidence at the 5% level to reject the claim that the median number of rooms in renter-occupied units is 4.

13. (a) H_0: median $=$ $11.63 (claim); H_a: median $\neq$ $11.63

    (b) Critical value is $z_0 = -2.575$.

© 2006 Pearson Education, Inc., Upper Saddle River, NJ. All rights reserved. This material is protected under all copyright laws as they currently exist. No portion of this material may be reproduced, in any form or by any means, without permission in writing from the publisher.

(c) $x = 16$

$$z = \frac{(x + 0.5) - 0.5(n)}{\frac{\sqrt{n}}{2}} = \frac{(16 + 0.5) - 0.5(39)}{\frac{\sqrt{39}}{2}} = \frac{-3}{3.1225} \approx -0.961$$

(d) Fail to reject H_0.

(e) There is not enough evidence at the 1% level to reject the claim that the median hourly earnings of male workers paid hourly rates is $11.63.

15. (a) H_0: The headache hours have not decreased.

$\quad\ H_a$: The headache hours have decreased. (claim)

(b) Critical value is 1.

(c) $x = 3$

(d) Fail to reject H_0.

(e) There is not enough evidence at the 5% level to support the claim that the daily headache hours were reduced after the soft tissue therapy and spinal manipulation.

17. (a) H_0: The SAT scores have not improved.

$\quad\ H_a$: The SAT scores have improved. (claim)

(b) Critical value is 2.

(c) $x = 4$

(d) Fail to reject H_0.

(e) There is not enough evidence at the 5% level to support the claim that the verbal SAT scores improved.

19. (a) H_0: The proportion of companies offering transportation is equal to the proportion of companies that do not. (claim)

$\quad\ H_a$: The proportion of companies offering transportation is not equal to the proportion of companies that do not.

Critical value is 5.

$\alpha = 0.05$

$x = 8$

Fail to reject H_0.

(b) There is not enough evidence at the 5% level to reject the claim that the proportion of companies providing transportation home is equal to the proportions of companies that do not.

21. (a) H_0: median ≤ 530 (claim); H_a: median > 530

(b) Critical value is $z_0 = 2.33$.

(c) $x = 29$

$$z = \frac{(x + 0.5) - 0.5(n)}{\frac{\sqrt{n}}{2}} = \frac{(29 + 0.5) - 0.5(47)}{\frac{\sqrt{47}}{2}} = \frac{6}{3.428} \approx 1.459$$

(d) Fail to reject H_0. There is not enough evidence at the 1% level to reject the claim that the median weekly earnings of female workers is less than or equal to $530.

© 2006 Pearson Education, Inc., Upper Saddle River, NJ. All rights reserved. This material is protected under all copyright laws as they currently exist. No portion of this material may be reproduced, in any form or by any means, without permission in writing from the publisher.

23. (a) H_0: median ≤ 25.3; H_a: median > 25.3 (claim)

(b) Critical value is $z_0 = 1.645$.

(c) $x = 38$

$$z = \frac{(x + 0.5) - 0.5(n)}{\frac{\sqrt{n}}{2}} = \frac{(38 + 0.5) - 0.5(60)}{\frac{\sqrt{60}}{2}} = \frac{8.5}{3.873} \approx 1.936$$

(d) Reject H_0. There is enough evidence at the 5% level to support the claim that the median age of first-time brides is greater than 25.3 years.

11.2 THE WILCOXON TESTS

11.2 Try It Yourself Solutions

1a. H_0: The water repellent is not effective.

H_a: The water repellent is effective. (claim)

b. $\alpha = 0.01$

c. $n = 11$

d. Critical value is 7.

e.

No repellent	Repellent applied	Difference	Absolute value	Rank	Signed rank
8	15	−7	7	11	−11
7	12	−5	5	9	−9
7	11	−4	4	7.5	−7.5
4	6	−2	2	3.5	−3.5
6	6	0	0	—	—
10	8	2	2	3.5	3.5
9	8	1	1	1.5	1.5
5	6	−1	1	1.5	−1.5
9	12	−3	3	5.5	−5.5
11	8	3	3	5.5	5.5
8	14	−6	6	10	−10
4	8	−4	4	7.5	−7.5

Sum of negative ranks $= -55.5$

Sum of positive ranks $= 10.5$

$w_s = 10.5$

f. Reject H_0.

g. There is enough evidence at the 1% level to support the claim.

2a. H_0: There is no difference in the claims paid by the companies.

H_a: There is a difference in the claims paid by the companies. (claim)

b. $\alpha = 0.05$

c. The critical values are $z_0 = \pm 1.96$.

d. $n_1 = 12$ and $n_2 = 12$

© 2006 Pearson Education, Inc., Upper Saddle River, NJ. All rights reserved. This material is protected under all copyright laws as they currently exist. No portion of this material may be reproduced, in any form or by any means, without permission in writing from the publisher.

e.

Ordered data	Sample	Rank		Ordered data	Sample	Rank
1.7	B	1		5.3	B	13
1.8	B	2		5.6	B	14
2.2	B	3		5.8	A	15
2.5	A	4		6.0	A	16
3.0	A	5.5		6.2	A	17
3.0	B	5.5		6.3	A	18
3.4	B	7		6.5	A	19
3.9	A	8		7.3	B	20
4.1	B	9		7.4	A	21
4.4	B	10		9.9	A	22
4.5	A	11		10.6	A	23
4.7	B	12		10.8	B	24

R = sum ranks of company B = 120.5

f. $\mu_R = \dfrac{n_1(n_1 + n_2 + 1)}{2} = \dfrac{12(12 + 12 + 1)}{2} = 150$

$\sigma_R = \sqrt{\dfrac{n_1 n_2(n_1 + n_2 + 1)}{12}} = \sqrt{\dfrac{(12)(12)(12 + 12 + 1)}{12}} \approx 17.321$

$z = \dfrac{R - \mu_R}{\sigma_R} = \dfrac{120.5 - 150}{17.321} \approx -1.703$

g. Fail to reject H_0.

h. There is not enough evidence to conclude that there is a difference in the claims paid by both companies.

11.2 EXERCISE SOLUTIONS

1. The Wilcoxon signed-rank test is used to determine whether two dependent samples were selected from populations having the same distribution. The Wilcoxon rank sum test is used to determine whether two independent samples were selected from populations having the same distribution.

3. (a) H_0: There is no reduction in diastolic blood pressure. (claim)

H_a: There is a reduction in diastolic blood pressure.

(b) Wilcoxon signed-rank test

(c) Critical value is 10.

(d) $w_s = 17$

(e) Fail to reject H_0.

(f) There is not enough evidence at the 1% level to reject the claim that there was no reduction in diastolic blood pressure.

5. (a) H_0: There is no difference in the earnings.

H_a: There is a difference in the earnings. (claim)

(b) Wilcoxon rank sum test

(c) The critical values are $z_0 = \pm 1.96$.

© 2006 Pearson Education, Inc., Upper Saddle River, NJ. All rights reserved. This material is protected under all copyright laws as they currently exist. No portion of this material may be reproduced, in any form or by any means, without permission in writing from the publisher.

(d) $R = 55$

$$\mu_R = \frac{n_1(n_1 + n_2 + 1)}{2} = \frac{11(11 + 10 + 1)}{2} = 110$$

$$\sigma_R = \sqrt{\frac{n_1 n_2(n_1 + n_2 + 1)}{12}} = \sqrt{\frac{(11)(10)(11 + 10 + 1)}{12}} \approx 14.201$$

$$z = \frac{R - \mu_R}{\sigma_R} = \frac{55 - 110}{14.201} \approx -3.873$$

(e) Reject H_0.

(f) There is enough evidence at the 5% level to support the claim that there is a difference in the earnings.

7. (a) H_0: There is not a difference in salaries.

   H_a: There is a difference in salaries. (claim)

(b) Wilcoxon rank sum test

(c) The critical values are $z_0 = \pm 1.96$.

(d) $R = 118.5$

$$\mu_R = \frac{n_1(n_1 + n_2 + 1)}{2} = \frac{12(12 + 12 + 1)}{2} = 150$$

$$\sigma_R = \sqrt{\frac{n_1 n_2(n_1 + n_2 + 1)}{12}} = \sqrt{\frac{(12)(12)(12 + 12 + 1)}{12}} \approx 17.321$$

$$z = \frac{R - \mu_R}{\sigma_R} = \frac{118.5 - 150}{17.321} \approx -1.819$$

(e) Fail to reject H_0.

(f) There is not enough evidence at the 5% level to support the claim that there is a difference in salaries.

9. H_0: The fuel additive does not improve gas mileage.

   H_a: The fuel additive does improve gas mileage. (claim)

   Critical value is $z_0 = 1.282$.

$$w_s = 43.5$$

$$z = \frac{w_s - \frac{n(n + 1)}{4}}{\sqrt{\frac{n(n + 1)(2n + 1)}{24}}} = \frac{43.5 - \frac{32(32 + 1)}{4}}{\sqrt{\frac{32(32 + 1)[(2)32 + 1]}{24}}} = \frac{-220.5}{\sqrt{2860}} \approx -4.123$$

Note: $n = 32$ because one of the differences is zero and should be discarded.

Reject H_0. There is enough evidence at the 10% level to conclude that the gas mileage is improved.

11.3 THE KRUSKAL-WALLIS TEST

11.3 Try It Yourself Solutions

1a. H_0: There is no difference in the salaries in the three states.

   H_a: There is a difference in the salaries in the three states. (claim)

© 2006 Pearson Education, Inc., Upper Saddle River, NJ. All rights reserved. This material is protected under all copyright laws as they currently exist. No portion of this material may be reproduced, in any form or by any means, without permission in writing from the publisher.

b. $\alpha = 0.10$

c. d.f. $= k - 1 = 2$

d. Critical value is $\chi_0^2 = 4.605$; Reject H_0 if $\chi^2 > 4.605$.

e.

Ordered data	State	Rank	Ordered data	State	Rank
25.57	CT	1	40.31	CA	16
26.42	CA	2	41.33	CA	17
29.73	NJ	3	43.26	NJ	18
29.86	CT	4	43.89	NJ	19
30.00	CT	5	44.57	NJ	20
33.68	CA	6.5	45.04	CT	21
33.68	CT	6.5	45.29	CT	22
33.91	NJ	8	46.55	CA	23
34.29	NJ	9	46.72	NJ	24
36.35	NJ	10	47.17	CA	25
36.55	CA	11	48.46	CA	26
37.18	CA	12	50.16	NJ	27
37.24	NJ	13	51.03	CT	28
37.39	CT	14	57.07	CT	29
38.36	CA	15	61.46	CT	30

$R_1 = 153.5 \quad R_2 = 160.5 \quad R_3 = 151$

f. $H = \dfrac{12}{N(N+1)}\left(\dfrac{R_1^2}{n_1} + \dfrac{R_2^2}{n_2} + \dfrac{R_3^2}{n_3}\right) - 3(N+1)$

$= \dfrac{12}{30(30+1)}\left(\dfrac{(153.5)^2}{10} + \dfrac{(160.5)^2}{10} + \dfrac{(151)^2}{10}\right) - 3(30+1) = 0.063$

g. Fail to reject H_0.

h. There is not enough evidence to support the claim.

11.3 EXERCISE SOLUTIONS

1. Each sample must be randomly selected and the size of each sample must be at least 5.

3. (a) H_0: There is no difference in the premiums.

   H_a: There is a difference in the premiums. (claim)

   (b) Critical value is 5.991.

   (c) $H \approx 14.05$

   (d) Reject H_0.

   (e) There is enough evidence at the 5% level to support the claim that the distributions of the annual premiums in California, Florida, and Illinois are different.

5. (a) H_0: There is no difference in the salaries.

   H_a: There is a difference in the salaries. (claim)

   (b) Critical value is 6.251.

   (c) $H \approx 1.45$

   (d) Fail to reject H_0.

   (e) There is enough evidence at the 10% level to support the claim that the distributions of the annual salaries in the four states are different.

© 2006 Pearson Education, Inc., Upper Saddle River, NJ. All rights reserved. This material is protected under all copyright laws as they currently exist. No portion of this material may be reproduced, in any form or by any means, without permission in writing from the publisher.

7. (a) H_0: There is no difference in the number of days spent in the hospital.

H_a: There is a difference in the number of days spent in the hospital. (claim)

The critical value is 11.345.

$H = 1.51$;

Fail to reject H_0.

(b)

Variation	Sum of squares	Degrees of freedom	Mean Squares	F
Between	9.17	3	3.06	0.52
Within	194.72	33	5.90	

For $\alpha = 0.01$, the critical value is about 4.45. Because $F = 0.52$ is less than the critical value, the decision is to fail to reject H_0. There is not enough evidence to support the claim.

(c) Both tests come to the same decision, which is, that there is not enough evidence to support the claim that there is a difference in the number of days spent in the hospital.

11.4 RANK CORRELATION

11.4 Try It Yourself Solutions

1a. $H_0: \rho_s = 0$; $H_a: \rho_s \neq 0$

b. $\alpha = 0.05$

c. Critical value is 0.700.

d.

Oat	Rank	Wheat	Rank	d	d^2
1.67	7	4.55	9	−2	4
1.96	9	4.30	8	1	1
1.60	6	3.38	6	0	0
1.10	1.5	2.65	3	−1.5	2.25
1.12	3	2.48	1	2	4
1.10	1.5	2.62	2	−0.5	0.25
1.59	5	2.78	4	1	1
1.81	8	3.56	7	1	1
1.45	4	3.35	5	−1	1
					14.5

$\Sigma d^2 = 14.5$

e. $r_s = 1 - \dfrac{6\Sigma d^2}{n(n^2 - 1)} = 0.879$

f. Reject H_0.

g. There is enough evidence to conclude that a significant correction exists.

11.4 EXERCISE SOLUTIONS

1. The Spearman rank correlation coefficient can (1) be used to describe the relationship between linear and nonlinear data, (2) be used for data at the ordinal level, and (3) is easier to calculate by hand than the Pearson coefficient.

© 2006 Pearson Education, Inc., Upper Saddle River, NJ. All rights reserved. This material is protected under all copyright laws as they currently exist. No portion of this material may be reproduced, in any form or by any means, without permission in writing from the publisher.

3. (a) $H_0: \rho_s = 0; H_a: \rho_s \neq 0$ (claim)

(b) Critical value is 0.929.

(c) $\Sigma d^2 = 14$

$$r_s = 1 - \frac{6\Sigma d^2}{n(n^2 - 1)} \approx 0.750$$

(d) Fail to reject H_0.

(e) There is not enough evidence at the 1% level to support the claim that there is a correlation between debt and income in the farming business.

5. (a) $H_0: \rho_s = 0; H_a: \rho_s \neq 0$ (claim)

(b) The critical value is 0.881.

(c) $\Sigma d^2 = 69.5$

$$r_s = 1 - \frac{6\Sigma d^2}{n(n^2 - 1)} \approx 0.173$$

(d) Fail to reject H_0.

(e) There is not enough evidence at the 1% level to support the claim that there is a correlation between the overall score and price.

7. $H_0: \rho_s = 0; H_a: \rho_s \neq 0$ (claim)

Critical value is 0.700.

$\Sigma d^2 = 124$

$$r_s = 1 - \frac{6\Sigma d^2}{n(n^2 - 1)} \approx -0.033$$

Fail to reject H_0. There is not enough evidence at the 5% level to conclude that there is a correlation between science achievement scores and GNP.

9. $H_0: \rho_s = 0; H_a: \rho_s \neq 0$ (claim)

Critical value is 0.700.

$\Sigma d^2 = 42$

$$r_s = 1 - \frac{6\Sigma d^2}{n(n^2 - 1)} \approx 0.650$$

Fail to reject H_0. There is not enough evidence at the 5% level to conclude that there is a correlation between science and mathematics achievement scores.

11. $H_0: \rho_s = 0; H_a: \rho_s \neq 0$ (claim)

The critical value is $= \dfrac{\pm z}{\sqrt{n-1}} = \dfrac{\pm 1.96}{\sqrt{33-1}} \approx \pm 0.346.$

$\Sigma d^2 = 6673$

$$r_s = 1 - \frac{6\Sigma d^2}{n(n^2 - 1)} \approx -0.115$$

Fail to reject H_0. There is not enough evidence to support the claim.

© 2006 Pearson Education, Inc., Upper Saddle River, NJ. All rights reserved. This material is protected under all copyright laws as they currently exist. No portion of this material may be reproduced, in any form or by any means, without permission in writing from the publisher.

11.5 THE RUNS TEST

11.5 Try It Yourself Solutions

1a. *P P P F P F P P P P F F P F P P F F F P P P F P P P*

b. 13 groups $\Rightarrow$ 13 runs

c. 3, 1, 1, 1, 4, 2, 1, 1, 2, 3, 3, 1, 3

2a. H_0: The sequence of genders is random.

H_a: The sequence of genders is not random. (claim)

b. $\alpha = 0.05$

c. *F F F M M F F M F M M F F F*

n_1 = number of *F*s = 9

n_2 = number of *M*s = 5

G = number of runs = 7

d. cv = 3 and 12

e. $G = 7$

f. Fail to reject H_0.

g. At the 5% level, there is not enough evidence to support the claim that the sequence of genders is not random.

3a. H_0: The sequence of weather conditions is random.

H_a: The sequence of weather conditions is not random. (claim)

b. $\alpha = 0.05$

c. n_1 = number of *N*s = 21

n_2 = number of *S*s = 10

G = number of runs = 17

d. $cv = \pm 1.96$

e. $\mu_G = \dfrac{2n_1 n_2}{n_1 + n_2} + 1 = \dfrac{2(21)(10)}{21 + 10} + 1 \approx 14.5$

$\sigma_G = \sqrt{\dfrac{2n_1 n_2 (2n_1 n_2 - n_1 - n_2)}{(n_1 + n_2)^2 (n_1 + n_2 - 1)}} = \sqrt{\dfrac{2(21)(10)(2(21)(10) - 21 - 10)}{(21 + 10)^2 (21 + 10 - 1)}} \approx 2.4$

$z = \dfrac{G - \mu_G}{\sigma_G} = \dfrac{17 - 14.5}{2.4} = 1.04$

f. Fail to reject H_0.

g. At the 5% level, there is not enough evidence to support the claim that the sequence of weather conditions each day is not random.

11.5 EXERCISE SOLUTIONS

1. Number of runs = 8

Run lengths = 1, 1, 1, 1, 3, 3, 1, 1

3. Number of runs = 9

Run lengths = 1, 1, 1, 1, 1, 6, 3, 2, 4

© 2006 Pearson Education, Inc., Upper Saddle River, NJ. All rights reserved. This material is protected under all copyright laws as they currently exist. No portion of this material may be reproduced, in any form or by any means, without permission in writing from the publisher.

5. n_1 = number of Ts = 6
   n_2 = number of Fs = 6

9. n_1 = number of Ts = 6
   n_1 = number of Fs = 6

   cv = 3 and 11

7. n_1 = number of Ms = 10
   n_2 = number of Fs = 10

11. n_1 = number of Ns = 11
   n_1 = number of Ss = 7

   cv = 5 and 14

13. (a) H_0: The coin tosses were random.
   H_a: The coin tosses were not random. (claim)

   (b) n_1 = number of Hs = 7
   n_2 = number of Ts = 9

   cv = 4 and 14

   (c) G = 9 runs

   (d) Fail to reject H_0.

   (e) At the 5% level, there is not enough evidence to support the claim that the coin tosses were not random.

15. (a) H_0: The sequence of digits were randomly generated.
   H_a: The sequence of digits were not randomly generated. (claim)

   (b) n_1 = number of Os = 16
   n_2 = number of Es = 16

   cv = 11 and 23

   (c) G = 9

   (d) Reject H_0.

   (e) At the 5% level, there is enough evidence to support the claim that the sequence of digits were not randomly generated.

17. (a) H_0: The production of defective parts is random.
   H_a: The production of defective parts is not random. (claim)

   (b) n_1 = number of Ns = 40
   n_2 = number of Ds = 9

   cv = ±1.96

   (c) G = 14 runs

$$\mu_G = \frac{2n_1n_2}{n_1 + n_2} - 1 = \frac{2(40)(9)}{40 + 9} - 1 = 13.7$$

$$\sigma_G = \sqrt{\frac{2n_1n_2(2n_1n_2 - n_1 - n_2)}{(n_1 + n_2)^2(n_1 + n_2 - 1)}} = \sqrt{\frac{2(40)(9)(2(40)(9) - 40 - 9)}{(40 + 9)^2(40 + 9 - 1)}} = 2.0$$

$$z = \frac{G - \mu_G}{\sigma_G} = \frac{14 - 13.7}{2.0} = 0.15$$

   (d) Fail to reject H_0.

   (e) At the 5% level, there is not enough evidence to support the claim that the production of defective parts is not random.

© 2006 Pearson Education, Inc., Upper Saddle River, NJ. All rights reserved. This material is protected under all copyright laws as they currently exist.
No portion of this material may be reproduced, in any form or by any means, without permission in writing from the publisher.

19. H_0: Daily high temperatures occur randomly.

H_a: Daily high temperatures do not occur randomly. (claim)

median = 87

n_1 = number above median = 14

n_2 = number below median = 13

cv = 9 and 20

G = 11 runs

Fail to reject H_0.

At the 5% level, there is not enough evidence to support the claim that the daily high temperatures do not occur randomly.

21. Answers will vary.

CHAPTER 11 REVIEW EXERCISE SOLUTIONS

1. (a) H_0: median = \$34,300 (claim); H_a: median ≠ \$34,300

(b) Critical value is 2.

(c) $x = 7$

(d) Fail to reject H_0.

(e) There is not enough evidence at the 1% level to reject the claim that the median value of stock among families that own stock is \$34,300.

3. (a) H_0: median ≤ 6 (claim); H_a: median > 6

(b) Critical value is $z_0 \approx -1.28$.

(c) $x = 44$

$$z = \frac{(x - 0.5) - 0.5(n)}{\frac{\sqrt{n}}{2}} = \frac{(44 - 0.5) - 0.5(70)}{\frac{\sqrt{70}}{2}} = \frac{8.5}{4.1833} \approx 2.032$$

(d) Reject H_0.

(e) There is enough evidence at the 10% level to reject the claim that the median turnover time is no more than 6 hours.

5. (a) H_0: There is no reduction in diastolic blood pressure. (claim)

H_a: There is a reduction in diastolic blood pressure.

(b) Critical value is 2.

(c) $x = 3$

(d) Fail to reject H_0.

(e) There is not enough evidence at the 5% level to reject the claim that there was no reduction diastolic blood pressure.

7. (a) Independent; Wilcoxon Rank Sum Test

(b) H_0: There is no difference in the amount of time that it takes to earn a doctorate.

H_a: There is a difference in the amount of time that it takes to earn a doctorate. (claim)

© 2006 Pearson Education, Inc., Upper Saddle River, NJ. All rights reserved. This material is protected under all copyright laws as they currently exist. No portion of this material may be reproduced, in any form or by any means, without permission in writing from the publisher.

(c) Critical values are $z_0 = \pm 2.575$.

(d) $R = 95$

$$\mu_R = \frac{n_1(n_1 + n_2 + 1)}{2} = \frac{12(12 + 12 + 1)}{2} = 150$$

$$\sigma_R = \sqrt{\frac{n_1 n_2(n_1 + n_2 + 1)}{12}} \sqrt{\frac{(12)(12)(12 + 12 + 1)}{12}} \approx 17.321$$

$$z = \frac{R - \mu_R}{\sigma_R} = \frac{95 - 150}{17.321} \approx -3.175$$

(e) Reject H_0.

(f) There is enough evidence at the 1% level to support the claim that there is a difference in the amount of time that it takes to earn a doctorate.

9. (a) H_0: There is no difference in salaries between the fields of study.
   H_a: There is a difference in salaries between the fields of study. (claim)

   (b) Critical value is 5.991.

   (c) $H \approx 22.98$

   (d) Reject H_0.

   (e) There is enough evidence at the 5% level to conclude that there is a difference in salaries between the fields of study.

11. (a) H_0: $\rho_s = 0$; H_a: $\rho_s \neq 0$ (claim)

    (b) Critical value is 0.881.

    (c) $\Sigma d^2 = 120$

    $$r_s = 1 - \frac{6\Sigma d^2}{n(n^2 - 1)} \approx -0.429$$

    (d) Fail to reject H_0.

    (e) There is not enough evidence at the 1% level to conclude that there is a correlation between overall score and price.

13. (a) H_0: The traffic stops are random by gender.
    H_a: The traffic stops are not random by gender. (claim)

    (b) n_1 = number of Fs = 12
    n_2 = number of Ms = 13

    cv = 8 and 19

    (c) $G = 14$ runs

    (d) Fail to reject H_0.

    (e) There is not enough evidence at the 5% level to conclude that the traffic stops are not random.

CHAPTER 11 QUIZ SOLUTIONS

1. (a) H_0: There is no difference in the salaries between genders.
   H_a: There is a difference in the salaries between genders. (claim)

   (b) Wilcoxon Rank Sum Test

© 2006 Pearson Education, Inc., Upper Saddle River, NJ. All rights reserved. This material is protected under all copyright laws as they currently exist. No portion of this material may be reproduced, in any form or by any means, without permission in writing from the publisher.

(c) Critical values are $z_0 = \pm 1.645$.

(d) $R = 66$

$$\mu_R = \frac{n_1(n_1 + n_2 + 1)}{2} = \frac{9(9 + 9 + 1)}{2} = 85.500$$

$$\sigma_R = \sqrt{\frac{n_1 n_2(n_1 + n_2 + 1)}{12}} = \sqrt{\frac{(9)(9)(9 + 9 + 1)}{12}} \approx 11.325$$

$$z = \frac{R - \mu_R}{\sigma_R} = \frac{66 - 85.5}{11.325} \approx -1.722$$

(e) Reject H_0.

(f) There is enough evidence at the 10% level to support the claim that there is a difference in the salaries between genders.

2. (a) H_0: median $= 28$ (claim); H_a: median $\neq 28$

(b) Sign Test

(c) Critical value is 6.

(d) $x = 10$

(e) Fail to reject H_0.

(f) There is not enough evidence at the 5% level to reject the claim that the median age in Puerto Rico is 28 years.

3. (a) H_0: There is no difference in the annual premiums between the states.
H_a: There is a difference in the annual premiums between the states. (claim)

(b) Kruskal-Wallis Test

(c) Critical value is 5.991.

(d) $H \approx 1.43$

(e) Fail to reject H_0.

(f) There is not enough evidence at the 5% level to conclude that there is a difference in the annual premiums between the states.

4. (a) H_0: The days with rain are random.
H_a: The days with rain are not random. (claim)

(b) The Runs test

(c) $n_1 =$ number of Ns $= 15$
$n_2 =$ number of Rs $= 15$

$cv = 10$ and 22

(d) $G = 16$ runs

(e) Fail to reject H_0.

(f) There is not enough evidence at the 5% level to conclude that days with rain are not random.

© 2006 Pearson Education, Inc., Upper Saddle River, NJ. All rights reserved. This material is protected under all copyright laws as they currently exist. No portion of this material may be reproduced, in any form or by any means, without permission in writing from the publisher.

Try It Yourself Solutions

1a. (1) 0.4857

b. (2) $z = \pm 2.17$

2a.

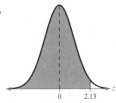

b. 0.4834

c. Area = 0.5 + 0.4834 = 0.9834

3a.

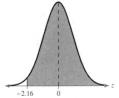

b. 0.4846

c. Area = 0.5 + 0.4846 = 0.9846

4a.

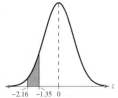

b. $z = -2.16$: Area = 0.4846

   $z = -1.35$: Area = 0.4115

© 2006 Pearson Education, Inc., Upper Saddle River, NJ. All rights reserved. This material is protected under all copyright laws as they currently exist.
No portion of this material may be reproduced, in any form or by any means, without permission in writing from the publisher.